Praise for

Elk Love

". . . a soul-soothing revelation of the innate connection between nature
and the human spirit."

—CHRISTOPHER WILSON,
director, Audubon Conservation Ranching Initiative

"A woman's new life in the western United States begets romance and a
welcome sense of connection in O'Connor's memoir . . . conveyed by
the author's exceptional prose. A superbly written true story of love
and self-discovery."

—*KIRKUS REVIEWS*

"O'Connor's exceptional writing style makes *Elk Love* a captivating
read. Healing and invigorating, this memoir is like a breath of fresh
air . . . . reads as a confession of a beautiful and artistic soul. The narrative is vibrant, poetic . . . ."

—*READER'S FAVORITE*, 5 STARS

"*Elk Love* is a beautiful memoir about love, grief, intimacy, and finding
one's place in the world. Throughout the vivid seasons and daily
rhythms of rural Montana, Lynne Spriggs O'Connor deftly illuminates
her own transformation through a unique relationship to this wild
place and a man who makes his home there. Art, ranch life, and romance converge in this remarkable love story that distills the truth . . .
and so much more."

—S. KIRK WALSH, author of *The Elephant of Belfast*

"In the midst of stampeding elk, mating birds, birthing cattle and all the viscerality of a working Angus ranch, Lynne Spriggs O'Connor has composed a lyrical memoir. I devoured this enchanting book about the sensual landscape of animals, budding love, and the intrinsic wildness of it all. This unflinching saga teaches the ancient knowledge that hope begins again as we traverse the cycles of life and death."

—NANI POWER, author of *New York Times*
Notable Book of the Year *Crawling at Night*

"Like a novel one can't put down, *Elk Love* takes the reader into a world few will ever experience—a world we risk losing. Savor the love story within this finely crafted memoir. Hold it close as you might a loved one, or as you might hold a rare and fleeting vision."

—PAGE LAMBERT, author of *In Search of Kinship*

"*Elk Love* demonstrates what it means to endure, to sustain, to adore the fierce wildness of the world around us, and to nurture that wildness in ourselves."

—KIM BARNES, author of Pulitzer Prize finalist *In the Wilderness*

"By turns sensual, expansive, nuanced, and spare, O'Connor brings clear-eyed and incandescent prose to skim the surface then dive deep."

— JENNIPHR GOODMAN,
screenwriter and director, *The Tao of Steve*

"If you long for a respite from the crush of this busy world... read this book. I basked in every page. You will be renewed and transported, and you will ask yourself: *What would it take for me to open my heart to true, and unabashed, wonder?*

—LAURA MUNSON, author of *Willa's Grove*
and founder of Haven Writing Retreats

Elk Love

ELK LOVE

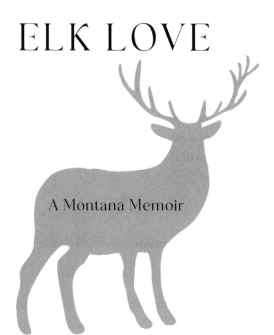

A Montana Memoir

Lynne Spriggs O'Connor

SHE WRITES PRESS

Published 2024
Printed in the United States of America
Print ISBN: 978-1-64742-640-8
E-ISBN: 978-1-64742-641-5
Library of Congress Control Number: 2024905778

For information, address:
She Writes Press
1569 Solano Ave #546
Berkeley, CA 94707

Interior design by Stacey Aaronson

She Writes Press is a division of SparkPoint Studio, LLC.

Names and identifying characteristics have been changed to protect the privacy of certain individuals.

For Phebe, Harrison, Moira, Gray, Isa,
Lucie, Owen, and Stanley

CONTENTS

III. WIND (2007–2008)

IV. EARTH (2009)

I.

WATER

(2004–2005)

WONDERSTRUCK

F all, 2004. Ten minutes outside of Great Falls, wide-open grasslands billow in the wind, unfolding effortlessly across rolling Montana plains. An empty two-lane highway stretches out in front of me. Somewhere in the distance is my destination—an isolated mountain range called the Highwoods. *This* is why I moved here. *This* is what I want for myself, this feeling of unfurling into beauty.

Huge round bales of hay speckle fields with autumn patterns of golden light and shadow. Painted clouds of pink, blue, orange, and purple drift in a never-ending sky. I crack the window for Willow, my one-year-old yellow lab and heeler mix riding in the back. We are on this adventure together. She raises her muzzle to fresh air, nostrils twitching to discern a thousand new secrets I will never know. Ten months ago, I lifted her small yellow body and placed her in my lap, trying to choose from a litter of eleven puppies. Only six weeks old, she picked up my keys in her mouth and stumbled away.

Dramatic light puts on a grand show today. Puffy clouds stacked to infinity float on either side of us. Distant mountain ranges punctuate the surrounding horizon in every direction. We pass only grazing cattle and horses, grain silos, and a few tiny towns. Forty-five minutes out, my written directions tell me to turn off this two-lane highway onto a country road and continue toward the Highwood Mountains. Willow hangs her head out the window, ears flapping in the wind. I'm taking her with me to interview a rancher and potential board member. My position as a museum director in Great Falls is *not* my heart's calling, but it's the job that brought me here.

The mountain range and two large separate rock formations come into focus as I proceed along the winding county road. A year ago, my friends back in Atlanta and New York couldn't understand. Why would I give up the prestige of overseeing one of the country's largest public folk art collections for a small museum in the rural West? But in an earlier decade of summers spent on Montana's Blackfeet Indian Reservation, this vast Rocky Mountain landscape had become my healing place.

Rounding a bend, I press down on the accelerator. In an imaginary liftoff, I fly over a blind hill, rushing straight into the heart of paradise.

But the road vanishes beneath me. Pavement gone, only gravel.

No ground will hold; the car swerves.

Gravel sprays out from beneath the tires. All four slip at once.

Fishtailing. Careening out of control.

Head for the right side of the road—a safe ditch, need traction.

I clench the steering wheel. A jackleg wood-and-barbed-wire fence now threatens just to the right. *Don't ram into it. Just hold steady.* But the shoulder is too steep. Everything snaps into slow motion. Bumpy. Rough. Loud slamming beneath me against hard ground. Tight grip. Banging. Rolling. I'm upside down now. My seatbelt is on.

I'm hanging upside down. Willow?!

A second later, the flipped car rights itself and sputters forward several yards before giving what sounds like one last gasp for air as the engine dies.

The stillness is shocking. Draw one deep breath. Then another. I call to Willow, who has disappeared from view. Unhooking my seatbelt, I open the door. My legs quiver. My stomach sinks. The top of my head throbs as I look; the entire right side of my car is destroyed.

I pry open the back hatch for Willow. She sits for one short second, shaking and terrified, then leaps out. I run after her, scoop her up, and hold her close.

I'm in the middle of nowhere. No cell coverage. I gaze at the destruction before me, squatting at the side of the long gravel road with Willow in my arms. We're shaking and cold.

"I'm so sorry, girl."

I look down the forsaken road and see a pickup truck approaching. An older man pulls over and steps out.

"Looks like you've got some trouble. You okay?"

"Yes, I'm okay. Thank you. I'm so glad you stopped."

His smile is kind. "Yes, ma'am. My name is Keith Crofton. I have a place just down the road here. What is it you're doing out this way? Do you know someone to call?"

"My cell phone won't work. I was going to see a man named Harrison . . ."

He tilts his head ever so slightly. "Harrison raises Angus cattle up there. Seems nice enough. But you don't ever see him." His shoulders shift. "I've already called the sheriff, so someone should be right along."

I nod with a shiver. Willow and I struggle on still shaky legs.

"Why don't you sit up in my rig where it's warm. You can use my truck phone to call Harrison if you like. I'll wait here for the sheriff."

I gather my long gray skirt in one hand before pulling myself up and into his truck. I leave Willow tied on a leash outside, imagining she prefers solid ground. Her brown eyes follow me. The smell of air freshener inside the truck is strong. I rummage through my purse, trying to find the number. A current board member at the museum named Fran suggested this friend of hers, Harrison, as a possible new board member. She'd said, "He's looking for ways to reconnect and might be persuaded."

I settle myself before dialing. Hang up. Dial again. *Beep, Beep, Beep, Beep.* Only a busy signal. This first meeting with a man who might support the museum is not going well. Finally, the phone rings. He answers.

"Where are you? Just stay put, and I'll be there as soon as I can. It will take me about twenty-five minutes."

I stare at my wrecked car. Stacked clouds still stretch like mountains across the open sky. From the front seat of Keith's truck, I spot what looks like an old farmhouse in the far distant hills. It's impossible not to think about what I left behind back East. I check on Willow. She's resting in the grass. I was alone at age forty-one in Atlanta when everything began to fall apart—a two-year-long perfect storm of extended ill health, growing bills, pressures at the museum, yet another failed relationship. Something finally snapped. In that crucible moment, my capacity to carry on as normal came to a screeching halt. Surrender felt like my *only* recourse. I thought about many of the artists whose works I had curated, who became my teachers—how they described the alchemy of surrendering to the fire of their own crucibles. I would let go of everything and follow my heart back to Montana. That fateful decision now appears to include letting go of the car I just totaled.

At last, a silver truck pulls up. A tall man steps out and walks over to Keith. Harrison looks like a giant next to his neighbor. He seems relaxed, smiling even. I push the heavy door open to lower myself out of Keith's truck. I gather up Willow and take slow steps in their direction, staring at the ground but listening as I walk. Harrison is doing most of the talking. They are *laughing*. I look up as I approach. He appears younger than Keith, with a prominent brow and a full head of brown hair. He thanks Keith after I do and sends him on his way with a pat on the back.

"You must be Lynne," he says, turning with an impish grin, eyebrows raised. "Are you okay?"

The sheriff pulls up, and Harrison says, "Here, you and your dog can climb into my truck. I'll go talk with the sheriff. You better give me your driver's license."

I hold Willow close and stroke her head inside Harrison's truck.

The two men talk. They walk all around my wreck, examining every detail before the sheriff is satisfied and returns to his patrol car. I've taken care of every damn detail of my entire adult life by myself. Not doing all this on my own is a welcome relief. Harrison steps up into the driver's seat of his truck and closes the door. He looks straight at me with bright blue eyes, hands me my license. "We'll have to wait here until the tow truck comes, so relax. Are you warm enough?"

As he reaches toward me to adjust the heat settings, his astonishing good looks begin to register, like smelling salts. He wears a plaid, button-down shirt—a crisp blue pattern, cotton, white buttons. Something about his good looks is slightly off. I secretly study him and notice his teeth are odd—jagged and very uneven, as if betraying some hidden wild state, as if his mother paid him no mind when he was a child. They're mangled, like my car. He delivers a few easy jabs, irresistible jokes about my driving skills on gravel. I fake a smile.

"I've never driven on gravel."

"Who is this?" he asks, leaning over to pet Willow. She is still sheepish.

"My Willow. Poor thing. She's as rattled as I am." I sigh, trying to keep it together.

"Thanks for coming," I say, squeezing my trembling puppy a bit closer.

We wait together quietly for the wrecker. Harrison focuses my attention on what is visible through the windshield in front of us. We begin to spot deer, then a group of antelope. Some are running. "See the way those deer are wagging their tails?" he says. "I bet you didn't know there are a whole series of different tail gestures to signal different things."

His voice is calm and steady.

"Once when I was checking calves out in a pasture, an eagle dropped from the sky, dove down to attack a Hungarian partridge. The dive looked magnificent, but the eagle missed. Slammed right into the ground and knocked itself out for a minute!" Harrison smashes the two heels of his palms together.

I flinch.

"If an eagle can't pull it off any more gracefully than that, then we're fooling ourselves. Look at that antelope over there," he says.

My eyes focus to follow his.

"I once watched a band of antelope running with a coyote, ears pinned back, in their midst. The herd wouldn't allow the coyote to turn left or right—ran him right out of the country."

This antelope is grazing peacefully, far enough away not to be concerned by our presence. I take a deep breath.

"How are you doing?" Harrison asks, reaching over to pet Willow. "Do you need more heat?"

"No, I'm okay. Your stories are helping." My eyes rest on the antelope, while I stroke Willow's head.

"Sitting in a tree stand in Virginia one time, the leaves were dead and deep, and I heard a strange sound of endless laborious marching. I'm looking for a deer, but this sound is too slow. Finally, I spot a big snapping turtle, following a dry creek bed, heading somewhere on a pathetic march."

I imagine that turtle and its steady determination to follow a long dry path that might, or might not, lead to water.

"Do you know about the license plate bird?"

I shake my head.

"Some birds and animals are specialists. This bird discovered that every license plate in the parking lot had fresh dead bugs attached. What a perfect example of adaptation for survival."

"That *is* smart," I say, beginning to question what is true. My eyes drift and settle on a group of small birds pecking at the road in front of us.

Harrison's gaze follows mine. "They're busy *gritting.*"

"What are you talking about?" I am so beat. Still out of my body.

"Birds eat gravel to help digest their food. Everybody knows that."

Finally, he succeeds in making me laugh. When I do, my head and ribs ache. "I like to *imagine* strange things like what you've been telling me. But birds eating gravel? That doesn't sound right."

"*Maybe* . . . but I can tell you all these things are true," he says, "because I've seen them for myself. But go ahead and doubt me. I'm certain you don't believe everything a complete stranger has just told you, do you? I rather like it when people can't figure out whether I'm telling the truth or not." He pronounces the word "*raw*ther." "It keeps things interesting." He smiles quizzically.

"I believe everything," I wager, "except birds eating gravel."

The lightness in Harrison's voice shifts; his blue eyes turn hard and distant. "I'm sure my stories sound strange. You shouldn't take anything I say seriously. But how would you know? People don't have a clue about what's real."

We spot the tow truck, and Harrison steps out to meet the guy, encouraging me to stay warm. I'm grateful for the easy way he handles things—a stranger who is willing to help me cope.

The remaining twenty-five-minute drive on gravel to Harrison's ranch is a blur. Willow attempts to burrow herself under the back seat. Jumpy myself, I lower the window for air.

"I'm sorry, Harrison, but would you mind maybe just slowing down a little? I'm still a bit nervous."

"Of course."

He slows a bit. Willow scratches at the truck floor. The sound of stones moving beneath the tires is too much for her.

When we arrive, I coax my poor puppy out of hiding.

"Why don't you bring her upstairs so she can be with you," Harrison suggests, as we walk through a mudroom, where two dogs rise from a nap. They bark and wag their tails with sleepy friendliness.

He leads the way down a hallway past a central outdoor courtyard, into a large kitchen. The trauma has settled into some deeper region of my body. I put Willow down. Harrison pours water in a bowl for her and sets it by a wood stove. Seated at his kitchen table, I can no longer hold back tears.

Harrison pours a glass of red wine and hands it to me. "Good for the nerves."

He has *no idea*. My nerves have been shot for the better part of a year, ever since (and long before) I arrived to begin this new life in Great Falls. During my first week here as museum director, I discovered the financials were not what I'd been led to believe. In fact, each year's budget hung in the balance. That same first week, a county commissioner critical to our annual funding made the front page for coming out of a bar with his fiancée, drunk. She stabbed him. He followed her to rehab. Good Lord! Museum employees have stories about their own experiences with gambling, drugs, even murder. Four weeks ago, missing petty cash and lapses in our security footage led to the discovery that a nice girl I hired recently is a young felon. Today was meant to be a rare escape.

Harrison is busy warming a pot of elk spaghetti on the stove. I wipe my eyes to see where I am. Windows on all sides of his kitchen offer an arresting view of a valley where evergreen mountains and hillsides of grass, buttery orange and reddish-brown, wrap themselves around the house before spilling down toward nearby buttes and far out onto open plains.

"That was quite a Thelma-and-Louise move," he says, stirring the pot.

I give a weak smile.

Harrison places a bowl of steaming spaghetti in front of me, then pours us both another glass of wine. Our anticipated lunch has become dinner. He scurries to set out a plastic bag with grated parmesan cheese. I sip my wine.

Harrison grabs something from a nearby bookshelf. "Look at this old photograph of three children. One of them is actually dead!

This was taken a hundred years ago—you're a museum person, you probably know more about old photographs than I do. But these are the three children of the guy who originally lived in this valley. One of them, Coe, drowned in the creek here when he was four years old, but they wanted to put him in the photo."

Harrison blows on his spaghetti before taking a bite.

"They dressed him up in what looks like a little girl's clothing, propped him up next to his sister sitting in the chair, and here, look closely," he says, pointing to the smallest child's eyes. "His eyelids had to be kept open with toothpicks. The postmortem makes him look like he's still alive, standing next to his siblings."

I don't quite know how to respond. Three magpies appear on a stone wall just outside the kitchen where we're seated. The black-and-white birds flap and dance in the wind as they try to maintain balance. Once, on the Blackfeet Indian Reservation, I watched a magpie approach the body of a dead magpie. It stood close for several minutes, pecked at the body, then flew off. A few minutes later, the bird returned with several strands of grass and laid them by the corpse.

The three magpies lift and leave. I turn to study the grim black-and-white photograph. Strong winds push against the house. It rattles in response. A loud squeaking sound—something persistently turning or swinging in the wind just outside the kitchen—goes unnoticed by Harrison. He mentions that two more young children, one from another family of early settlers, also died in this valley around the same time and are buried here. I push my bowl of spaghetti aside.

Light is becoming softer outside. A hawk soars low along the ridge of a nearby hillside.

"Once I was hunting over there," he says, pointing to the far side of the valley. "I'd just fired off a few shots at a coyote, and I heard the sounds of children laughing at the creek. I was alarmed—how dangerous to be shooting when there were people around! I called out and looked everywhere, but no one answered. I believe it was the laughter of ghosts of those three dead children, playing in the creek where Coe drowned."

Willow lies on the floor next to us, twitching in her sleep. I remember Keith's subtle tilt of the head, his comment about this man named Harrison whom no one seems to know.

"Coe's father, J. Y. Warren, was the first character to build a homestead on this site back in the late 1890s—moved here from Missouri. He was a hard man by many accounts. Once he placed a live rattlesnake in a pretty box and sent it to someone in the mail—his way of settling an argument."

Harrison inhales his spaghetti. It smells good, and I need strength. I pull my bowl closer and take a first bite. "This is delicious, Harrison. It's so sweet. I've never had elk before." I eat more and feel better.

Bright light illuminates the large buttes we can see out his kitchen windows, but the sun must have dropped below the mountains behind us. Daylight is leaving this higher valley.

I have no idea what time it is.

"After Coe drowned, J. Y.'s young wife just couldn't take her life here anymore. They buried Coe on an east-facing hillside where the other children were buried. Soon after, she left him and took their remaining children back to Missouri. A few years later, lonely old J. Y. went on a walkabout, and somehow found his wife. Her response when she met him at the door: 'Shall I go get my gun?'" Harrison takes another sip of wine. "I can almost channel J. Y.'s spirit."

"What do you mean?"

"A guy can go nuts being in a place like this by himself for too long." He continues in a voice that drops away like his distant eyes. "The silence can tear at you."

There's an odd vulnerability to this man, who turns over stories of suffering like an elephant turning over the bones of its dead.

"I guess I better be getting you home. Look at Willow," he says.

She opens her eyes at the sound of her name.

By the time Harrison delivers us to my house in Great Falls over an hour later, Willow and I are both weary to the bone. My body melts into bed. I drop backward in time, into the comfort of those winding (paved) country roads I used to travel, making visits to meet the creators of works I exhibited back East—a professional career devoted to celebrating both Indigenous and self-taught artists as shapeshifters, powerful storytellers, and visionaries. As a museum curator, I was drawn to artists whose works invited conversations about the invisible, interwoven, and imperfect qualities of life. I felt inspired by what was stunning and unexpected. Some artists were informed by visions or dreams. In unusual depictions, plants and animals became sentient messengers.

Willow jumps up and turns in place before lying down next to me on the bed. The majority of unschooled artists I worked with across the Southeast—many African American—hadn't blossomed as artists until later in life. Their passionate devotion to creativity was often precipitated by a devastating tragedy of some kind, a personal crisis, or the ongoing oppression of poverty and/or racism. In response to pain that seemed insurmountable, they had surrendered their lives to follow Spirit. Many described their journeys as a calling.

I looked to the lessons of those intrepid artists when my own life came crashing down. Their indomitable convictions and transformative works gave me courage to follow my own calling, to place all my faith in this place called Montana. One year and one car crash later, blind faith is still all I've got. I slip off to sleep with Willow in my arms.

SPARRING

I see my board member friend Fran a few days later. Without mentioning my crash, I joke with her about Harrison's good looks.

"He might be too distracting in a board meeting," I muse. "What's his story?"

"I think he's involved with a woman from Virginia."

Just as well.

But Harrison begins calling me at work to check on how I am faring. He enjoys joking about my grandiose "crash-and-burn" debut more than I do.

"Can we keep this little secret just between us? *Please?*"

"Sure. But I can guarantee your lovely loop de loop is no secret. Nothing stays a secret for very long in Montana."

My mind circles back in time. At nine years old, I'm already thin and tall like my mother. I have the same green eyes as everyone in our family. The four of us are seated at the heavy, round, antique dining room table. I'm next to my father, and Laurie, my younger sister, sits close to Mom. My mother seems unhappy but tries to look otherwise. She has that perfect flip hairstyle like Mary Tyler Moore. I'm picking at the potato chips on top of her tuna casserole. My father is gossiping again about some colleague in the clergy. When Mom doesn't respond, he pulls me into his ritual of ridiculing her. "There she is," he says, "little Miss Perfect. *So dainty.* Dabbing those little corners of her mouth to stay tidy." I join him in laughing at her. Mom stops, puts down the napkin without a word. I'll pay for this later. When he then lays into my sister for something, a part of me wishes I could disappear. *She is only seven*. Laurie looks sheepish and little at this heavy table. She scoots closer to Mom.

Harrison is right about secrets. News travels fast in small towns. But I'm attempting to keep my private life quiet. There's no reason anyone here needs to know about my past relationships—or my present ones, for that matter. Six months ago, soon after I got my new puppy, an acquaintance introduced me to a tall, virile, long-haired Croatian wheat farmer with a finely honed libido. *A wheat farmer of all things*. We were at a bar–restaurant. What began as a one-night frolic with a divorced farmer turned into occasional nights of earthy clandestine pleasure.

Harrison's calls are sporadic. He disappears without a word for weeks at a time, until my office phone rings again.

"Hello, Madam Director."

I am reserved. All business. Yet his silliness and that hushed raspy voice are refreshing on the other end of the line. When he can hear one of my employees in the background, he is quick to cause mischief. "What did it feel like being up in the air, upside down? Could you speak up and *describe it* for me again?"

Before long, I am laughing out loud. He invites me to join him for lunch, and I accept.

Our first few meetings for lunch in town begin with nervous jokes and darting eyes. We are intrigued to be together again. I climb into his truck in my skirt and heels, determined to hide the fact that I am delighted by his flashing blue eyes and full shock of chestnut hair, the latter more reminiscent of a preppy adolescent than a fifty-something-year-old man. I find it impossible not to appreciate those boyish brown locks when they fall lavishly over his protruding brow and hide one eye. Except for his wild-ass teeth, Harrison's countenance is dashing.

He enlivens our fifteen-minute drives to local establishments with amusing stories about his hermit life. He sets the stage with self-deprecating (and often hilarious) descriptions of ranch life and of himself as someone "from away" who is hopelessly uninformed. He is agile with language; he attributes this to his Irish blood. His improvisations are full of surprises. More than once, he gets lost while talking and driving. My laughter gives way to gasps when he heads the wrong way down one-way streets.

"Okay. It's your turn now," he announces one day as we sit down for lunch. "I want to hear details—everything you're encountering here. Give me all the good gossip!"

I'm still assessing him as a possible board member. I want this to stay professional.

After we order, he cajoles and interrupts: "I'm not interested in that. Tell me something juicy!" He's restless and easily bored. A part of me would love to cut loose. But gossip means trouble. So far, Harrison seems hidden and enigmatic. Possibly nuts. Best to maintain my professional role as a stalwart spokesperson for the higher aspirations and promising future of the arts in Great Falls. I smile politely when our food arrives and continue my informal interview.

"Tell me about your own interest in art," I suggest, bringing a spoonful of tomato soup to my lips.

"Well . . . I took art classes in college. Basically, I rejected everything about school from eighth grade on. My only real interest was hunting. Art classes seemed the easiest to skip."

"Ah, you missed out! Anybody can benefit from exposure to the arts. This is my lucky calling. We're working toward something brand new in this community . . . "

"Sounds to me like your head is in the clouds."

Swallowing, I ignore him and go on. "I'm really excited about some major new plans at the museum . . . "

"I'd suggest you not plan things in life," he interrupts again.

Every turn of optimism meets raised eyebrows. Each enthusiasm is dismissed as silly, irrelevant.

"My goodness you're a real can-do girl," he says.

I grimace.

"Sounds to me like you've got an unrealistic approach to life in Montana."

"Tell me about you. Do you have a family?"

He pauses. "I have three grown children, three boys. They all live on their own now. All far away."

"And how did you end up in Montana?"

"I moved here fourteen years ago from Virginia. It's a long story. But you didn't finish telling me about your big plans for Great Falls."

My jaw grows tighter. I swallow hard. Ears pop. The waitress has taken our plates away, and I barely remember what I've eaten.

"All I can tell you," I finally allow, "is what I know to be true. Being open to possibilities—no matter how unlikely something may seem, *does* make a difference. I've experienced undeniable grace in my life, and I've witnessed it in others'. In my experience, the worst situations have always, eventually, led to something better."

He cocks his head. He stares straight into my eyes. One eyebrow rises. "Are you *sure*?"

What is *with* this guy? Optimism is all that's *left* of me. I've given him nothing to suggest how hollowed out I really am, body and soul: A wanderer with no home. A woman with no womb. Still waiting for my next something better.

Almost every day of my last two years in Atlanta, a red river of menstrual blood poured from my body. Large gelatinous chunks of clotted blood made me gasp. I saw doctors. Tried acupuncture, castor oil, and heating pads. Disappeared from meetings to hunch over in pain. Anemia set in. While juggling the stresses of a demanding job, I quietly began interviewing for four separate museum positions in Montana. Like a wounded animal, I sought refuge in nature. My boyfriend agreed to help me move to Montana. We found a house there together. After two major surgeries back in Atlanta, the bleeding and pain finally stopped. But I was burned out, and my blood trail was long. I'd lost my uterus. It was then my boyfriend sent a Dear Jane letter. He'd met someone else.

We finish lunch without my telling Harrison any of this. I'm not even sure *how* I actually got myself to Montana. By the time I arrived, I felt suicidal. Yet one year later, here I am, surrendering to life—trying hard not to resist or judge *anything*. This new life here, now—*whatever it is—has got to work.*

I'm quiet on our short ride back to the museum. I can hardly wait to escape. With the help of strong winds, I slam Harrison's truck door behind me and wave goodbye. Obviously, my sales pitch is not moving him one bit. Did our mutual friend ever *really* think he might make a good board member?

The town crematorium is next door to the museum, which used to be an old high school. I trudge up the last set of stairs, back to my office that was the principal's office, back to this strange grind of believing that many people in Great Falls even care about contemporary art. Outside, the smokestack from the crematorium's furnace juts like a finger into a granite sky.

Over ten years living in New York City during my twenties and thirties, I worked in feature film, codirected an art gallery, and pursued a Ph.D. in Native American Art History at Columbia University. Whether it was Native American or African art, folk art from Yugoslavia or from Mexico, I explored refreshing perspectives in visionary works created by individuals considered "outside" the (white male) mainstream. The contemporary museum where I curated folk art exhibitions in Atlanta for seven years was spacious and full of light, modern and world-class. This 1896 three-story gray sandstone structure I now oversee features a cavernous basement, where an ancient boiler malfunctions in subzero weather, and a haunted high-ceiled attic infested with brown bats, reeking of pungent guano.

If bats in the attic and a broken boiler aren't enough, I'm told the plumbing throughout our three floors of public space is failing. Pipes are clogged, requiring something called a "full flush." The thought of closing the museum so our entire plumbing system can be "soaked" for six to ten days, like dirty dishes in the sink, ties my stomach into tighter and tighter knots. Imagine—a local fire suppression team sending high pressure blasts of water through a network of ancient piping in a 108-year-old building.

Staring out my third-floor office window, I see a few dark puffs of smoke rising from the crematorium's chimney. I pause, witness to a stranger's passage. It doesn't take long. A few hours later, I step outside. Another old window has fallen from a gallery on the museum's second story. I kick at its broken framework of rotting wood and shards of glass in the parking lot. If I smoked, I'd be lighting up.

I head to the grocery store after work to look for comfort in food. I've been yearning for New York City cuisine. Bumper stickers on the back fenders of souped-up Chevy trucks scream local sentiments: DON'T TAILGATE ME OR I'LL FLICK A BOOGER AT YOU; I'M DRIVING THIS WAY BECAUSE I'M A BIG BAD BITCH; FAST TRUCKS, BIG GUNS, LONELY WOMEN; FUCK OFF.

I ask the grocery clerk anyway, "Excuse me, where can I find some lox?"

He looks at me as if I'm nuts, walks me out to the sidewalk, and points down the street to a locksmith. I start walking, searching for some glimmer of hope along this town's main drag of neon-lit casinos and bars, pawnshops, gun shops, liquor stores, a "Tokyo Shampoo" parlor, endless car dealerships, and fast-food chains.

The Missouri River courses straight through the middle of town. Some sixty miles of beautiful trails and protected green space along both sides of the river are Great Falls's saving grace. Each day I rise early and walk portions of this trail system with Willow before work. A short six-minute drive from my house allows us to meander through an arid landscape, step out into high meadows where deer graze, wander along dramatic sagebrush- and cactus-covered bluffs where hundreds of cliff swallows return to nests of mud in sandstone cliffs each spring. Other days, we drop down to stroll close to the river, hiking through willows and cottonwoods, spying geese with goslings, great horned owls, snakes, beavers. Whistling marmots and rabbits set Willow wild. In these colder months, I still force myself to walk in the dark of mornings and evenings, sometimes along the edge of frozen waters.

Two weeks later, up pops Harrison again.

"I'm going to be in town tomorrow to pick up some ranch supplies. Thought I'd swing by the museum."

We've met four times by now. It's been three months since my crash. For some reason, I still get butterflies at the thought of seeing him. I'm of two minds. But I'm lonely. I suggest a local pizza place on the river.

"So, tell me stories about your time spent with Indians on the rez." As he speaks, he scratches his scalp vigorously, like a dog with mange.

"If you're talking about the ten summers I spent on the Blackfeet Indian Reservation up around Browning, Montana," I say, "I found the people there to be incredibly kind. I met Southern Piegan or Amskapi Pikuni filmmakers and scholars, artists and educators. As members of the Blackfoot Confederacy that spans the U.S. and Canada, they call themselves Niitsitapi, which translates to Real People." I pause, recalling my first summer. "The physical beauty of that vast open country along the Rocky Mountain front was stunning to me. The *grack-grack-grack* of noisy magpies caught my attention right away—I'd never seen such a bird. During my first few years up there, the roof over my head was a rickety one-story shack known by locals as 'the chicken coop.' It was all I could afford. Each June, I'd sublet my apartment in New York to pay for three months out West. I became like a finch or a robin, establishing an annual migration pattern. All those summers on the reservation. That's when I first fell in love with Montana." I hesitate, not sure how much he wants to know, wary of how much I want to share.

I tell him a little about my time with Native American friends and elders; how I value the perspective Native cultures afford. Harrison listens to my stories without interrupting.

"Now that's really interesting," he says, reaching for his glass of lemonade. "I thought maybe you'd just gotten yourself swept up into one more hokey storyline."

"Have you ever noticed how insensitive and cynical you can be," I proffer, "mocking things you really don't know anything about?"

We pause. The waitress is here with our pizza and lemonade refills. Harrison reaches for a slice.

"Yes, I have noticed," he says. "That's the one thing I do well. I figure I better hang onto it." He pauses for a moment, chewing, then drifts off again to some other place.

"Look," I say, "Indigenous practices have taught me a lot. And I'm a minister's daughter. Ceremonies and rituals can bring an elevated consciousness to life. In my own experience, they've helped me cultivate a relationship with pain. To recognize it as a catalyst for growth."

Harrison blinks once, adjusting himself in a booth that needs new foam stuffing. "I know that's the way it's supposed to work. I suppose it's happening here for me, in the place where I'm completely alone most all the time."

"It *is* pretty amusing," I reflect. "I work on an advanced degree and study Indigenous cultures in books and museums. Then I live on the Blackfeet Indian Reservation, where I come to know Native community members and I learn much more. Yet *this* culture has got me completely stumped."

Harrison's face lights up like a Cheshire cat.

I continue, "I'm sure this is no news to you, but I know nothing at all about farmers, ranchers, and all the other conundrums of this place. I'm supposed to be raising money for the museum; most folks here have no reason to care what the word *philanthropy* even means. They're too busy just trying to get by. They have little interest in most contemporary art."

"*Aha*," he flashes, "such optimism."

My gut tightens. "Look at you. You're delighted with yourself. And all I'm looking for is a little compassion."

"You should meet my friend Phyllis," he suggests. "Her mother came out here on a stagecoach. She's a lot of fun. You two would really hit it off."

He finishes the last piece of pizza. I'm still fuming.

"You like to play this weird game of attrition, don't you? You disorient people with negative pushback, doubting and challenging *everything* until they're exhausted. Completely worn down."

"Well," he says, "that might be true. I think people are often much more interesting when they're off balance and undone."

"You're like a cat playing with a mouse before devouring it."

Late one afternoon at the museum, I fall into talking about my previous life with a nice older plumber who has just finished fixing one of the building's ancient toilets. I'm still putting off the "big flush."

"New York City is amazing. Living there makes it so easy to know people from anywhere in the world. I loved working with Atlanta's huge Mexican community. Such rich traditions. So much kindness. And all the talented African American artists across the South. I was constantly inspired. Life here, without direct access to those perspectives, feels like something essential is missing."

The born-and-raised Montanan listens politely while packing up his tools. Kneeling on one knee, he pauses before rising, then cocks his head to one side, as he looks off down the hall. "You know," he says, "I don't think I've ever met a Black person."

Three, four, five beats pass. I search his eyes for a twinkle, his mouth for an upward turn. Any signal that this is a joke.

"Really? *Never*?"

He sets his jaw, shakes his head slowly. "Nope. Never have."

I have been confiding in this kind man as if he were the old friend I do not have here. He has listened to my life story as a single woman from an entirely different planet. I still forget where I am: that many men here (including this one, perhaps) might not be all that open to listening to the perspectives of someone outside of their own community. But he spoke skillfully, politely, with an almost puzzled objectivity. He modeled what a Buddhist might refer to as "virtuous restraint."

Socializing has always felt awkward, often nerve-racking. But never like this. When I first arrived on the Blackfeet Indian Reservation, I undertook my work with humility. I learned about reciprocity, and I was made to feel welcome. Artists here in Montana—and anywhere—make me feel alive. But unlike Atlanta or New York, this sparsely populated Western state is 87 percent white, 6 percent Native American, and less than 1 percent any other ethinicity.

It is three weeks later in November when Harrison calls again, just enough time for me to forget what a knot-head he can be. This time at lunch, I throw decorum out the window.

"You know, you're a real asshole sometimes!" So much for virtuous restraint.

He looks up from his half-eaten hamburger as if he has just been awarded a badge of honor. "*Yes!* I know I am. Can't help it. The more 'together' someone seems, the more I want to blow their lid off. Thank you!"

"I've just about had it with you blowing *my* lid off. I've endured enough of these boxing matches. What makes *you* such an expert on *my* life and everyone else's? Why do you push so hard and sound so cold-hearted at times?"

It seems as if the entire restaurant has grown silent. He pauses, takes another long drink of coffee, and puts his cup down.

"Three years ago, I found out that my wife of thirty-two years had leukemia. In eight weeks, she was dead. That same year, my best friend died from a sudden lung condition that might have been hantavirus. By the time my father died a few months later, I was cold as ice."

I sit in silence.

"This is why I don't believe plans and decisions make the slightest difference. Life is nothing more than a fire. We can tell ourselves anything we want. But really, we're just caught up in flames, in a swirl of what we can't ever understand. We're just burning along with everything else."

Harrison's jaw flexes tight as he pushes his plate away, hamburger half-eaten. I take a long deep breath. For one moment, his eyes had softened before turning hard again.

He waves for the bill and changes the subject. I observe him with compassion, still listening.

The next morning, I stand by the river along its icy banks with Willow. Harrison's words ring in my ears. He's not made of ice after all. There's a shattered heart beneath all that cynicism. My dog sets off ahead of me to the river trail. We pass the familiar stretch of trees with gnawed trunks, where nearby, a beaver packs mud and makes progress in renovating an old lodge. Each morning, Willow follows its scent with a start.

My own heart feels chilled as I wait for her return. Harrison seems bewildered by the losses he must face. But I know everything about how to start a new life. Five years after my parents divorced, my father died. Five years later, my NYC loft and everything I owned went up in flames. By age twenty-six, my own life felt like a swirling fire. As I migrated from one place to another, my friends extended from Minnesota to Michigan, Maine to New Mexico, Atlanta to New York. I've stretched my adult years over thousands of miles of American soil. But I could never tap a place that felt nourishing enough to put down deep roots—not until I arrived in Montana.

I stop to search a stand of old cottonwood trees for the family of great horned owls that I know live here. Farther along the path, the empty nests of cliff swallows extend like a series of abandoned winter villages of small cliff dwellings. Since day one of my job here, I have carried the dead weight of what I alone cannot fail at doing for a struggling museum. These trails are the only place I can breathe. Strolling along the banks of this river grounds me.

Lunches with Harrison lead to occasional dinners in town. He keeps reaching out. I remind myself of his ailing heart. He seems to need a friend as much as I do. Like magnets, we attract and repel.

"I bet you don't know another person on earth who has gotten an F+," he boasts one November evening at a local steakhouse. "The only way I made it through college at University of Virginia was because of Professor Peter Taylor, a great writer. He provided all the A's I needed to squeak through."

"I gather you've gotten away with a lot over the years."

"Basically, from eighth grade on, I rejected everyone's ideas about how to behave. I was fearful of everything. Except when I was in the duck marshes, hunting."

"That wouldn't work for a first-born PK—preacher's kid—from the Midwest. While you were rejecting everything, I was busy pleasing and placating. I got straight A's."

"It's a better path. I told myself very early in life: the fewer experiences you have, the fewer people you know, the better."

He confirms what I've already surmised. He has no interest in ever joining my board of directors. Maybe that's a good thing. Harrison places his fork and knife on his empty plate. Only the bone of his T-bone steak remains.

"I feel like a Martian from another planet," I confess. Our waiter arrives to clear the table. Tonight, I need something for dessert. Something sweet. "The fruit tart, please, and a cappuccino. You have cappuccino, right?" The waiter nods. "Thanks."

I turn to Harrison. Then look around to see who might be here before speaking.

"Somehow I've landed in a place where it feels like music can be playing and no one will get up to dance. You talk about *your* isolation and loneliness. Try being a single professional woman from a big Eastern city in this rural farming and military town. *Nothing* feels familiar or welcoming. I've never lived in a place where people keep to themselves like this. Where is the *joy*? Everybody seems frayed at the edges."

My neck is sore, shoulders tight.

"I'm someone who lives for diversity. Joie de vivre! I enjoy different foods and music and languages of other cultures. And here I am, having moved to one of the least diverse states in the country because I loved the landscape. No one here wants to look or act *different* from the next person. Seems to be a rule. I haven't found anyone here who likes spicy food. Except you."

"*Now* we're getting somewhere," Harrison says, beaming.

"I spend so many years, work so hard, and spend so much money getting an advanced degree—"

"And then you come to a place where mediocracy attacks excellence. Brilliant!" He cheers.

I cast another glance at the tables near us. Harrison folds his napkin, lines up one edge to the edge of the table.

"This place *is* tough," he concedes. "When I arrived here fourteen years ago, I'd bought the ranch and knew nothing at all about ranching. There were no fences, no farm equipment. I immediately had to deal with a terrible blizzard that killed a lot of cattle and a ranch hand who keeled over dead from a shifting blood clot. About all the help I got was one neighbor throwing me two tablets for scours—sick calves with diarrhea—and the words: '*Good luck!*'"

His own beginnings make mine sound easy. I do the math. The year after he bought his ranch and moved here was my first summer in Montana's Blackfeet country.

Harrison grits his teeth and confides: "Locals referred to me as 'Hollywood.' But I've lasted a lot longer, and I know a hell of a lot more about cattle than anyone thought I would."

I take a sip of the cappuccino, cradling the cup in my hands. I catch myself imagining what it would be like to kiss this gorgeous man. Breaking off a piece of fruit tart with my fork, I bring it to my mouth. It is so full of sugar it hurts.

"You really would love this woman named Phyllis," Harrison insists.

"I'd *love* to meet her," I say. "But you've got to make it happen!"

Three weeks later, I ask more about his childhood when I'm halfway through my salad at lunch. Forget talking about work. I'm still wondering why his mother never thought to fix his teeth.

"Growing up in Thailand, I hardly spoke English. When I returned to Virginia, my aunt Rebecca worried I was a heathen. She took it upon herself to help me grow up to be a Christian gentleman. She would implore me to be like George Washington. 'It's very important that you always tell the truth,' she would say. She had a strong, sure character."

He pauses. "Now I see she was trying to tell me that if you don't protect your own inner honor, it will haunt you like a pack of wolves.

And she was right. I've been incredibly lucky. I've had a lot of strong women in my life. My mother would always tell me, 'Every time you walk into a room, remember that you are the equal of everyone there, and the superior of most.'"

"Which you believe—"

"The Harrison coat of arms is *Vincit Qui Patitur*: He Conquers Who Perseveres. It was certainly true for my mother and father. After forty-plus years of drinking and fighting, they finally decided to love each other. That's how I've survived. Life is simply endurance. Not with skill. Just persistence."

His mother, I learn, had perseverance in spades. She had multiple miscarriages and four children: one mentally disabled son, one schizophrenic son, Harrison, and his older sister, who hasn't spoken to him in many years.

"That last part is familiar. My sister hasn't spoken to me in years either."

"Aunt Bec was right to be worried about me. When I was a boy in Siam, I played with lepers. My mother would put me in a bath and pop boils. My foot had a hole in it caused by some burrowing worm. I remember watching cobras come out from under the house until a servant would pour boiling water on them, and they'd slither back under."

I'm no longer wondering about his crooked teeth.

"We had this number two girl named Tawi. She was wild from the jungle of Chiang Mai. A woman with a gold tooth who would climb a tree to get lunch. I had a pet monkey who slept beside me in its own bed. My amah slept on the floor."

"Amah? Number two girl?"

"Domestic workers. They came with the job."

"Yikes. How long did you live in Thailand?"

"About five years. We moved there when I was one or two years old. One day Tawi invited me to come into a small room. She undressed, lay down on a bed, and lit her pubic hairs on fire."

"*What?* This happened when you were a small boy?"

"Probably four years old. I remember just standing there thinking: *This is something interesting that human beings do. But I think I will not tell anybody.*"

I don't tell Harrison about an early memory of my own. When I was an eleven-year-old safety guard, wearing a bright orange diagonal sash standing on a street corner outside my grade school before recess, a thin, dark-haired man with haunted eyes walked straight up to me and exposed himself. I stood frozen as he turned to walk away. I didn't move until he was out of sight, still afraid I might be killed. I struggled to find the words while whispering into the principal's ear. *"What?! You mean he exposed himself?!"* Everyone in her office turned to look at me in horror.

Weeks later, I was called off the playground in front of the whole school. Police had found a Vietnam vet exposing himself to young girls and nuns, and they needed me to identify him. I rode in the front seat of an unmarked car between a plainclothes officer and my mother. When he pulled up to the gas pump, the officer rolled down his window and struck up a conversation with the attendant. Instantly, I recognized those haunted eyes.

My parents and I never spoke about that incident. Much later in life, I would learn why my mother was so quiet that day. She had been a silenced victim of rape and incest during her own childhood, from ages eight to twelve years old.

Harrison is gazing off into space.

The waitress clears our lunch plates.

"My mother shot a gun at my father once," he tells me. "He dug the bullet out of the wall like the good CIA agent he was. They owned two identical Smith and Wesson 38s. She beat my father with a cane more than once. She loved to start fights. There was a lot of screaming. To this day, every time I hear a martini shaker, my body knows it's time to duck and hide."

He notes my startled expression.

"Oh, you'll like this one. Once my mother used a can opener to cut my father's chest open in a Z just like Zorro. Another time, my father hid in a locked bathroom during a fight, and she lit the bathroom door on fire."

"Is this all part of why you moved to Thailand? Was your father really CIA?"

"He worked for a while as an editor for Scribner's publishing house, in the days of Hemingway, Fitzgerald, Thomas Wolfe, Marjorie Kinnan Rawlings, and Max Perkins. Later he worked for the United States Information Agency and then Radio Free Europe. Through a friend in Bangkok, he got involved with Cold War propaganda strategies. Started dropping balloons over Eastern Europe, releasing pamphlets to incite revolt against Russian authority, work that all ended up being for the CIA. After Thailand we moved to Uruguay, then to Germany."

"Were you and your father close?"

"No. He perfected the art of staying as hidden as possible as a means of self-preservation. So did I."

I have no idea what is true. But the more stories I hear, the more I understand why someone with such a childhood might want to move 2,300 miles from their family to hide away in a beautiful wild landscape, stark and empty.

At another dinner several weeks later, Harrison has recently returned from a bird-hunting trip in Texas. He sits down next to me at an Italian-style restaurant. His eyes are wild. He's unusually present. Alive.

"You look wired," I say.

"I am. I haven't slept well, ever since I got home."

He is amped up. Downing black coffee. No wonder he's not sleeping.

"This was the greatest year of birds many hunters have ever experienced. We put up thirty-six coveys of quail in one day. It was blazing, intense."

I cringe at the thought of hunting birds. He sips more coffee.

"I still can't believe it. It's like I just got back . . . I can feel the blood trilling in my arms. It isn't the blood. It's me! I can literally feel my old self again."

I'm still trying to feel like *my* old self again. I tell him about an exhibition we're mounting that juxtaposes African American quilts by the women of Gee's Bend, Alabama, with Native American quilts by Lakota Sioux women from the Dakotas. He likes talking about art and asks a few questions, then settles into silence. He is no longer listening. Just watching. Syrupy music plays loudly in the background. The lighting is awful.

"What's going on?" I ask.

His eyes are buggy. He's sitting and staring as if in a trance.

"What's up? Why aren't you responding to anything I say?"

He smiles. "You stupid idiot! Your facial expressions and your body gestures make you interesting, not your practiced presentations."

"Did you call me a *stupid idiot*? I've sort of enjoyed our times together. I kind of like you, Harrison, but . . . "

His eyebrows raise.

"I've reached the end of my rope with your incessant teasing and insults. All the insane resistance. What I really need right now is a *friend*. Not someone who calls me names like a five-year-old and picks me apart like a bug under a microscope."

The music is awful. Harrison's lunacy dials down a few notches.

"I'm the stupid idiot," he says. "My words are like confetti; they don't mean anything. They just spout out of me. I'm not very good at *easy*. So, I try to stir things up. Keep things lively. I really don't think before I speak. You shouldn't take anything I say seriously."

The waiter arrives with our pasta dinners and offers cracked pepper that comes out of a grinder that lights up like a flashlight. I begin to eat in silence.

"I really *am* interested in getting to know you better," he insists. "I just can't stand trivial, trite, social niceties. I want to burrow in, uncover your weaknesses. Discover your blind spots. I'm curious about your flaws, your vulnerabilities. What really makes you tick."

I'm taking in his surprising words as I eat.

"I see you as a million little drawers, like one of those Japanese cabinets—"

"*Tansu?*"

"Yes! I see a *tansu* with a million drawers, and I want to open them all and see what's hidden away inside."

From anyone else, this would hit my ears like tin: completely canned. But Harrison doesn't do "canned." His perspective strikes me as refreshing.

Later that night at home, as I'm about to crawl into bed with Willow, I come across something a cartoonist friend made for me as a surprise back in Atlanta. I had shared my sad little story with him almost as Harrison would, as an amusing badge of honor. I had made light of how, just days after I'd gone under the knife a second time, I'd dealt with the shock of being jilted by mail. Pulling up the sheets, I get comfortable before admiring my commemorative ink drawing: the gesture of a kind young man honoring the depth of what I was juggling when everything fell apart. A skinny young woman with long hair and glasses stands facing the viewer with a puzzled look. In the palm of one hand, she cradles her heart, anatomically rendered. Her exposed belly shows a long vertical stitched scar that disappears beneath low-cut jeans. On the wall beside her, a framed image of a uterus hangs like a family portrait. In the fingers of her other hand, she holds an opened FedEx letter with the words: "Dear Lynne, I've found someone else. Sorry, Mark."

Two weeks later, one hundred friends gathered at a friend's rustic home in Atlanta to say their goodbyes. Sitting alone the next morning on the floor of my empty Atlanta apartment, surrounded by packed boxes, I had called and listened carefully to a wise old therapist.

"Let's be straight about this," he said. "The only thing you should be lamenting is how many men are pig's asses and how rare it is to find a good one. The best hope one has in life is to spend time with those who can help you learn more about how to take better care of yourself. You suffered pain for a few years and had two major surgeries. But you're healing now. You're cured. And you can work anywhere you want. Forget about this jerk. Do whatever you need to do to be happy."

When Harrison calls again five weeks later in January, his voice sounds timid. I suggest he stop by my place after work. Willow barks as he walks up stairs to my front door.

He steps inside. She hasn't seen him since the crash.

"Hey girl, remember me?"

She wags her tail.

"Hi there," I say, smiling. "Make yourself at home."

Harrison bends to pet Willow. He hates visits to town. He's always anxious to return to the ranch. But this afternoon he seems fine talking to Willow and looking at art books on the couch while I make tea. I'm shy about the humbleness of my tiny house. He seems perfectly comfortable, even relaxed.

"Hey, look at this funny portrait someone did of me a few years ago." I hand him the cartoon and explain.

"Oh dear," he says, sighing. "I'm sorry. That must have been so hard."

"It was . . ."

I sit down on the couch.

"Harrison," I begin, pouring tea into two cups. "*Almost everything* about my new life in this place *still* seems exhausting and hard. Then I meet up with you, and more times than not, *you* tire me out. I'm not interested in arguing and defending myself all the time. Can you understand that?"

"I know. It's funny. My wife, Moira, and I never once argued."

"Okay. Right there, that's crazy talk. *No couple* is married for over thirty years, has three children, and never quarrels."

He puts his cup down.

"You know *nothing* about our marriage. There were never cross words between us. What we had was a rare kind of love, something few people will ever know about or experience. We didn't *need* to talk about things. We understood each other."

"I've never been married. I can only imagine," I say, hand to my heart. "It sounds like you were incredibly fortunate. But I'm curious: Why make love sound so rarefied, so exclusive? It's been what—four years now? Beautiful, amazing, true love stories are happening everywhere, all the time. Long- and short-lived, profound, ridiculous, transcendent, impossible. Deferring all hope for happiness only to your past, only to someone who is gone . . . that seems like a tough way to live."

Harrison looks prickly. I pause, but only for a minute.

"And your childhood—it sounds so rough! Some terrible shit happened. I'm amazed at how easily you tell those stories, like it was all a joke. Like it happened to someone else."

I glance at my cartoon. I've done the same thing myself. But nobody tops a few Native American artists I know who are absolute masters with humor. Having permission to laugh often with Native friends on the rez was a tremendous gift.

"Oh, I haven't told you even a fraction of the insanity," Harrison assures me, still prickly.

I reach over to touch his shoulder and he pulls away.

I fill his cup with more tea. Willow has decided to camp out next to him.

"What is it about *you*," he asks, "that has caused you to stay single all these years?"

"Well. A good man *is* hard to find. But also, in my own fucked-up childhood, I got the message loud and clear: You need to be completely independent. Depend on no one. Never fully trust. And, from my mother, especially men. I'm sure that has something to do with it." I take a slow sip of tea. "I prefer spending time alone to being with most people anyway. But at this point, it feels a lot less like a choice. More like my assigned post in life."

"Don't you get lonely? I don't know how you do it. But you've got your work. You see people all day." He strokes Willow. "I'm not normal—out there mourning in nowhere land. For a long time, staying on the periphery of life worked for me. Until now. Now I'm barely hanging on."

"I know that feeling. The grief *will* pass. Have you tried talking with a professional?"

"I handled therapy like I handle everything. I didn't take myself or the process seriously enough to ever give it a real chance." He gazes down at Willow, then in my direction. "You'd make a good therapist. I like talking with you. Thanks for not giving up on me. *Yet*, anyway. You're my only human contact, my only chance to talk. When we're together, I feel better. The rest is misery."

"What about your friend Fran on the museum board?"

"She was my wife's best friend. Not mine."

Aha. I inhale. "Living alone is *not* all that bad, Harrison. It teaches you *a lot*. But yes. Always having to be courageous and strong, pushing through the pain, picking yourself up to carry on, alone, is all I've ever known. It's not for the faint of heart."

"*I am faint of heart*." He sighs deeply. "And *I'm* exhausted now, from all this talking. I've got to get back tonight with feed for the dogs and cattle . . . "

I scoot closer. "Can I give you a hug?"

His upper torso falls, limp and heavy, into mine. We stay in each other's arms for what seems like a long time.

Standing at the door before turning to go, he stares straight into my eyes with a puzzled look.

"You speak so directly. You're speaking with me in ways that my wife and I never spoke in our thirty-two years of marriage."

I lock the door and reach down to pet Willow. We look out the front window together as he walks to his truck. She holds her gaze as he climbs in and drives off into the night. Her presence is so kind and peaceful. In our silence, I imagine what she is feeling—an easy acceptance of his visit tonight. Willow seems to know all she needs to know about Harrison. I aspire to be more like my dog.

GIANT SPRINGS

W inter, 2005. On a sunny cold Friday afternoon in February, after a busy week at work, I leave the museum early to meet up with Harrison. He's been in town running errands and picks me up for dinner. We go for a drive first along the section of river where I walk with Willow while there's still daylight.

Giant Springs State Park is my favorite spot on the southern bank of the Missouri. I've heard Harrison talk about how much he loves spring creeks. This park's main feature is a huge spring whose waters bubble up to form a small gin-clear pool, then flow out some fifty yards into the Missouri. Described in journals by Lewis and Clark during their exploration of the Louisiana Purchase in 1805, Native people utilized these springs in winter. Their constant temperature is fifty-four degrees.

Originating sixty miles away in the Little Belt Mountains, these springs discharge some 150 million gallons of water per day. According to chlorofluorocarbon dating, snowmelt from the Little Belts takes fifty years to travel underground before returning to the surface here. Fluorescent-green algae and specialized plant life thrive in these active waters.

This is Harrison's first visit. He observes huge trout as they weave their way through their well-aerated environment. "Probably introduced here by the adjoining hatchery," he says.

On walks with Willow along the river in late May to early June, I often stop here to watch goose mamas bring their waddling families down the grassy hill to float in these waters. Eventually, their offspring graduate to the adjoining Missouri. Only a few geese are here today.

"I love how the adults form circles around their young when they first move them out into the river," I tell him. "It's a smart way to prevent their little ones from being carried away."

"That's wonderful you and Willow spend time here. The Missouri is a special place."

We wander out onto a promontory to feel the cold power of the river. Harrison tells me how much he enjoys taking his boat out to fish and float the Missouri in the summertime. I lead the way back as we step out to walk along a narrow cement land bridge, stopping for a moment in the middle. On one side is the pool of bubbling spring waters with its neon-green plants and trout. On the other side, its relatively warm waters pass beneath us under the bridge, flowing down and out into the bed of the Missouri River.

When we reach the far end of the bridge, in the cover of overhanging cottonwood trees, Harrison rests his hand on my shoulder. I stop and turn around. Before I know what has happened, he gently leans in and steals a first kiss. I don't pull away. When his warm lips leave mine, I feel stunned and slightly embarrassed.

"You don't need to look so surprised. This is exactly what you had planned when you brought me here," he says, smiling with soft eyes.

"Not really," I confess, rolling my own.

In fact, this kiss was never part of my plan, which was to keep a certain distance with Harrison. I had not consciously allowed myself to anticipate his advances. This place *is*, however, a romantic spot. It *was* a pleasant surprise, the affectionate touch of his lips.

Our breath creates steamy clouds between us, while bubbles percolate and mist rises from the surface of underground springs. Still flushed, I fumble to button up my coat and check my watch.

"Time for our dinner reservation!" I announce, pulling away.

A COMFORTING DISCOMFORT

Great Falls's primary employer is Malmstrom Air Force Base. A large part of their mission is to manage 150 intercontinental ballistic nuclear missiles hidden in underground silos throughout the counties that surround Great Falls. I'm told these missiles would only be launched when there was no other option left—an *end-of-the-world* scenario. Equally distressing are Malmstrom's loud fighter jets, huge military cargo aircraft, convoys of armed fighting vehicles, and helicopter pilots who fly low over town during frequent training exercises.

But what if the enemy is within?

My mother often felt like the enemy when I was a young child. She had learned from men in her childhood to be fearful and secretive. From her mother, she understood she was to be a perfect daughter, then a perfect wife and mother with perfect children. No wonder she was high-strung. Each Sunday before church, she would dress my little sister and me in matching dresses. After hairspraying herself, she would cover our eyes with one hand to spray our matching permanent-curled hairstyles. Our nails were always clean and cut. We always smiled. As the minister's family, we were models of perfection. Back at home, she was a dutiful housewife. I never understood why my mother seemed so angry and resentful. So guarded. The burden of her constant judgment—of herself and us—was stifling. I resented her limitations and tried my best to stay out of her way. My sister became her loyal helper.

My father—a six-foot-three-inch, heavyset man with a rounded button nose and face I've inherited—was my refuge. Our alliance was our escape. In shared company, we did our best to feel comfortable.

Only after his death did I learn he almost certainly had lived as a closeted gay man. He stayed hidden—even from himself—at a time when homosexuality was looked upon by most Americans with disgust, discomfort, or fear. During those same years, I was also unaware that he emotionally punished and blamed my mother for their lack of intimacy. Looking back now, I see them both depressed at home each evening. But I preferred—and needed—to see my father as church members did: a warm, kind, and generous man. A sensitive man who loved to joke around. The parent whose love felt generous and unconditional, for whom I could do no wrong. He was proud of my excellent grades. He featured my artwork in his church's published newsletter. We would cook delicious fancy meals together after he had taken notes watching an episode of Julia Child's *The French Chef*. When he had to be the disciplinarian and spank us as little girls, I was allowed to hold a pillow between my bottom and his hand, while my sister, Laurie, felt the full sting of his slap. I never asked why.

When my mother and father met at Princeton Seminary, they carried their respective secrets into a marriage of convenience. I don't have a single memory of them showing affection for one another. When my father suffered a fatal heart attack at age forty-seven, it was my first experience of death. I felt somehow responsible. At his funeral, several people came up afterward to tell me what I never had allowed myself to absorb. "You were always his favorite. *You were his smile.*"

Cold winds rage outside my window tonight as I lie in bed with Willow, aware of the military base just thirty blocks from here and nuclear missiles only miles away. My mother never remarried. We are cautiously reconnecting. Two determined spirits seeking wholeness, each living alone. My father never felt free to love whomever he wanted—without fear of persecution or judgment. Aspiring to purge every last judgmental bone in my body, I fall off to sleep wondering if I will *ever* find *my* own freedom in love.

SIP 'N DIP

W hen Harrison picks me up from work the following Friday, the energy between us is charged. That first kiss has changed everything. We sit in his truck in the museum parking lot. He looks flashy in a parrot-green, thin-wale corduroy shirt.

He goes first: "What would two people living around here do, I wonder, *if* they were going out on a date?"

"*Hmmm* . . ." I respond, eyes shining with his. "How about the Sip 'n Dip? Let's go there!"

Harrison pulls out like a teenager, with a slight screeching of his truck tires, while asking directions.

Nowhere in the world is quite like Great Falls's Sip 'n Dip Mermaid Bar and Tiki Lounge. Up narrow stairs, one enters a dark lounge with a Polynesian-style thatched rattan ceiling that twinkles with Christmas lights, netted glass fishing globes, and hanging dried blowfish. Servers bring huge bubble-shaped glasses filled with blue and pink signature cocktails. The "Sip 'n Dip fishbowl" features ten shots of different liquors mixed with fruit juices and arrives with multiple straws, paper umbrellas, a slice of fruit, and a maraschino cherry. At the center of this large room, local entertainer Pat Spoonheim sits at an old three-layer electric keyboard, smoking like a fiend, during a short break. Pat's been working here since 1963. At seventy-six years old, this tough old gal with a gravelly voice, big earrings, thin body, and towering hairdo is a living legend. She plays organ music late into the night, four nights a week. Happy to take requests, she uses her husky alto voice and jazzy style to make every cover song—Elvis Presley, Neil Diamond, Frank Sinatra—uniquely her own.

Two busy barmaids are surrounded by kitsch: black velvet paintings, fake plants, hemp fishing nets, and a bamboo ceiling with more
strings of lights. But the most unusual feature is the huge glass window
in front of us. We gaze straight into the bottom of the adjoining Motor
Inn's swimming pool. Like some campy R-rated human aquarium, women in mermaid
costumes gyrate giant fishtails back and forth, talking with one another
above water, their upper bodies out of sight. Every so often, these
ladies in bikini tops hold their breath and dive theatrically under the
surface. Three women submerge tonight. They smile and stare right at
us through glass, their long hair wavy liquid as they tread water with
arms and green fishtails. One mermaid does lazy flips and swivels
around, while her two friends blow bubbles.

One dives to the bottom of the pool to retrieve a rubber lobster,
which she shakes with her teeth like a dog with a bone. Everyone at our
end of the bar cheers as the three wiggle their way back up for air. Two
cowboys in tall hats rise from their seats. Each sticks a five-dollar bill to
the glass window, hoping for more.

"This place is outrageous!" I holler over the din. "I've heard about
it since I first moved here."

"Did you know this was originally an old cattlemen's bar?" Harrison shouts, ordering a second margarita.

I'm still working on my first. "All I've heard is the Daryl Hannah
story. Remember her in the 1984 movie *Splash*?"

He nods.

"I've heard she turned up here three or four years ago." I speak
straight into his ear. "She slipped into one of the fishtail costumes and
dove in to reenact her own role as a mermaid. *GQ Magazine* gave this
place a number one rating two years ago when I arrived: 'the hottest
bar/nightspot *on earth* worth flying to see.'"

Piano Pat has put out her cigarette and is singing a soulful classic I
almost recognize.

"She'll play anything you want," Harrison says, raising his new drink for a toast. "On my fiftieth birthday, she sang a rendition of 'Danny Boy' for me I'll never forget. When she takes her next break, I'll introduce you."

Over at the keyboard, I shake Pat's bony hand as she drinks something with the other. I suggest a song we both like. A few minutes later, Pat is singing us a rousing upbeat keyboard version of Johnny Cash's "Ring of Fire." Every table in the house is packed with raucous locals ordering blue fishbowl drinks. Harrison revels in "the ghoulish avidity of so many women with heavy eyeliner and balding men in big hats."

We stay for dinner and order their famous homemade fish and chips. Before Harrison drops me off and heads back to the ranch, he comes inside for a proper good-night kiss.

Just one. He leaves me, closing the door on his way out for the long drive home.

Other than the Sip 'n Dip, the bar scene in Great Falls is less than alluring. I've never spent time in bars, but a few Fridays later, we give this idea of "conventional dating" one more try. I'm nervous as Harrison pulls up to park in front of an eight-foot-high pink neon sign above the Flamingo Lounge along Great Falls's ugliest main drag of casinos and nightclubs.

"I'll give you fair warning," he says, slipping his arm through mine. "The minute we open the door and walk in, everybody will turn around to check you out because you're wearing a skirt."

"Oh boy," I say. I still like wearing skirts in the West, especially since no one else does. But now I'm regretting my choice for tonight of something short and black.

The Flamingo is a classic Western bar, complete with its own mechanical bull. Sure enough, the gaze of many eyes follows us as

Harrison leads me to a table. We sit down and try to blend in. A beer doesn't help.

"Have you ever seen one of those?" Harrison asks, pointing. "Ready for a try on the old bull?"

I'm not budging. A bar fight between rough-looking guys might break out at any moment.

He leans in. "Just look around you and imagine you're doing research for a movie."

I begin to soften.

After a few beers and some amusing brainstorming about actors to cast for scenes in my movie about an imaginary doomed museum, which Harrison names *The Big Flush*, he grabs my arm and pulls me out onto the empty dance floor where a band called Mad Dawg is playing rockabilly.

Harrison stares at me with a precocious smile as he lifts his left hand, inviting me to rest my fingers in his palm. I place my left hand on his shoulder as he slips his other arm around my waist and pulls me close. His warm palm remains open as it pivots like a rudder, guiding me and steering my body with the music. With great embarrassment, I almost step on his feet twice. He steps on my toes once. Soon we move easily. Everything softens as he holds me.

By the time we emerge into the fresh night air, large early spring snowflakes are falling. Fumbling in the dark under the giant pink neon sign, Harrison grabs my coat and pulls me close. His lips fall into mine, like an eager puppy dog. I offer to make him a strong cup of coffee at my house before his long drive home. Willow is curled up fast asleep on the couch. By the time coffee is brewed, I find Harrison passed out next to her.

SAND MANDALA

It is reported that tens of thousands of people have been traveling east to west for the past two years as part of a nationwide Lewis and Clark bicentennial celebration across North America. We anticipate huge crowds in Great Falls this summer. My curator and I work hard to fund and prepare a major summer exhibition. Lewis and Clark mapped their journey and helped define the American West. Our show explores diverse ways in which others from different cultures have chosen to visually "map" their identities. The show includes an installation by Northern Cheyenne artist Bentley Spang, dreamtime paintings by several early Australian Aboriginal artists, and a sand mandala to be created on the premises by Buddhist monks.

I've arranged to bring four lamas here from India: Lama Rabje (Rapjee), Lama Tashi, Putong Jong (lama-in-training), and Khenpo Tenzin Norgay. These "lamas," I mention to community members who sound puzzled, are not the animals that some local sheepherders use to guard their flocks from coyotes. They are Tibetan monks or spiritual masters of high rank. In the Nyingma tradition, *khenpo* refers to someone who is very accomplished, a senior monk and teacher. The lamas have been preparing for this event back in India with special rituals and prayers. I have been meditating, trying to stay the course. But my nerves are shot; the path has not been easy. There are funding snags and local naysayers along the way. A majority of board members cannot believe anyone in Great Falls will be remotely interested.

Stress levels rise with a string of strange occurrences. A small fire breaks out in the museum one month before the monks are to arrive.

Then 70-mph windstorms tear down several trees and rip out a few windows on museum property. Steady rains have been falling for five weeks straight before my new friends from India land safely in Great Falls. Their arrival seems a minor miracle.

As their sponsor and hostess, I call the private home in Great Falls where they are staying to invite them for breakfast and a tour of the town. I feel protective in this place where outsiders are often shunned. I want to show them my favorite spot on the river, Giant Springs. They will appreciate its beauty, I imagine, and might like to use it for their closing ceremonies. "No individual in the group proceeds with any action until the group as a whole comes to a consensus," their translator explains to me on the phone. "Nothing" is done for long periods of time.

Each morning I wait patiently while the translator checks in with the monks. Finally, she returns with their response: "It has not yet revealed itself." It takes a few days to break me in. Soon I come to rather enjoy this mysterious response.

An hour before our auspicious opening event, we discover (to my great horror) that an alarming amount of water is gushing through a closed window of the museum. Water splashes onto hardwood floors into the gallery where food is about to be served. Piles of wet leaves have created a small dam in our rooftop gutter system. Moments before businesses in town close for the weekend on a rainy Friday evening, we make desperate calls. I plead with a local equipment rental company to loan us a cherry picker so a volunteer who doesn't mind heights (a rock-climbing brother of one of my employees) can hopefully stop the flooding.

During the first forty minutes of our opening reception, museum guests enjoy hors d'oeuvres while gazing out the window at this heroic, drenched young man as he teeters above us trying to clear piles of mushy leaves from a third-story gutter pipe in pouring rain. The monks arrive in brilliant saffron robes, steady and calm.

For the next three days, working in a large gallery space, these lamas create a beautiful sand mandala. With focused attention, they take turns tapping long copper funnels to apply grains of colored sand and create intricate patterns that follow a preordained design, while hundreds of visitors watch. Mandala is a Sanskrit term meaning "container of essence." After many hours of painstaking work, the details of their sand painting make symbolic reference to the whole of the universe in its ever-shifting subtleties and complexities.

Over the course of its creation, I get a few chances to speak with Putong Jong, the youngest lama-in-training. When I bring Willow to work one day, his eyes light up. He follows me outside and asks if he can hold her leash. As we walk, I admire the beautiful orange color of Putong's robe and Willow's golden coat in the light. I tell him how I had stared into my new puppy's brown eyes and had asked her what she wanted to be called. The name Willow popped into my head. I tell him I learned from Native American friends that the bark of a willow tree can be used medicinally, as a natural aspirin or mild painkiller. Putong tells me that in Buddhism, a willow branch is one of the chief attributes of Kuan Yin, the bodhisattva of compassion. When I ask him to tell me more about Kuan Yin, he describes her as "The One Who Listens to the Sounds of the World with Ease."

More than a thousand people attend the final day's ceremony; a sudden clanging of loud urgent bells signals the impermanence of everything. Some onlookers gasp, most watch in silence as the beautiful mandala is ritually destroyed. Exquisite patterns—so carefully planned months in advance, requiring three full days to create—vanish in an instant. Kaleidoscopic flecks of colored sand are ritually turned and swept, then gathered into an urn and taken away.

A thousand bystanders follow us out of the museum and down to the banks of the Missouri. Harrison is tethered to the ranch; I'm sorry he can't be here. I walk behind the lamas in their robes of saffron and crimson as they step out onto the land bridge over Giant Springs. This is where the sacred sand will be ceremonially released. As the urn is tipped, particles of orange, turquoise, yellow, and pink blossom into the river's current. Prismatic rainbows swirl and dance before dispersing. What hours earlier was a discrete work of art is ephemeral and formless, now carried along by the flow of life.

At our farewell dinner, I am seated across from Khenpo Norgay, the highest ranking of the group. This is my last chance to have a personal audience with these practitioners. I thank them again for all they have done and present braids of sweetgrass as tokens of my appreciation. I tell them about its ceremonial significance for Native Americans as a means to purify and summon positive energies, to bring protection and healing. After our food arrives, I address Lama Tashi, whose name is a Tibetan word meaning "good fortune" or "auspiciousness." "May I ask one question of Khenpo?"

He speaks to Khenpo Norgay, who nods. The table becomes quiet.

"I am confused about something. I thought I was going about everything with right mind, with compassion and gratitude. I tried to have no expectations or desires. I felt great humility as I was preparing this event and asked that the experience might benefit all beings." I take a breath and continue. "But many very difficult things have been happening. Several strange and unexpected events have seemed like obstacles. Why is that? What does this mean?"

When Lama Tashi hears about the fire, strong winds, and flooding waters, he laughs knowingly, offers kind eyes. The lamas lean in and speak among themselves. Tashi explains to me that one "nickname" for this *khenpo* has something to do with the Sanskrit words for fire, wind, water, and earth.

"Yes," explains Lama Tashi, with a bemused smile and comforting nod, "many people have these experiences. Wherever he goes, they often encounter these forces. Do not worry. They are all manifestations of purification."

Before they leave, I ask Khenpo Norgay if he might bless my mala.

Taking my string of Tibetan prayer beads in his hands, he sits in the passenger seat of their rental pickup truck and chants prayers for perhaps ten long minutes. I don't understand a word, but the beautiful sounds wash like light over and through my being.

I can't help but smile when, just days after the lamas depart for India, my bookshelves begin rumbling. A 5.6 earthquake has struck in Dillon, Montana, two hundred miles to the south. A final nod from Khenpo Norgay and his fellow monks. Somehow, I believe, we might all still be benefiting from the purity of his kindness and clarity.

NELL

Harrison has a surprise; a tiny eighteen-month-old English setter puppy bounds straight into my lap as I climb into his truck in my skirt and heels. Before I can even touch her, she flies back to Harrison. From this strategic vantage point, chest out, feathered tail wagging, she instantly presents herself as a force to be reckoned with.

She's a gorgeous tricolor, white with black-and-tan ticking, elegant auburn eyebrow markings, and floppy jet-black ears, soft as corn silk. Harrison tells me he's had other bird dogs, long ago, but little Nell is special. He's smitten.

"She's small; I think she was the runt. But when I went to see the litter, I watched her dash to the garden, pick up a big chunk of watermelon in her mouth, and run off with her head high. I knew right then she was the one!"

Nell has just arrived in Montana after nine months in Texas with a professional bird dog trainer. Harrison went to Texas to pick her up with a new friend named John, who lives in Great Falls. John hunts with bird dogs and is a falconer.

"She's so small. Is she really ready to hunt?" I ask.

"This dog is not like any dog you'll ever meet," he says, stroking her. "She was already steady to wing and shot at one year. You're looking at the very best there is. As soon as wild coveys of little cheepers are big enough to fly and crisp fall is in the air, my Nell will get a next chance to express who she really is!"

Nell came from a couple in Virginia who have bred this bloodline of setters for generations. The original sire was named Chief. His daughter, Miss Chief, was tough, like her daughter Nell. The most esteemed females in this line are endearingly described by their breeders as "dykey bitches; powerful, pushy, overbearing, and brilliant." I imagine Nell never really being completely with you, always on to the next thing. She seems a perfect match for Harrison. As Willow is for me.

FLOATING THE MISSOURI

One hot afternoon in June, Harrison calls me at the office.

"How's the Big Flush going? Are your office walls dripping yet? I keep looking for you in the headlines."

"I'd love to talk," I say, "but I'm super busy. I've got two grants to finish, three of my five employees out sick, and a budget due before my board meeting tomorrow. Some of us still have to work for a living, Harrison."

"Sounds to me like you need a break. All you *do* is work. Would you like to join me this weekend for a float down the Missouri River?"

The invitation drops into my body like food to a starving belly.

Rivers and wild places came alive for me as a child only through the powers of my own imagination. I grew up in Kansas City, Missouri. Dad helped set up new churches, and Mom was a social activist in the sixties. They lived admirable lives in service of America's impoverished and disempowered. Dad marched with Martin Luther King Jr. in Selma when I was five years old. Their call to be models of moral and civil righteousness seemed all-consuming. For a time, inner-city neighborhoods were their habitat of choice.

As a young girl, I finally convinced them to take my little sister and me on a camping/canoe trip. I was giddy. Just when we got ourselves on the water, and my father was figuring out how to paddle, a torrential rainstorm cut loose. The canoe tipped over. I watched his wallet, my mother's sunglasses, and any hopes of this ever happening again float down the river.

From his early days in Virginia, Harrison has spent most of his life hunting and fishing in wild places. Nature has provided what he has always sought: a retreat. Wilderness is his familiar place. When spring snows begin to melt, he aches to get back on the water.

My personal fishing guide arrives trailering his own boat. He steps out of the truck wearing his straw cowboy hat, looking irresistible. He smiles at the sight of me leaving the windows cracked for Willow, then watches as I walk toward him across Albertson's parking lot.

"Let's do some shopping." He kisses me on the cheek like a husband.

We are hasty to gather all his favorite traditional river trip man-foods: hot salty fried chicken from the deli, tins of Pringles potato chips, a box of Cheez-Its, a few apples and bananas, a box of ginger cookies, cold drinks, and two bags of ice. Everything gets packed into a cooler on his boat. I fetch Willow while Harrison makes room in the backseat of his truck. Willow squeezes in next to a pile of rods and reels, waders and wading boots, spools of leader, boxes and more boxes of fancy flies.

Willow's breathing becomes labored as soon as we leave town. Her body quivers with post-traumatic fear. It's been like this ever since our rollover. Even sedatives don't help.

"My God, look what you've done to her!" Harrison exclaims.

"I know, it's terrible. I don't know what to do, poor girl."

Scratching as if digging a hole beneath my seat, she seeks cover until the ordeal is over. I reach down to rest my hand on her quivering head.

This two-lane highway that runs south from Great Falls toward Helena follows the path of the Missouri River, first through flat open plains, then rising, as the road winds through a deep mountain canyon where the river flows below. (South of Helena is the town of Three Forks, where the confluence of the Jefferson, Madison, and Gallatin rivers forms the rushing headwaters of the Mighty Mo.) Today we are headed to the tiny town of Craig. Unlike many small towns across Montana, the future of this one seems secure. With one fancy fly shop, one café, and a boat launch, seasonal visitors come from around the world each summer and, for a few lucrative months, transform this sleepy place into fly-fisherman central.

Willow is thrilled to jump out and shake off the ride. I tie her leash to the banister of the fly shop's wooden steps while we go inside to purchase fishing licenses. Harrison hires someone to drive his truck to a favorite takeout spot called Pelican Point so it will be there waiting for us. I walk Willow the short distance to the water. Harrison backs his truck down the ramp and slides his craft into the river. We watch as he tethers it to a large rock along the bank, then drives back up the hill to leave his truck and keys.

Large cottonwood trees line the river's banks. To the left of the launch, a one-lane bridge stretches 150 yards over the water to where large fields of bright yellow flowers are in full bloom. While Willow investigates the grassy bank where we wait, it occurs to me that some forty-five years ago, I was born at the far eastern end of this very river in St. Louis. I came into this world only a few miles from where these same waters of the Missouri join with the Mississippi on their way to the ocean.

Across the water, a bald eagle sits high up in a huge old cottonwood tree on the opposite bank. *Did my mother and father ever walk along the banks of the Missouri, carrying me as a baby?* It's strange to suddenly recognize my own relationship with this river as one of the oldest of my life.

When Harrison returns, he is in waders and boots. This is the first time since meeting him almost a year ago that we have ventured out of town together. *This is so much better than a bar.*

"Ready to go?" He bends down to hold the boat steady as Willow and I climb in. "Put Willow in the space between your back and the cooler so she can feel comfortable. She'll need to stay put."

A breeze moves the boat. Harrison snugs down his cowboy hat before stepping in. He takes the oars.

After four weeks of heavy rains, the water is high, the current dynamic. I sit in the bow. Harrison rows from the center. An osprey cries as it passes overhead. Red-winged blackbirds sing in the reeds. Water laps as oars dip and stroke, dip and stroke. The current carries us, and we give ourselves over to it. As we travel along slowly, things happen. A heron lifts from marsh grasses. A trout rises for a caddis. At some point farther along, the splash of a beaver's tail smacks the water's surface.

Stroke by stroke, Harrison maneuvers the boat. Along one side of a muddy bank, a long dark mink slinks through brush. Nearby against the opposite bank, an enormous beaver lodge of piled logs and ancient branches rises like a pyramid. At a bend in the river, swallows dance over our heads. They make ticking sounds as they dive-bomb, devouring bugs midair. Harrison notes, "You can usually see the beginning of a hatch by the activity of swallows."

Willow rises from a nap in the middle of the boat behind me. She prefers boats to cars. She is quick to understand how to balance her weight. Leaning over one side to stretch her neck, she dips her tongue for a cool drink from the river. Harrison is on constant lookout for rises on the water's surface or fishy-looking pools where brown trout or rainbows might be hiding.

We settle into each other without effort. We notice everything as we travel. Another eagle's nest is just ahead on the right. A kingfisher scoots by our boat overhead, *chit-chit-chit-chit*, parading himself like the feathered royalty he is. Farther along, a blue heron stands still and silent in riparian grasses. We find a spot that looks especially inviting. Harrison pulls the boat onto a patch of land in the middle of the river. Willow jumps out and refreshes herself, standing in cool currents of water before setting off to explore the island.

On land, I pull on waders. Harrison and I step out into the river together. He stands behind me and wraps his arms around me so his capable hands can direct mine. He moves my right arm and hand to lift the rod up and back, up and back.

"There, that one was good. Did you see that? Watch what's happening to your line. You're trying to create a tight loop in midair. No, you're bending your wrist." He wraps his large hand around my wrist and squeezes tight. "Keep your wrist straight and still; don't bend it at all. It becomes an extension of your forearm. Now stretch up through your arm and reach higher. As if you're painting the ceiling of the sky with a long paintbrush."

He steps downriver to fish, leaving me to practice on my own.

Later, I'm glad when he sits down next to me on the bank and leans in for a kiss. But when his hands get a little too busy unhooking straps on my waders, then fumbling awkwardly to unhook my bra in broad daylight, I pull back.

Defiant, he demands, "Are you a lesbian?"

I laugh. "No," I say, thinking of the lovely extended tryst with my long-haired Croatian wheat farmer that recently fizzled out. Harrison has no idea. "Are you gay?" I tease, one eyebrow raised. "You're unusually keen about the aesthetics of things."

He scowls. "You're so reserved, I wonder sometimes."

"I like men," I say. "I like you. But at the moment, I *love* being *here*! Is it always this peaceful?"

Harrison answers with a slow kiss. He stands and extends a hand. With shining blue eyes, he helps lift me to stand in awkward waders and boots.

"Shall we get back on the river?" he says.

Later in the day, we feel hungry enough to bring the boat onto the banks of a larger island and drop anchor. A picnic lunch is Willow's favorite part of any day. She crunches a salty potato chip, devours scraps of chicken, settles in the grass beside us to chew on a chicken leg bone that Harrison offers her. After a swim, I notice Harrison's legs have no hair.

"Here," he says, "feel how silky smooth these calves are. Long ago, I pulled out the last hairs growing on both legs, one by one."

Ouch. I've heard of birds, highly stressed, who pull out their own feathers. I know that a pregnant doe rabbit will pull hair from her own belly and chest to line her nest. I worry for Harrison and the slow drip of secrets he is sharing with me while we nap side by side under an old cottonwood tree, lulled by the sounds of the river.

Driving home at day's end, I look down on the Missouri as we follow its path back down through the canyon. My body is quiet, still feeling what it was to be there.

HARRISON'S RANCH

B y the time I see Harrison in town one week later, he has cycled back to feeling anxious. He seems pleased, however, when I accept an invitation to come visit him. This will be the first time I've been to his ranch since my accident one year ago. He picks me and Willow up early Saturday morning.

Driving the last thirty minutes beyond Geyser on *the* county road, we approach and then trace the outer eastern perimeter of the Highwood Mountains. These mountains are one of many discrete island ranges that define the topography of the open plains east of the Rockies.

"What's that?" I ask, as we pass by a strange but innocuous-looking area, about the size of two swimming pools, and surrounded by high fence with barbed wire, indicating restricted access.

"That, my dear, is a missile site."

Ah, yes. The 150 nuclear missiles hidden underground across these beautiful grasslands. "It's disturbing," I say. "Heavy weapons of war, right in the middle of paradise."

"If it's time for the ultimate rodeo, I guess this is as good a place as any to be. Out here, right next to the big boys."

"True enough," I nod. "If it's the end of the world, better to go fast."

"Just think," he says, "if it weren't for Malmstrom's road crew and their MX missiles out here, I'd be up to my ass in mud every spring."

It must have been Malmstrom who laid that nice fresh gravel that sent me swerving. I'm quiet as we continue our drive along the meandering road.

I observe more about this surrounding landscape now than I did a year ago. As the next ten miles unfold, two distinct volcanic rock formations loom large in the distance. Square Butte, with its long flat top, has buttresses and steep, vertically ascending spires with jagged pinnacles. Its wide girth of craggy rock sits heavy like the bottom of an anvil, commanding and ominous. Approaching this magnificent butte feels like we're approaching a grand fortress, a castle, or a great ship. A half mile farther, the domed shape of Round Butte to its west appears slightly smaller and softer in appearance. These two forms rise side by side, two giant rock monuments surrounded by open space.

Harrison follows my gaze. "Over here east of the Highwoods, those two buttes are visible from nearly one hundred miles in any direction."

As he drives on, I imagine the grandiosity of their ancient volcanic union perhaps belies deeper intimacies, those that have defined life on Earth long before us and will long survive us. Fire and ice, male and female, yin and yang, a complement of opposites. Their location in space feels undeniably powerful. Sacred ground.

We pass a pond where three swans and a group of geese look content. All sorts of waterfowl stop to gather here; Harrison has seen mallards and teal, wigeons, snow geese, and even pelicans, at the same time of year I see them along the river on my walks. Farther down the road, a line of cottonwoods frames another pond.

"Are those nests up there?" I ask.

"Blue herons."

Ten to fifteen great blue herons arrive and settle into the bulky stick nests perched high atop this rookery each spring. As we travel through spacious grasslands, I'm amazed. Signs of human habitation are absent except for fencing and a few farmhouses. These swales and coulees are all verdant habitats rich with wildlife. Last time I was here, I was in a stupor. I realize now that this is one of the most beautiful roads I've ever traveled.

Rounding the next curve, I can't believe my eyes. "Watch out!"

A group of twenty-some cow elk, large and dignified with several calves, appear from nowhere and are crossing the road right in front of us. Harrison slows to a stop. In silence, we watch them pass. The adults jump a fence without effort. Young ones race up and down the fence line anxiously before slipping under to rejoin their herd.

"What elegance," I whisper.

"Nearly two hundred graze in my valley," he says. "It's quite a sight."

Ten minutes later, at the crest of a hill, three pronghorn antelope are grazing on a flat near Arrow Creek. Whitetail and mule deer, elk, and coyote all live in this expansive world, as do over one hundred bird species.

"In the spring," Harrison tells me, "you'll see meadowlarks, swallows, snipe, long-billed curlews, and even the occasional sandhill crane pair. Great horned owls, magpies, golden and bald eagles, sharp-tailed grouse, and Hungarian partridge live here year-round."

"This is a grasslands heaven," I say.

"I imagine all these birds thrive and find shelter here, in large part," he says, "because of their symbiotic relationship with elk and cattle who graze these lands. There's good water here. But without all that stomping around, soil and grass can go stale."

The road continues upward into the mountains. Hillsides at greater altitudes afford groves of aspen and cottonwoods, forests of lodgepole pine and Douglas fir.

"Do you have bears?" I ask.

"Black bears. No grizzlies yet, like your glacier country. But they've been spotted not too far away, traveling across the plains. It's probably a matter of time. We've got mountain goats, mountain lions, even moose in this higher country. Some folks say they've seen wolves."

As we climb and curve along the gravel road, open prairie stretches out behind us as far as the eye can see, incised by the deep purple ravines of the Arrow Creek breaks. Still farther out across the plains, other mountain ranges appear. They float in a sea of prairie grasses: the Judiths, the Snowies, the Moccasins.

"I was with a wilderness group on the other side of these High-woods just last week," I recall aloud. "We trekked all the way up to Baldy. The interior of these mountains—basically your backyard—almost felt like part of Glacier Park. But with one huge difference. All the way along, we had to avoid stepping in cow manure. Instead of finding bear tracks or moose scat on trails, cattle had been hanging out everywhere. It didn't feel like I was moving through *wild* at all."

He flinches. "If not for the cows and cattlemen living here today, what do you think this country would look like? This entire place would be full of A-frame cabins like so much ruined country. Or worse. The fact that ranchers are here is exactly what *keeps* this place beautiful, quiet, and wild."

I must admit this perspective had never occurred to me until that moment. I thought only of Native people who lived here long before any ranchers and so honored this land.

We rumble over a few cattle guards after turning straight into the mountains. Harrison stops the truck several times, getting in and out to open and close gates that keep his cattle in pastures. We continue past the red barn and the kennel, where Nell and two other bird dogs are barking. We turn by a large pond before driving right through a ford of Cottonwood Creek to arrive at his house on a hillock. I let Willow out to reacquaint herself with Harrison's two house dogs. Oscar is Harrison's gray-and-tan Airedale, and his daughter, three-year-old Tula, a poodle–Airedale mix with kinky curly black hair gone wild. We head to the kitchen for tea. Walking upstairs from the mudroom, I remember that Harrison's house is no ordinary house.

"How, when, did this all happen?" I ask. While he makes tea, I sit at the same kitchen table surrounded by windows where, one year ago, he fed me elk spaghetti and took care of me. "It's so beautifully de-signed. Everything seems brand new."

"After ten years of living in the old bunkhouse down by the barn, Moira wanted a real home. I saw something I liked on the front of a magazine—simple lines, made of stone, wood, and glass. She encouraged me to call up the architect. We wanted something similar to Bhutanese houses built high in the mountains that we had seen while visiting there. Something that would blend easily with its surroundings in nature, blurring the lines between outside and in."

He sighs, his jaw tightens. "Her dream house was little more than finished sketches on paper when her leukemia was diagnosed. She died sixty days later. Fifty-three years old."

One and a half years after she was laid to rest on the east-facing slope of the ranch, right above the grave of J. Y. Warren's four-year-old son, Coe, Harrison was still numb. His three sons, having just lost their mother, helped him decorate this new house, formally and elegantly, with intricately carved furniture and large painted ceramic pieces from China, passed down through their mother's family. Photos of Moira— a kind-looking woman with short dark hair in a black helmet, riding jacket, and boots on horseback—and of their three boys when they were young hang over Harrison's desk along a corridor that serves as his office, outside his bedroom. I purse my lips. She is everywhere.

We move through other rooms and corridors. I admire hand-painted Thai figurative works on paper, traditional Indonesian wayang kulit shadow puppets, a large exquisitely detailed painted narrative screen, two old elephant bells, and other rare objects that came from travels when young Harrison lived with his family in Thailand. A small green Inuit stone sculpture of a mermaid sits on the windowsill over his kitchen sink. Harrison tells me it came from his mother, who collected Inuit art.

Time to lace up our hiking boots, call the dogs, and head out before the day slips by. But horses grazing high in various pastures on both sides of the valley catch my attention. Before setting off on foot, we drive up to meet a few. A brown gelding named T gracefully approaches.

He is regal and elegant, a gentleman. Bows his head as he arrives. T is Harrison's horse; they have a connection. When T eventually decides to leave at a fast gallop, his power is striking. He is more horse than I could ever handle. Harrison must be a good rider. A multicolored gelding named Spoon is a bit standoffish, but Harrison eventually gets him to let us come closer. This is the same horse I saw in a photo hanging at one end of Harrison's desk, his youngest son with his first horse, a paint he named Teaspoon. Down by the dog kennel, we spend time with a sweet brown gelding named Andre, who walks right up to us and lifts his head whenever we stop stroking him, asking for more.

Harrison tells me a little about each of these horses and points to an older black mare named Brise, Andre's mother. She's the oldest horse on the ranch. Another senior mare, named Rocky, has trouble walking with arthritic knees. Harrison is quiet and reserved around these horses. He takes me inside a charming cabin upstream from his house along Cottonwood Creek. Referred to as the Red Nose, rumor has it the Western painter Charlie Russell liked to come into this valley (like so many other valleys in Montana) to drink with friends.

After lunch back at the house, we head out on foot into the mountains for a three-hour hike with dogs. When Harrison stops to work a lock and open a gate, he mentions the combination. It is Moira's birthdate. We follow an old irrigation ditch that wigs and wags through one pasture after the next, up and down rolling foothills that extend from the top of this valley, all the way to the bottom, a drop in altitude of some fifteen hundred feet.

Along one extended stretch of channeling, we follow water as it travels *up a hill.* "This is brilliant!" I say. "How did J.Y. and Max figure all this out?"

"Little by little, I suppose. Noticing where water gathered, carving trenches to direct its flow. All the water that feeds into our buildings and water tanks for livestock is gravity-fed."

We stand together at a fence line with three dogs, high on the crest of the hill, the summit point, where this water—pushed to climb uphill by the force of so much charging down the mountains behind it—finally falls back into its own gravitational flow.

Afternoon light begins to change. As we turn to travel down the hill, the dogs pick up energy, running and playing all the way back to the house.

"I suppose Willow and I should be getting home," I say. "Thanks so much for bringing me out. Maybe we can have dinner in town before you head back?" A horseshoe of mountains wraps around us as we stand in tall dry grass near his truck. I cup my hands to inhale deeply. "I love the smell of horses, don't you?"

He nods with a distant gaze. "Dinner in town sounds nice."

I settle Willow into the back of the truck before Harrison pulls out and we head down the long gravel road that both links and separates us—back toward Geyser, and the highway to Great Falls. I reach around to comfort my dog, still thinking about water. Churning down through mountains. Gurgling over rocks. Whirling past old beaver dams. Rushing into creek bottoms. Digging pools for trout. Irrigating and nourishing everything along its path.

Water flowing *uphill*.

Some part of me doesn't want to leave Harrison tonight. I feel the same desire in him. Without speaking of it over dinner, we agree: respecting still-tender memories takes precedence.

II.

FIRE

(2005–2007)

THIS LAND DEEP WITHIN

"Phyllis is back in Montana," says Harrison on the other end of the phone. "She invited us to stop by for a visit tomorrow. Want to go?"

"Yes!" I say without missing a beat.

He proposes a road trip to her Lonetree Ranch on the other side of the buttes where Phyllis spends each summer. She lives in Arizona the rest of the year. This is the invitation I've been anticipating for months.

Early the next morning, Harrison picks me and Willow up, and we drive the familiar forty-minute trip from Great Falls to the small river town of Fort Benton. We've shared a few lovely dinners at its 1882 Grand Union Hotel overlooking the Missouri. As we travel on, I ask Harrison to tell me more about the person I'm about to meet.

"Phyllis and her three sisters are granddaughters of the Fontana family, who homesteaded and have owned property near my ranch for three generations. Phyllis's Italian mother, Mary Fontana, first arrived at Lonetree with *her* mother and sister by stagecoach in 1908, when Mary was five years old. And Mary is still alive."

We wind our way through cattle country and rolling fields of wheat and barley with the Highwoods, Square, and Round Buttes in the distance. After another half hour, we approach the small town of Geraldine. Just before the next small town of Square Butte (located at the foot of its namesake), Harrison turns right across railroad tracks onto a deeply grooved gumbo path that barely seems a road at all. Square Butte towers to our left. The Highwood Mountains stretch out to the west.

As we bump along on this red dirt path, Willow tries desperately to jam under the back seat. We enter a wide-open valley, driving along a channel of low flat land with cliffs rising on either side, part of what is known as the Shonkin Sag. "The Sag" was once a huge river channel, one of the most famous prehistoric glacial meltwater channels in the world. This same ancient pathway was formed by an earlier version of what we call, in these modern centuries, the Missouri River.

Harrison points to crop fields to our left along this flat bottom. "That's where Phyllis's father used to land his small planes when she and her sisters were growing up."

"Did you ever meet him?" I ask, one hand on Willow's trembling body behind my seat.

"I never met him. But Phyllis's mother is really something. I once saw Mary walk across an airport, her step was so lively and animated. She caught my eye even at ninety-something! A real looker and sharp as a whip. Before my time, she used to come up to the valley when it belonged to J.Y. She'd check on him and clean his cabin after his wife left him. One day, after my wife had died, I came out to Lonetree to visit, and Mary was there. She said, 'Hi, Harrison. Are you batching it up there in the Red Nose? Here, take an extra cookie.'"

He laughs. "I'm sure Mary's offer was a symbolic gesture. Taking care of another man in the same place, same situation, squirreled away in his own insanity. Look over here," he says, pointing toward dramatic vertical cliffs to our right. "That's all shonkinite granite up there. This used to be a famous quarry."

Just as volcanic activity created Square and Round Buttes eons ago, it also laid down a substantial granite deposit here known as the Shonkin Sag laccolith. I recognize this same gray stone in high ridges on Harrison's ranch. As we approach the site of the old quarry at the foot of the cliffs, we pass by a small building with clothes hanging out on a line. The shed is abandoned, but the outsides of its windows have been brightened with paint. Upon closer inspection, I see a full-size painted cardboard cutout of a woman's body, made to look as if someone were standing inside the shed, gazing out its window. What appeared to be a pair of red long johns, a blue dress, a striped shirt, pink petticoat, and a pair of socks hanging out to dry in the wind are actually pieces of canvas that have been cut, painted with bright colors, and pinned to a clothesline to *look* like real articles of clothing.

Just past this old quarry shed, we turn right and head straight toward the towering cliffs. A metal cutout sign, blowing in the wind over a cattle guard, marks the entrance—LONETREE FOUR SISTERS RANCH 1890. There is a compound ahead: a large painted tepee, the remains of two wooden stagecoaches, and several handsome old buildings scattered among ancient cottonwood trees, all situated in a narrow vertical canyon that cuts down through the cliffs. This canyon is the pathway where the stagecoach once made regular stops.

"There she is," Harrison announces with a smile.

A stylish five-foot-tall woman wearing a hat, a hip-length leather vest, and lots of Southwestern jewelry rises from a chair on an open house porch. A calico cat stretches in the sun as she waves to greet us. Even from a distance, Phyllis sparkles. On her own terms, she is fully marvelous. Pixie-cut gray hair and ruby-red lipstick look smart under a fancy Western hat adorned with two pheasant feathers. As she steps down the porch stairs and onto the grass, her hat feathers dance. She's luminous, like lemon zest. Despite her small stature, everything about her seems larger than life. Phyllis approaches us with smiling green eyes and gives me a hug.

"Lynne, I've heard so many wonderful things about you! It's so nice to finally meet you. I want to hear all about your work at the museum."

My spirit lifts instantly in her presence. She speaks in caroling notes, nimble and fresh, like a cheery robin. Even before that first hug, strong feelings of some dearness and devotion seemed to flow from her to me.

"And handsome Harrison! How are you?"

Harrison leans down to give her a kiss on the cheek. She looks pleased.

"Now who is this?" she asks, patting Willow's head before waving us on. "Come on in! Can I pour you both a glass of homemade chokecherry wine?"

As we follow her up the steps of her sitting porch, I stop to examine a large figure made with old tree branches to one side of the stairs. The figure wears a top hat made of black duct tape and wood. Its eye sockets are a cow's partial skull, its mouth has an extended wooden tongue painted red, and its gesticulating arms have white gloves for hands. With a black bowtie and a red sash around its waist, its long legs look as if this four-foot-high stick man is dancing up a storm. Willow takes a sniff, then trots off. A hand-painted sign next to the figure reads: IT DON'T MEAN A THING IF YOU AIN'T GOT THAT SWING.

There is a splendid feeling of celebration as I step inside "the Meriwether" for a tour. (Phyllis likes naming things. This building is named after Captain Meriwether of the Lewis and Clark expedition.) What was once the old family granary has been transformed into an eye-dazzling ranch cabin. "You can still see grains of wheat in between these logs," Harrison notices. Every wall of the high-ceiling interior of this grand space is covered with Phyllis's bright paintings of magpies, big yellow sunflowers, Native Americans, and her family members. Opera music is playing from painted speakers. A red, black, and white Navajo blanket and a bear hide hang beside her paintings on one wall. I see animal skulls Phyllis has painted and a stuffed chicken. Funky wood tables and a desk have been fashioned of logs, twigs, leather, and paint. Phyllis shows us one "embellished" table that has been in the family since her childhood.

"My sisters and I made all these pieces. They look exactly like the Western style of Thomas Molesworth, the famous American furniture designer, don't you think?"

At one end of this large living space is a grand stonework fireplace built by Phyllis and her son. "We picked up each of these stones on our walks together here over the years." The metal frame around a large television screen is painted with a pattern of orange and brown crosses. Lampshades are decorated with hand-painted designs. Even the rugs beneath our feet are pieces of canvas, painted to *look* like Navajo weavings and taped down onto the old wide-plank wooden floors of the granary.

In a whimsical kitchen at the other end of this room, high above on a central wall, hangs a stunning six-foot-high painting of oranges and pinks, purples and blues. The image is one of many Phyllis tells me she has "borrowed" from favorite artists as inspiration for her own works. This one is a boldly embellished scene from a Maynard Dixon painting: a cowboy and horses spill down a hillside into the foreground. In the distant background she's added her beloved Square Butte. Her kitchen refrigerator is covered with painted geometric designs.

Wandering into back rooms, we come upon a washer and dryer, several dressers, even a claw-foot bathtub, all painted with juicy colors and bold patterns. A collection of adorned hats hang on deer antlers against a purple wall.

"I decorated all these myself. You should do this with your hats!" she cheers.

One made of straw, like the straw hat I wear today, has a band of old snakeskin and bear claws. Another, a brown felt hat, has a band of white porcupine quills woven right into the felt, and another jazzy straw one is decorated with a ring of fringed leather and silver conchos.

The three of us return to the kitchen, where Phyllis takes fresh bread, baked in a cast-iron pan, out of the oven. "Isn't this fun, and it's so easy! You don't have to knead it at all, and you can use the same dough to make your own pizza crust. I'll send you home with a copy of the recipe if you like," she offers.

By the time we settle ourselves outside on her sitting porch, with warm bread and homemade chokecherry wine, I feel dizzy with joy. Harrison looks happy.

Everything around us is decorated with more bright colors. There are painted bison skulls. Tree-trunk stools provide extra seating and tables. A large, old, painted metal funnel hangs from the edge of the porch ceiling as a flowerpot, as do several homemade bird feeders. Adjusting my straw hat to block the sun, I tell Phyllis I'm still thinking about all those wonderful hats of hers.

"Have you ever noticed how wearing a hat makes everything better? I'll tell you a little secret," she says. Placing her wineglass on a tree stump, she leans in my direction. "For any special occasion or travel off the ranch, be sure and add one or two of the longest pheasant tail feathers you can find. If they're placed at just the right angle, you can have loads of fun. Just last week I was in a crowded elevator, and my feathers were accidentally tickling the ear of the man standing behind me. I didn't notice, and I suppose, *maybe*, he was a *little* irritated at first. But when everyone in the elevator suddenly burst out laughing, he couldn't keep a straight face."

She winks.

Unconcerned birds visit feeders while the three of us visit on the porch. I put Willow on a leash when Phyllis's friend Bambi and a few other deer approach an old wooden trough where she puts corn out for them. Each one has a name, she tells us. All of nature seems to know Phyllis as a friend.

"Do you need a refill on wine before we continue our tour?" she asks, standing up to stretch in the afternoon light. "That first stone building up the hill is Lonetree. That's where I grew up. Come on, I'll show you!"

As we stroll up the canyon along a path following Phyllis, I hook my arm in Harrison's and give him a strong squeeze. He looks at me and whispers, "I *knew* you'd love this."

The Lonetree stone house, built in 1890 to serve as a stagecoach stop and post office, stands in the shade of several beautiful old cottonwoods. Towering shonkinite granite cliffs are its dramatic backdrop. A large hollowed-out granite trough serves as a catchment for fresh spring water. Nearby is an outdoor grill made of more stonework. A National Register of Historic Places sign hangs over the front porch. This two-story building was the inn where folks stayed when they arrived by coach. Many years later, Phyllis's family turned the house into a living museum.

In the parlor, a large stone fireplace has a half wagon wheel on its mantel. Period wallpaper and original furniture decorate the room. More fresh spring water pours out of the ground and through a pipe right into a copper sink in the kitchen, just as it has for generations. A few of Phyllis's paintings depict childhood memories. One pictures Phyllis and her two sisters collecting meadow mushrooms just up the hill from here with their grandmother in 1939. Upstairs, where folks riding the stagecoach could stay overnight, her father's old study has copies of early newspapers laid out on a heavy oak rolltop desk that came from the office at the old quarry. Another one of the upstairs bedrooms contains Phyllis's grandmother's beaded gown and button-up boots.

We stop to look at framed photographs on the walls—her mother and father, Mary and John, when they were newly married; Phyllis and her sisters when they were gorgeous little girls. I imagine them running around this house, hair flying and feet dancing. At the bottom of the stairs in the front foyer, we stop in front of a large nineteenth-century portrait of a woman with an enigmatic smile and arresting eyes.

"Who is this?" I ask.

"That's my great-grandmother, Sarah Cooper DeLoss. I think she was born in 1842 or '43. She was a fascinating woman—worked with Louis Pasteur and then became a very famous doctor in her own right. She's been written up in books. She was quite well known for curing people with tuberculosis and rabies in the early days."

We step outside and venture farther up the steep road where, so many years ago, the stagecoach from Fort Benton would sometimes lock its wheels to prevent a runaway when it slid down along a wet canyon to its Lonetree stop. While Phyllis and Harrison walk and talk, I stop to stand quietly with Willow in the sunlight. One of many hand-painted signs along this canyon passage commands my attention. It reads: THIS LAND IS DEEP WITHIN ME. I CAN FEEL IT IN MY BONES. IT IS MY ROOTS AND MY SOUL. The words vibrate in my throat as I read them out loud. Back on the Meriwether's sitting porch, the three of us gaze off toward Square Butte and Geraldine, enjoying the peacefulness. I can't stop drinking in the details of everything she has created.

"Phyllis, you remind me of the visionary self-taught artists I worked with back East—ingenious recyclers who love turning the ordinary into something extraordinary. I visited huge outdoor environments where *thousands* of found objects were transformed into magical works of art." I glance again at her dancing stick figure beside the porch stairs. "One artist, Bessie Harvey, would see souls trapped in twisted tree branches and roots and create figures to liberate them."

"Like Michelangelo, seeing a form inside a block of marble, carving until he set it free."

"Exactly," I say with a laugh.

"My goodness! What fun you had. They sound like such interesting people."

"Shining souls, full of grit and humor. *Anything* could be reimagined. They were like you."

"Well, I've taken a few art classes . . . but I kind of do my own thing, don't I? I suppose I *might* be a visionary artist. You never know!" She laughs at herself. Willow drinks from a bowl. "My sisters and I have loved this part of Montana our entire lives. We were always making things and having adventures." She looks at Harrison. "We all have such fond memories of hopping on our horses to fish on your Cottonwood Creek when we were young. We used to visit old J.Y. there a lot after his wife left with his children."

Harrison pipes up, "I bet you young things sure brightened his days when you came to visit."

"Oh, we had a lot of fun with him! We'd catch trout, cook it up on a grill outside, and have a picnic. And he always loved Mother's cookies."

Harrison flashes a knowing glance my way from across the porch.

"We don't want to take up your whole day, Phyllis," he says, motioning to me that we should go.

A pang, a sudden sadness surprises me.

"I'm so glad you could come. Here, before you go . . ." Phyllis stands up and motions for me to follow. She leads me through a screen door into a screened-in sleeping porch that runs along the other end of the granary, complete with six beds and more art.

"This is the best sleeping porch I've ever seen, Phyllis. It's all *so* perfect."

"It is wonderful, isn't it? This is where I like to fall asleep under the stars, after evenings of homemade wine and some dancing."

Phyllis and I give each other a big hug at Harrison's truck. Before I climb in, we hold hands and say we can't wait to see each other again. Willow jumps into the back seat. I promise Phyllis I'll call next month before she leaves to fly back home to Arizona.

Closing the truck door, I wave, then turn toward Harrison. "You were right. I adore her."

"I admire how Phyllis enjoys life," he says, rumbling over the cattle guard. "And she works at it."

He may understand more than I realized. Our time with Phyllis felt like coming home.

I gather my courage. "What is it, exactly, that you admire about *me*, if anything?"

Harrison pauses as we weave our way along the bumpy road.

"Your curiosity," he finally answers. "And your tenacity. You've survived repeated upsets in your life. I can see that you're resourceful. Diligent, like a beaver. You know how to keep starting over again."

"Thank you for that," I say, aware of his own struggle to reset his life.

"I can see you're also a woman like Phyllis. You know how to be excited and happy about things in life. I need to be around that."

On the highway to Great Falls, I comfort Willow in the back. The colors and textures of Lonetree are still dancing in my head. A strong longing not to leave behind all the passion that Phyllis lives, not to return to the cold loneliness of my own house, lingers. What *is* home for me now? A six-hundred-square-foot house in Great Falls, painted white with black trim, and a tiny backyard with a chain-link fence? My very first "starter" house, bought when I was forty-two—so small that I've kept everything packed in the basement—still doesn't feel like a home. Except for bare essentials—plates and silverware, pots and pans, a bed and a couch, sheets and blankets—my house after two years remains empty.

Harrison pulls up to the curb. I give him a big hug as we say good night.

"I'm glad you finally got to meet Phyllis," he says with a smile.

Later, climbing into bed, I set my teacup down next to a braid of sweetgrass on the night table. I think about a moment with Harrison on our drive home from Phyllis's, appreciating the beauty of mare's tail clouds in a salmon and lavender sky. I recall the vibrant purples and reds, oranges and yellows of Phyllis's spirited world. The saffron orange and crimson robes of the monks during their healing ceremony. The rainbow kaleidoscope of sand dancing in the river.

OPEN FIRE

F all, 2005. A lot of killing happens here. When late summer turns to fall, masses of men (a few women and young teens) turn into armed predators. The talk is about locations of gophers, coyotes, game birds, mountain goats, deer, elk, lions; how to measure a deer for its value (non-typical attributes, inches of antlers and points), how much meat a cow elk might yield. Camo and guns are everywhere. I find this jarring, unsettling. My primary experience of Montana's wilderness prior to moving here was vast peaceful empty plains and national parks. Hunting is unfamiliar territory.

At Harrison's suggestion, I wear orange when walking along the river with Willow after work. I've bought an orange jacket for Willow too. Hunters arrive now to shoot the very ducks and geese I have come to care for. I shudder when gunshot rings out. It occurs to me that Harrison, my first-ever hunter friend, might help me address this discomfort. One evening, he reads aloud an apt E. B. White quote to consider.

"It is plain that I now reside in a friendly community of killers, and that until I open fire myself, they cannot call me brother." [1]

He elaborates on this male perspective over a dinner of elk spaghetti and red wine at his house. Willow lies at my feet.

"It might help if you think of hunting as one of the last and only opportunities for an ordinary person to feel connected to the land and feel no boundaries. For someone like my contractor, Steve Kirschner, taking his boys hunting is like taking them to church. Most people don't know anything about their environment—its joys, complexities, subtleties, magic. Hunting affords feelings of connection."

I come at it from a different angle. A lifelong fascination with Indigenous cultures is rooted in my own desire to feel more connected. As a curious young girl, I discovered stories about people who lived as an integral part of nature. Everything had a spirit, a name, a tradition of personality, and an unfolding drama. At the center of all stories were animals. For as long as I can remember, I'd secretly imagined myself much more at home in a world of animistic perspectives than with what conventional adult behavior told me to trust, admire, or value.

"How can you live life and *not* know these experiences?" Harrison muses. "Is a house cat and a bird feeder *it*? What about the experience of a mountain lion swishing its tail sideways at you or the prehistoric sounds of a sandhill crane flying overhead?"

Harrison's entire life has been centered in these experiences, where the threads of hunting and spirit have always been interwoven, where hunting's convergence between life and death is implicit. As he talks, I see figures in cave paintings that conjure the magic of the hunt. I recall stories about early forest shamans and ancient hunting societies, stories centered on nature's constant cycles of transformation.

"I still have a hard time with the fact that it is premeditated killing."

He gobbles up his spaghetti and continues.

"We're not angels ascending to some higher state. We're animals. Predators." He pauses. "If you really want to understand, you should come bird hunting with me some time."

When weekends arrive, I happily take leave of my tiny house in town. Sometimes I travel to Harrison's ranch. When he invites me to visit this

Friday after work, I'm surprised to meet his oldest son and daughter-in-law. Burr looks very much like a younger version of Harrison. But his brown eyes are those of a gentle soul. Even so, he is reserved at this surprise meeting, as am I. We sit down somewhat awkwardly on the kitchen couch, me on one side of Harrison, Burr on the other. His wife, Robin, holds onto the small hands of their baby girl who is learning how to walk.

This young couple is visiting from Maine with their first child, Phebe. Harrison's first grandchild. I'm told this wee girl with a blond bob and bangs was born last year on March fourth. Harrison was in Maine at the time. I study Phebe carefully as she takes practice steps. Harrison remarks on the beautiful shape of her ears. Her piercing blue eyes remind me of photographs I've seen of Harrison's mother, Nancy. Her grandfather seated next to me has the same blue eyes.

Harrison is clearly proud. Happy for his son. Yet he, too, seems strangely reserved. Aloof with me. Quietly admiring, yet somehow uncomfortable in the presence of this beautiful small soul. After an early dinner, Phebe's parents head upstairs to put her to bed. Harrison walks me downstairs to my car with Willow.

"Why didn't you tell me you had family visiting?" I ask.

"I didn't see the point. I suppose it seemed easier to just let it happen." He leans in, gives me a kiss. "I'll call you later. Drive safely."

My phone rings ten minutes after I get home.

"I like Burr," I tell Harrison. "He has a lovely way about him. But it felt like everyone was so uncomfortable."

"My boys are still tender about their mother. Our world revolved around her," he says, pausing. "I suppose it feels disloyal to bring another woman into a dead woman's life. You can understand that."

"I can understand your son's discomfort. But you? Look, you should take as long as you need to heal, Harrison, but . . . " I cut myself off. "It's hard when you spring a surprise on everyone. I enter feeling like an outsider, and then *you* act weird and distant."

"I wanted to be with you. I'm really glad you came. I miss you already," he says.

"And you were so hands-off with your new granddaughter. Just watching her from a distance. Little Phebe is spectacular! I wanted to pick her up and hold her so badly. But I was definitely the unwelcome stranger in the room."

"I always feel like the stranger in the room," he says. "Phebe is *something*, isn't she? I had boys. I don't know a thing about little girls."

On subsequent weekends, when Harrison and I are alone again, we spend all our time outside. These luscious days of fall have always been my favorite time of year. Here, high winds often rip leaves from trees as soon as they turn colorful. We visit with Harrison's horses, whom I am coming to know. Powerful T, sweet Andre, dear arthritic Rocky, mysterious black Brise. A darling brown three-year-old mare with a white blaze named Burna. And we begin to spend more time with his English setters.

September through December is upland bird-hunting season: the time when Harrison takes these hunting dogs out through his valley in search of Hungarian partridge, sharp-tailed grouse, and the occasional pheasant. I am intrigued by a second invitation to join him. I have no idea what bird hunting is. I don't like the idea of killing anything. But I'm glad for an opportunity to know more about his three young bird dogs: Nell, Drum, and Dollar.

When I arrive at the ranch this morning, Harrison's truck is parked across from the barn.

"Well, what do you think?" he asks. He's standing in front of a beautiful new kennel for his setters. "The builders just finished every-thing yesterday. Like it?"

Three large outdoor spaces allow his dogs to enjoy fresh air, feel the sun's warmth, and keep an eye out for pheasants. Two indoor spaces, one for the girl and one for the boys, will keep them warm and comfortable all winter. There is also a sink, plenty of cabinets, a place to sit down, and enough space to park his dog trailer inside.

"Wonderful! *Much* better accommodations than before."

"Yes. My contractor said my dogs now have a better place to live than some people he knows."

He's right. Harrison must have more wealth than I know. But what if true abundance is a state of mind? During the happiest years of my life, I was working four jobs to afford living in New York City while putting myself through five years of full-time graduate school. Always working hard and just getting by made me the person I am today. I share Harrison's desire to care well for the animals he loves.

Inside the kennel, I say hello to Drummy, a tricolor male like Nell, but larger. I'm told he is very much a "gentleman's" hunter in that he moves through the country at a slow and even pace, checking in often and staying close to Harrison. Petite Nell, of course, is at the other end of the spectrum, always determined to be far ahead. The two of them are barking and wagging their tails, clamoring for atten-tion, while Harrison sits to hold Dollar's frozen all-white body close to him between his legs, hugging his chest.

I sit down next to them. "Tell me about this guy. How long has he been here?"

"Dollar arrived five months ago. He was a one-and-a-half-year-old when I got him." He strokes Dollar's chest as he talks, hugging and patting him. No response from Dollar. "I had to physically pull him out of the travel kennel. He stood there without moving, frozen in place, eyes to the ground. Immediately, I knew this puppy was not the dog I had chosen."

"What do you mean?"

"Good boy, Dollar," Harrison says, still rubbing him. I do, too, as I listen. Dollar's eyes remain vacant.

"I'd speak to him and stroke him, like this, but his body stayed rigid, tail still and low. No response. When I pulled out a collar, he dashed to hide under my truck. When a collar beeped, Dollar shot straight to me, body quivering, pressed hard against my legs."

"What happened to him? Why didn't you get the right dog or send him back when you realized?"

"I had carefully selected my third English setter puppy from a highly recommended breeder/trainer who turned out to be rotten. I paid the man to ship the puppy after he was trained."

Harrison pulls Dollar up and cradles him in his lap between us. The other two setters are quiet. We both keep hands on Dollar's body as Harrison tells the story.

He found out too late that this unscrupulous breeder/trainer was teaching classes in which he repeatedly zapped the hell out of a "school dog" to demonstrate his skills at dominance with the use of electric collars. That dog was Dollar. The animal abuser then swapped out Dollar's litter mate—the new hunting dog Harrison had paid for—and sent Harrison his traumatized brother, Dollar, instead. When Dollar arrived, he was severely shell-shocked—a puppy who only knew the fear and terror of being punished. Had Dollar not come to Harrison, he might well be dead.

"Wait a minute. You're telling me that someone you paid—a 'professional trainer'—repeatedly fried a young puppy to boost his own ego? Then, he pulls a sneaky switcheroo on you? Did you report this monster?" I lean in and hug Dollar. A far-off stare is all he can manage.

"I got boondoggled. But I got the genetics I wanted. It will be okay."

I squat next to Harrison's legs and stroke Dollar's soft white belly. He is still catatonic.

"My first goal is to have him lift his head to meet my eyes."

Harrison places his hand under Dollar's chin and gently lifts his head, encouraging eye contact as he talks. Gestures like this remind me of why I return here, to Harrison, again and again.

"You can help me. We're just going to keep showing him love, no matter what, for a long while. I won't ask anything of him. Just tell him how great he is and encourage him to meet my eyes. We'll take him along with us today. But I want to keep him on a leash or in the truck until he can meet my eyes."

"How long do you think that will take?" I ask.

"I have no idea. We just need to give him nothing but love, no pressure, for as long as it takes for him to trust us. Then he can hunt."

I like the idea of showering Dollar with love. I take him in my lap and stay at it, while Harrison starts gathering things for our hunt.

"The most important thing is that he's safe now."

Once GPS collars are placed around Nell and Drum's necks, Harrison dons an orange hunter's cap and vest, throws a couple bottles of water in the back pocket, and a whistle and the GPS tracker around his neck, ready to head out. We crack the truck windows for Dollar. Bird hunting consists of spending countless hours trekking through open spaces, quiet together, following his two hunting dogs with Willow on a leash.

Occasionally, Harrison loads his shotgun and shoots a bird to reward a "point." He is careful to have me stand back with Willow. I hold her with a leash in case the sound of a shotgun seems scary, but she does fine. A bird falls from the sky as its relatives fly away. I'm shocked. Harrison shows me the dead body before placing it in his vest pocket, as if it is something to be admired. The sharp-tailed grouse is indeed beautiful, feathers soft and mottled, body limp, still warm. I am touched by its beauty. But we must walk on; our canine kestrel, Nell, has already swooped out to hunt the next covey. I listen to the sound of tall grasses moving beneath my feet, brushing against my ankles and calves. I listen to the beating of my own heart, as I struggle to keep up with someone thirteen years my senior. He has the powerful stride of someone who has walked this way his entire life.

"Look at that cast—isn't it beautiful? Most people would be uncomfortable with a dog running that far out, but it's really okay," Harrison assures me as he observes Nell, ears flapping in the wind as she flies. "And so wonderful to watch them moving in this country, so comfortable when they're following the coordinates they're getting from the wind."

Eventually, when the dogs are beset by mystery—half pointing, checking this way and that, tails half-wagging, heads raised searching the wind for possible scent—I can almost see what they see: the hen grouse that has disappeared, the old cock pheasant outwitting them. We name these places in Harrison's valley. "*The place where the rooster befuddles.*" Gary Snyder had it right. The significance of place names is intimacy.

From time to time, Harrison reminds me of his "disdain for anyone who heads out just to take a walk." I am getting used to his contrarian perspective. Even when surrounded by breathtaking beauty, Harrison will think and speak of what he does not like.

"I *love* following Willow on hikes along a river's edge trail," I say.

Harrison argues. "I'm sorry . . . only hunting can draw one into an ancient walkabout of mysterious experiences."

We find peace in these autumn weekends, comfortably strolling arm in arm as we feel the textures of the land beneath our feet. I'm surprised today when I reach down to hold his hand and he pulls away abruptly. A short time later, I hook my arm through his again and give his wrist a little squeeze as we walk on. This time, he doesn't pull away. With the opening of every lock on every gate, I'm reminded that Moira is still with him. With us.

Moving my body through a windy prairie that stretches out in every direction, following dogs who track small birds in an ocean of grass— these things bring a depth of pleasure that catches me by surprise. One cold afternoon, we step through native thigh-high needle-and-thread grass. Sun illuminates every blade. In the chilly air of another morning in October, we tromp through a country where rosehips flash strawberry red against bright white patches of snow. Food, water, shelter. Everything makes these grasslands ideal bird habitat.

The sun is often setting by the time we turn for home. Tonight, we spot several deer grazing. Harrison taps me on the shoulder. "Look, I'll show you something funny. Walk exactly like I do," he whispers.

He bends from his waist and begins to swing hanging arms lazily, bobbing his head, and wobbling sloppily along. I watch with disbelief.

"Come on . . . just do this, make yourself look like a complete fool!"

So here we are, the two of us, jouncing down the hillside looking like wooden Pinocchios learning to walk.

"And do this too sometimes. . ."

Harrison bends even lower to grab and pull noisily at grass with one hand. We have become something less threatening. Then he leads me in waving the other hand behind us in a way that a whitetail deer would switch its tail as if to say, "It's okay." And his crazy game works. The deer stand still, watching us carefully, calm enough to lower their heads and continue grazing as we pass.

After tired dogs get dinner at the kennel, we sit with Dollar outside. We stroke him, speaking with kindness and love. We lie next to him, rubbing his soft fur, before Harrison puts him up for the evening. I still seethe at the thought of that abusive trainer. Back at his mudroom, Harrison cleans our quarry. He invites me to stand next to him at a sink now filled with feathers and blood, where he will use two thumbs to gently draw open a thin sack of skin to reveal the contents of this bird's craw, the area in its throat where food can be stored. This one has been eating lots of grasshoppers. Harrison separates the breast meat from the feathers and bones as if he were unzipping a jacket. We prepare a grand feast with our fresh wild fowl upstairs in his kitchen. I discover game birds carry a special fullness of flavor when one has been present for the hunt.

A few weeks later over coffee, I tell Harrison a story I haven't thought of for many years: My first and only exposure to guns. My first time ever seeing something killed.

"When I was ten years old, I remember vaguely noticing my best friend's father, a policeman, as he stepped out of their house in pajamas. Carrying a gun! Many of the young children in our neighborhood had gathered in his front yard. We'd formed a circle around an unusual event: a small brown bat was giving birth to a tiny baby bat right there in the grass."

Harrison holds his coffee cup, listening.

"I noticed the father's large bare feet. He smelled like beer. But nothing could distract me from the wonder of what I saw. The small-winged mother bat had just begun to lick the tiny face of her new baby. The burley unshaven man standing next to me lifted his arm, aimed his gun into the center of our circle, and fired. He shot the mother more than once as we watched in terror. He shot the baby. 'God damn bats,' he muttered as he turned to walk back into the house.

"Our circle of children stood frozen. Someone was screaming. An eight-year-old squeezed her younger sister's hand. My eardrums were ringing. What remained of a mother bat and her pup lay in the grass. I fled to one of my secret hiding places. I pushed in through the lowest boughs of our backyard's big old pine tree until I was invisible, curling up in a ball on hard ground next to its trunk and weeping. I don't think I ever told my parents."

"Why wouldn't he just pick up a stick?" Harrison asks in disbelief. "Are you *sure* that happened? Men just don't pull out pistols and shoot something in front of children. Something's not right there."

But they *do*.

"If that really happened, that's the behavior of a profoundly disturbed man," he says, pausing. "Tawi lighting her pubes up in front of me seemed pathological. Life is full of pathology. You can't avoid it. No one can. You just have to be sensitive to it. And act accordingly."

ELK

F all's bird-hunting season overlaps with bowhunting season for elk. Harrison can hardly wait. If you want to see elk in the wild, they're often in the hills all around his house. We gaze through a scope from the ultimate tree stand, his glass kitchen. Sometimes we sit for hours watching the valley's herd.

One Saturday he invites me to head out with him around three in the afternoon. Harrison dresses in camo and "quiet hiking boots" and insists I do the same. He pulls something out of his mudroom closet for me. "This should fit! Here, let me paint your face with some of this green stuff."

We laugh. Looking in a mirror, I flinch. What would people from my previous life think of me now?

We trek up a mountainside to a place in the pine forest where he shows me a series of elk signs: markings on tree trunks where bulls have rubbed their antlers, a complex network of trails, tracks, and droppings. He carries a beautiful traditional bow with arrows. We travel silently, whistling if we need to get one another's attention. We stop in a high aspen grove when it is still early, around four in the afternoon.

"This is the place. We'll stay quiet until the light fades and every-thing begins to move. I'll get you close to some elk tonight," he promises. "We'll be here for a while, so take a nap if you like."

Lying down on yellow leaves, we nestle in next to one another. The earth is warm beneath us. A slight breeze carries fragrances of nearby juniper and sweet pine. I listen to chickadees, hear two crows talking. Far off in the distance, a mother cow calls for her calf. Cold wet air touches my cheeks and fingertips. A spider lowers itself from an over-hanging tree branch onto my chest. A bird lights on a higher branch of another tree, just above Harrison. How soon we become invisible in this quiet stillness. Larger creatures begin to travel by, including a group of five deer.

As afternoon changes to the chill of evening, I am glad for my gloves and hat.

"I've done this for almost forty years, fifteen of them here in this valley," he says. "I know these places now as other animals do."

"Ah," I say softly, turning to clear some thorny wild rose branches so I can readjust and lean back. "You're lucky to have such a strong connection with this place."

"The other part of returning to these familiar places again and again is becoming comfortable with what you *don't* know. Suddenly seeing animal behavior you've never seen before."

"I can't imagine how anyone would ever tire of this."

"Are you warm enough?"

I nod. "Every time we step out, amazing things happen," I whisper.

"I'm always surprised to find that a certain aspen patch has hailed out, all beat up and dying, trees down. Later on, a dense jungle of five-foot aspens appears in exactly the same spot. What is thick at one point suddenly thins. What is barren becomes loaded."

He gazes out from the shelter of aspens into open pastures below. The light of the day has become soft, like our voices.

Everything feels potent.

"There they are!" I whisper. We observe a group of elk arriving in the meadow where the old beaver dam is, just below us.

"Watch. Those cows are going to cut out soon and head right up here into the woods. And that bull will follow them."

We watch shadows running across grass.

Three minutes later, two large females are the first to run right toward us, up the hill and into the woods, exactly as Harrison predicted.

I sit cross-legged with my head down, perfectly still. Harrison is ready with his bow. In a split second, two huge animals *jump right over my back!* Astonished, I look up carefully to watch them leave.

Here comes the bull. How does something with such large antlers manage to travel through woods? He stops along the trail where we are, only ten yards away. We don't breathe, don't move. I watch his eyes, his nostrils; listen to the sound of his breathing. Harrison silently, incrementally, pulls the arrow back without the bull noticing.

Ping! The bull hears the sound of the bowstring being released. But in the excitement of the moment, Harrison didn't pull back far enough. The arrow impales the bull's flank but doesn't penetrate very far. The injured elk runs off.

"What just happened?" I ask. "Was that enough to kill him, or will he just work the arrow out and heal?"

Harrison speaks in a hushed voice: "We need to wait here and be still before getting up. He'll soon lie down." When we rise to find him, he is gone.

I worry for this gorgeous wild creature, just harmed in front of my eyes and perhaps suffering now somewhere, all alone. As we undertake an initial search, flashes of intimacy ripple inside me. I feel drawn to Harrison, walking ten feet in front of me. He is both hunter and protector. Instinct warns me to hold back—to protect myself from being too vulnerable. *Don't be touched by this moment as much as I am. It might all go away.*

We begin to track a very slight trail of blood along the forest floor. Harrison's style for doing this seems haphazard; he finds a spot of blood and moves on. I look too, as if this beautiful now-wounded elk's life depended on it. Drop by drop, I discover a few spots of blood on a fallen branch along the animal trail, a single red drop on a yellow leaf. I leave my hat as a marker on one, a mitten on the next. We stay and look for hours. We never find him. I feel somehow complicit in this act. I am learning about the imperfect nature of hunting.

Back at the house that night, standing in the mudroom with Harrison and the dogs before I head home, I continue to worry for the bull.

"But when one, then two of those cow elk jumped over me, it was the most amazing, deeply peaceful feeling in my body."

Harrison slides his arms around my waist and pulls me close.

"I wasn't scared at all! It seems strange, but I felt no fear. It was just the opposite."

I pull away to look into his eyes.

"I suppose they could have hurt me," I wonder. "But I only felt awe."

He kisses my hair. I snuggle in closer. Outside, I listen to the sounds of strong winds I'll need to battle on the long drive back to town.

A STORY OF BISON

W inter, 2006. The director of a larger museum in Great Falls invites me to join her staff as curator to oversee a special three-year project. I jump at the opportunity. I'm hired to research some two thousand Native American objects in storage and to use the collection to create a major new permanent exhibition to tell a story about the bison of the Northern Plains. I assemble a large panel of Native American advisors to guide our work.

We head to the collection to examine the Native objects found there. Before research can begin, we confront the horror of what has happened to these personal works of art. Each morning for months, my assistant and I don gloves, face masks, and disposable body suits before entering the museum's storage area. We must protect ourselves from exposure to potentially high levels of arsenic, mercury, DDT, and other toxic elements commonly used (for much of the twentieth century) to fumigate Native American objects for the purpose of preservation. A spectrometer informs us of each piece's potential dangers. The worst are bagged and set aside.

Awareness of pesticide poisoning makes everything poignant. We discover stunning dresses and headdresses, elegant tools, pipe bowls, saddle blankets, drums and rattles, varieties of containers from quivers to tobacco bags. Objects are examined with Native American consultants and advisors and blessed in the appropriate manners. A tool made of an elk antler used by women for scraping bison hides registers its heft in my hands. The smooth shiny patina of its handle tells me this beam of bone had long and continuous use. Pictographs of horses are incised along its rounded surface: references to the tool owner's most beloved horses, perhaps.

A pair of small, beaded moccasins remind me of an afternoon long ago spent with Molly Kicking Woman, a Blackfeet elder who taught me how to make hide moccasins. We used a one-piece pattern, stitched together with a vertical seam at the heel. These little shoes are constructed the same way, probably by a child's relative.

More children's moccasins come to light the following day. Each is adorned with bright-colored beads, several with floral designs. No two pairs are alike. My friend George Horse Capture, a member of Montana's A'aninin tribe who attended Berkeley, encouraged me years ago to look at *eighty* pairs of moccasins side by side. Only then, by studying their construction and decorative features, could I learn to distinguish one tribe's work from another. During a break today, I find myself daydreaming about being at Harrison's ranch again, learning to distinguish individual horses and cattle. These chemical smells of collection storage make me yearn all the more to re-experience the fragrance of elk, the scent of a horse.

One day while doing research, my assistant and I examine photos of regalia worn in a traditional Blackfoot dance that imitates the springtime mating behaviors of prairie chickens. It is called the Chicken Dance, something I will learn more about later. The outfit includes a head roach (a headdress with a tail made of the long guard hair of a porcupine, deer tail hair, and two eagle feathers) and a bustle of hawk and eagle feathers. I think back to that bird falling from the sky when Harrison took me bird hunting. Part of me wishes now that I had held that beautiful sharp-tail grouse in my hands for just a few moments.

One remarkable pipe bowl—shaped in what non-Indigenous people refer to as a tomahawk-style and carved of red stone called catlinite— becomes a personal favorite. Stone would not have been sprayed with chemicals; that was only for perishable materials like hide and feathers. I remove my mask and bring it to my nose, never imagining I would feel so moved by the faint earthy scent of tobacco. Its lower flat surface—carved in the shape of a hatchet blade—has an incised tableau of a bull elk with large antlers. He stands under a giant plant, nose lifted. A huge snake whose head shape and extended tongue recall male genitalia drapes itself around the bull's body like a serpentine necklace.

Native people have told me that their artworks contain agency and sometimes when working alone here, I also think I can *feel* the spirits in these objects. I try to listen for their stories. A horse mask made of thick bison hide and fur has red trade wool around its eyeholes; bison horns and feather pendants are positioned at the horse's ears. A galloping horse wearing such a mask must have appeared supernatural. A woman might have made this for her husband's prize mare or stallion to wear when they went bison hunting or to war as a prayer for their swift success and safe return. Native American friends, scholars, and artists continue to bring valuable insights throughout this work. Holding these objects is a reminder of where this path of learning about Native art and perspectives began for me, fifteen years ago.

Over all those summers of doctoral fieldwork on the reservation, I was lucky to be able to work with Darrell Kipp. He is an Amskapi Pikuni member of the Blackfoot Confederacy who returned to his reservation after receiving a scholarship and graduating from Harvard. I watched him fund, build, and fill three new immersion schools as a means to preserve and revitalize the quickly disappearing Blackfoot language of the Blackfeet Nation, based on a prototype he had learned about from Maoris in New Zealand. Molly Kicking Woman taught me how to make sarvisberry soup, its taste like a warm pudding of sweet blueberries and almond. I was shown how to apply yarrow leaves to bee stings. I learned about beaver bundle ceremonies and buffalo jumps and the behavior of young owls. I hiked high mountain passes and saw bears, moose, mountain goats, bighorn sheep.

Wilderness was the magnet that always drew me back.

DELIVERING BULLS

S pring, 2006. I stand ankle-deep in muddy pools of slippery brown cow shit and frothy urine. The truck next to me is splattered from top to bottom.

"Glad I borrowed these boots," I say, looking down.

Rick, Harrison's ranch hand, is working with Harrison as they try to load three bulls into the trailer so Harrison and I can take a pretty drive together and deliver stock. I carefully step back from the action to clean splattered eyeglasses.

Normally, this valley's aromatic fragrances of juniper, cottonwood buds, sweet pine, and wild roses are wells of refreshment. I adore the grassy perfume of horses on my hands. But this full-body immersion is hard to embrace.

Not so for Harrison. "I love the smell of burning plastic, animal shit, embryonic fluid, underarm sweat."

"Yuck, are you kidding?!" I think he's crazy. "Why on earth would you find those pleasant?"

He thinks for a minute. "Maybe it comes from when I was a boy ... "

Yesterday, he told me a story about the Howdershells, tenant farmers who lived and worked on his mother's land in Virginia. To escape the fireworks at home, Harrison spent a lot of time with the Howdershell family in his youth.

"I remember sleeping with three brothers in the cold tenant house after a long day of making hay. Stinky socks and sweat weren't half of it. There was no indoor plumbing. There was an outhouse. But we tended to shit behind a shed where the hogs ate. And I don't recall too much bathing ever going on there. One of the brothers when he was dating would wash his feet, splash on aftershave perfume, and off he'd go."

One hour later, Harrison and I are on our way. Halfway to Geyser along the gravel road, he spots a neighbor approaching in his white truck and suddenly reaches over with his right hand, grabbing the top of my head. He pulls me down onto the seat, out of sight.

"What are you doing?" I ask, his hand still on my head as he drives. When his neighbor is past, he lets me sit up.

"What was that? Were you just *hiding* me?"

"Just trying to keep things under wraps," he says, slightly embarrassed, eyes on the road. "That was my friend Harvey. He jumps at any opportunity to give me a hard time."

I pick up my hat from the seat, place it back on my head. What a kook!

A few miles farther down the road, I'm told we don't yet have the necessary brand papers for the animals we're towing. Beyond the town of Geyser, we pull off to the shoulder. A herd of cattle clog the center of the road near the brand inspector's ranch. Harrison rolls down the window and spots Clooney, the inspector, who is helping move the group on horseback. He waves for us to continue and rides beside us as we inch along.

"Hey, Harrison. How you doin'? A whole lot of early rain this spring. Can you believe all the flooding? Hasn't flowed like this since 1986—pocket gophers all drowned. Wish I'd had a dog, but the eagles are doing a damn good job of it," he chuckles.

Harrison and I are soon en route again, traveling papers in hand.

"He sure looked comfortable on his horse. You do too. Did you have horses when you were growing up?"

"Well, I was in Middleburg, Virginia, known as 'The Nation's

Horse and Hunt Capital? I'm sure it has the largest population per capita of excellent riders. It was all fox-hunting culture when I was there. Now it's all about three-day eventing. But I don't know anything. Moira was the one who knew everything about horses."

"Your old horse Andre is so kind. I'm sure Brise was something in her day. It must have been fascinating when you and Moira were breeding horses."

Harrison waits before speaking. "It's really something to visualize Foxlease. She was a thoroughbred with the eyes of an eagle. That's where everything started. Her daughter, Maid of Erin, produced Musical River. Willie was a remarkable thoroughbred stallion for passing on his integrity to many daughters. Then we got Brise. The first black Trakehner mare. She was Andre's dam. Then came his sister, Montana, with the thumbprint of Allah on her neck."

Something about his cadence makes me think of a recording I once heard of a man referred to as Ishi, the last known member of the Yahi people. After every other member of his family and his entire tribe had been killed, Ishi recounted in his Native language a long tale of creation and survival.

"Six generations I've known," Harrison continues, "and all bred for one purpose: trustworthiness."

There is a palpable mix of pain and pride when he speaks of her horses. Here are the genetic combinations, the pictures he sees, the attitudes he still admires. What began with his wife he poured into his own breeding of cows. When he first moved to Montana with his family, he fell into cattle ranching through necessity. Now cows are his lifeline. For the past five years, ever since his wife's death, he tells me relatively little care has been extended to their eighteen horses—horses who previously lived as the center of someone's life. This is not a place I want to insinuate myself.

As we round the bend toward Loma, he turns down the radio. "What Indian name would you give me?" he asks.

"Stays Away," I blurt out.

He smiles. "Fair enough. My father used to call me the Artful Dodger."

"Well then, what would mine be?"

"Blood Sugar," he declares. "I bet your friends on the rez would love that name! I still suspect all you really did there was get high with the guys."

I roll my eyes. "Give me a break!"

"I've come to see that you are one of those women who arouses physical attraction—I'm not sure if it is in both men and women. But it seems problematic. As does the fact that while I was married and loyal for my entire adult life, from age twenty-one to fifty-eight, you were out dating and experiencing the world."

I wince. "I've been a single woman my whole life. That's not a crime. Don't you think it's a *positive thing* I've come to know a few good men? Had some fun?"

"No, I don't," he says. "It creeps me out. And I particularly didn't like it when you mentioned the term 'fuck-buddy.'"

I sigh, drawing back again like a turtle. I've had a lifetime of experiences with men, none of which can I share openly with this one.

"Look," I say. "There's plenty about *you* that seems problematic to me. Besides, if you knew me at all by now, you'd know that I'm quite shy. With all that experience, I'm still clueless about what makes men tick." I turn to study Harrison's handsome profile as he drives along. "Maybe you can shed some light on the subject for me."

He turns to squint his eyes. "I'm coming to understand that you flash between a much more beautiful, softer person and one who by habit is always on the march."

He's right, but there is something about Harrison that makes me want to stop the march.

A few minutes later, he brings family into the conversation. "Did I tell you Phebe has a little sister now? She was born two days ago."

"That's exciting." I smile in my memory of wee Phebe learning to walk. "And everything went okay? What's her name?"

"She has big brown eyes like her dad. Like his mother had. Her name is Moira."

SPRING FEVER IN
PARADISE VALLEY

Moments after I step out of my car one Saturday in early May, Harrison arrives with mischief in his eyes and a sly lift of one brow.

"Are you ready for an official tour of my cattle operation?"

I've barely stretched my legs after the hour-and-twenty-minute drive. The cup of black tea he hastily made for me inside is still too hot to drink. "Bring your cup along," he insists. My antsy tour guide heads out the door and loads his two dogs and Willow into the back of his truck.

Even before I've climbed into the cab next to Harrison, Oscar, his jolly gray-and-tan Airedale, is busy humping Tula. "The beginning to any good journey," Harrison says with a smile, looking in his rearview mirror. "A fella's gotta have his habits!"

This "fella" thing, I learn, is a manner of speaking Harrison has adopted recently from his older neighbor Leroy.

As we ford Cottonwood Creek, pass the pond, then curve left to drive along the lower hay field and down the hill toward the dog kennel, he continues his shtick.

"When a fella comes from the East and finds a place like this, he thinks of it as his little piece of paradise. I'm pleased to provide you with a personalized tour of my Paradise Valley, which I'm hoping you'll enjoy," he announces with a silly grin.

Harrison parks in front of two very large black creatures (his prize bulls, 801 and 301) who look quite interested in three cows next to them. He tells me ranchers who want early spring calves turned bulls out with their cows May first.

My next thought instantly vanishes with the jarring appearance of a long red spear-like phallus that, right before my eyes, is thrusting toward a cow as one of these huge bulls attempts to mount her. Leave it to Harrison. Before I even know what's happening, we've got front row seats at a live X-rated bovine tango. I squirm in my seat, bug-eyed with curiosity. His bull's bravado delights Harrison, who begins mimicking hip gyrations and grunting noises. He casts a glance my way, loves to see me caught off guard.

"Isn't this great?!" he insists. "Now . . . see that cow," he says, pointing. "That's Annie. She's the first registered cow I ever brought onto the ranch. She always hides her new calf for three days. And she is the best kind of cow. She won't allow that bull . . . cows won't allow bulls to mount them until they're exactly ready in their chemistry to have it work. So when bulls approach them, a cow keeps moving away and carries on eating. Meanwhile, the bull is faking a series of mounts, like a slow-motion basketball game. The opponent knows where you want to go, but you lull them into a complacent guarded anticipation of your moves—like some boxers do, creating a regular rhythm, so they'll think it's just another fake move. But suddenly it's the real one." He turns to address the bull. "Come on, buddy. You almost had it that time!"

"Why are they putting their noses up in the air like that?"

"Ah, that's flehmen. Flehmen is when a bull lifts his upper lip into the air, curls it back and wrinkles his nostrils, usually with a cow's urine dripping off his nose." Harrison curls back his own upper lip and lifts his head in my direction to sniff the air. "He's receiving the chemistry of the oncoming estrous and discerning hormones. Sniffing out information about when to get serious."

These bulls are pushy and insistent. Competitive. Sometimes they seem to forget about the ladies altogether.

Overcome with their own virility, they make monstrous grunts. We watch as they dig huge holes in the earth, sending clouds of dirt and clods of mud into the air all around them. (I later learn that dirt on the bodies of horses, bison, elk, and cattle becomes a natural insect repellent.) Then the two begin to headbutt and push hard in a show of strength.

"These assholes can be fast; could kill you in an instant if they wanted to. They easily weigh a ton or more. And you better not forget it for one minute."

Art historians make references to fecundity and fertility rites in scholarly treatises. Here is an actual biology lesson in the field.

"The next time I see an image of a bull in a work of art, I'll notice if his lips are peeled back and his snout is high in the air. I'll be the only one at the next art history conference who knows what that means from personal experience."

Harrison tells me his herd is made up of various strains of registered black Angus. After forty-five days of mating from May first into June, bulls are pulled away from the cows. They protest vociferously, then fight among themselves to relieve tension. All cows are gathered from various pastures. Mothers with young female or "heifer" calves and those with male bull calves are separated. Cows with bull calves are turned out to graze in the adjoining National Forest lease from July tenth until their calves are weighed and replacement bulls are chosen in September. Mothers and their heifer calves are kept closer to home in Harrison's pastures, always in view, since he considers heifers to be more valuable.

"How did you first get involved with all this?"

"Through a series of flukes," Harrison tells me over lunch, "including my being told by the Forest Service when I first moved here to get into the cattle business if I wanted to retain grazing rights in the National Forest. I didn't arrive in Montana with any intention of ranching. But I've found, to my great surprise, that cattle are now my favorite source of calm. Being here alone is hard. Evenings are the worst. I lie in bed, try to find comfort, and I always fall into being with my cattle. Others count sheep. I count cattle. Looking at them, imagining them, thinking about their ear-tag numbers, their pedigrees, their proportions. They bring peace."

We gaze out the windows that surround his kitchen table. He is pleased.

"This view, this place, wouldn't be half as interesting without cows on it. *So* much better to look at a grassy hillside with cattle on it, than just empty hillsides, isn't it? Wonderful to think that cattle have provided this kind of deep satisfaction since biblical times. It's meaningful to know I'm part of something ancient."

We sit together, watching. I notice one mother sniffing different babies until she finds her own. Several lie quietly with their calves, giving them little baths, licking their small ears, eyes, noses. I find one cow–calf pair staring at each other as if hypnotized, completely infatuated. One energetic youngster runs circles around her mother. A group of others team up in a gang to zoom down the hill, racing and kicking up their heels.

I'm happy to drive around again in his truck together after lunch.

"I know how to handle you, baby," Harrison proclaims, completely out of the blue. "Ply you with ideas and let you run like a bird dog. Feels like flypaper, don't it?"

"Excuse me? *What* did you say?!" Nostrils flaring, I stare cold and hard with disbelief in his direction.

He sits in his seat smiling at me, smug with delight. I turn away in silence, indignant.

"That bull over there looks like he's limping," I report, still avoiding Harrison's gaze. "Watch. See that? He looks hurt."

"I see. You're right. Let's drive over and check it out. Probably foot rot."

"What's foot rot? Can you treat it?"

Harrison pulls up next to #910. The bull hobbles a few feet in the opposite direction before stopping.

"Yep. Looks like foot rot. We'll get Rick and help him get this guy in so we can look after him."

By the time we coax the lame old boy to hobble down the road and into a corral for doctoring, the last light of day has left the valley. Harrison drives me back to the house and my car. I'm ready to head home with Willow.

"I'm glad we could help that guy. Do you think he'll get better?"

"Yes, I do. We'll give him some LA200 and some sulfa boluses, and he'll be fine. It's good you spotted him. You're getting to be a real rancher woman."

My smile is tight as I load Willow into the back of my car.

"Thanks for the crash course," I mumble, tired and still annoyed.

Harrison leans in to kiss pursed lips. I climb in behind the wheel.

"Good night," I say, as Willow and I pull out.

"Sweet dreams," he says, before turning toward the mudroom door with Oscar and Tula.

When Phyllis and I talk by phone the next day, she asks about Harrison. The cheeriness of her voice makes me happy. And she'll be back in Montana soon.

"You are always so *up*, and he can be so insensitive and gloomy sometimes . . . " I want to tell her more, to *ask her more*.

"But you two are still having fun, aren't you? I'm sure he feels very lucky to have you in his life, living up there all alone."

"He *can be* a lot of fun," I admit.

"Hey, I have some great news," Phyllis says. "I found a sweet little house right on the river, on Lower River Drive. When we leave Arizona this June, we'll be moving to Great Falls!"

Finally, a dear friend nearby—a soul sister and collaborator in this desert of conservative men.

"Well, Willow," I say after hanging up. She wags her tail and lifts her head. Beautiful kind brown eyes stare straight into mine. "We'll soon be able to visit our friend Phyllis more often."

TIME

M ost every time I visit Harrison, he suggests we drive around the ranch. I'd rather walk. He wants to drive, cover more territory. There must be a reason, so I tag along. He has no specific destination in mind. We travel no faster than five miles per hour in a small red lightweight Kubota utility vehicle, more akin to a golf cart than a truck. I am impatient. This seems trifling. He points things out. A goose nest in the hollow tree by the pond. An old beaver dam upstream. He jokes and teases as we ease along. Merriment is fine, but why aren't we *doing* anything?

We drive off road, something I have never done before. Slowly, we edge over plants as they bend and snap beneath our tires, roll over heavy brush as it scrapes the underbelly of Harrison's vehicle. We travel up and over foothills, careful to avoid large rocks.

"I love being out in all this, don't you?" I say, as if this is common practice.

"This is how I check on what's happening," he answers. "An animal that needs help, a fence that needs mending, poachers during hunting season. But we never do this during fire season," he cautions. "It's green now. But anytime there's dried grass, one little spark could set a whole field ablaze. You saw what happened last year to Leroy Strand down the road. Before anyone knew anything, 20,000 acres were on fire."

We talk about the driven trail on the hillside, left by the heavy tractor used to feed animals each day, and even the smaller footprint of this vehicle. We recall the stage-wagon tracks still visible at Phyllis's Lonetree stage stop.

"I don't like it," he says. "But why live in a place like this if you can't relax and enjoy it? I care about this valley. We are still low impact compared to most."

As we approach creek crossings when water is high, he stops for dramatic effect.

"Can we make that? What do you think?"

I invariably say *no*. He persists.

"Should I try it or not? It looks pretty tricky, but *here we go!*"

He guns it, and we crash through a fast-flowing creek as it washes up around us, wheels spinning to gain purchase. I gasp. Harrison glows. We laugh.

But we discover more serious things, situations that require us to act. Going slowly, we notice a heifer's face covered in porcupine quills; a young calf with bloody diarrhea. We count horses to make sure they are all together. We observe a bull's movement to scan for lameness. We find sick or injured animals, something dead. We see cows roaming around where they shouldn't be. They've escaped through an open fence that's been knocked down by traveling elk. It needs fixing. We notice a mother cow standing on a hillside by herself, crying for a lost calf. Where is it? I soon see this is not trifling, driving without purpose. The *only* way to see is to slow down. Something is *always* happening.

Nothing seems to faze Harrison: we encounter a situation, and he shows me how to help. We get busy. My first reaction to any animal in distress is empathetic alarm. My heart quickens when I see dogs chase a barn cat. My jaw hardens when we notice a horse favoring one leg. My gut twists when we come upon a small, half-eaten body of a dead calf under a tree.

Sometimes, our aimless driving takes us beyond cattle and horses, paddocks and pastures, into the surrounding wilderness. Harrison drives slowly through grasslands and swales. I feel the pleasure of being in wide-open fields with mountain streams, around protective patches of hawthorns and willows. In draws and coulees, hollows and hillsides, the land seems to fold in upon itself. He shows me soggy meadows with underground springs. We pass groves of aspen, higher forests of evergreens. Every part of this valley is home for wild creatures.

On a high hill with many views, we stop and leave the vehicle to stand quietly. We scan everything around us. If we spy something wild and are downwind, we hide in the grass and watch its movements. Harrison's vision is impressive. He can pick out animal forms from far away. He points to elk grazing in a high meadow, mountain goats on a rocky cliff, whitetail deer sneaking off into distant brush. We bring out binoculars, set up the spotting scope, and relax.

I like to imagine what this steppe region must have been like for the ancestors of the contemporary Blackfoot Confederacy and other Indigenous people who relied on bison and other wild game for their survival. When Prince Maximilian de Wied of Prussia traveled to what is today Montana in 1833 with a Swiss artist, Karl Bodmer, he wrote in his journal:

> "The Indians' bodies are strong and hardened from living in the open air; they walk with a vigorous, long stride and make a forceful appearance; young people proud and erect; the elderly stealthy and quick but stooped. Their gaze into the prairies is trained; they distinguish objects at a great distance." [2]

Harrison and I sit outside for hours, just looking. He invites me to sit closer, puts his arm around me. He smiles, tucking a strand of hair behind my ear.

The more I look, the more settled and attuned my own vision becomes. I grow to recognize familiar shapes of different birds and animals. Sandhill cranes flying overhead look and sound different from herons. Mule deer travel with a distinctive hop. I begin to recognize fur colors as they change with the seasons, how they reflect light at different times of the day. I see the hair of white goats flash bright in sunlight like reflective mirrors against the rocky cliffs of high mountains where they live. I admire the warm red coats of grazing cow elk in the dimming light of a fall evening; the bright white of antelope trotting off through open prairie; the lope of a coyote dashing toward a hidden ravine. I scan the landscape for shapes and movement, looking for whatever stands out, in places where I know animals might prefer to be.

Like those first stories Harrison told me the day of my wreck while we sat in his truck, I am always on the lookout now. When we drive at his slow and steady speed, my senses cannot help but engage.

THE LANTERN

One clear cool afternoon in late spring, Harrison and I pull on our boots, grab large clippers and leather gloves, and head out with the dogs to collect willow branches near the stream by the house. Harrison has some Tibetan prayer flag fabric he got when he was in Bhutan many years ago and wants to make a large lantern to hang over his dining room table. As we work by the stream, I think back to what Putong, the young lama-in-training, told me about willow branches being associated with Kuan Yin, the bodhisattva of compassion. I say silent prayers of thanks to each plant I cut. Tula, Oscar, and Willow seem fascinated: suddenly *we're* the ones interested in sticks. When we have enough, we gather and carry our long branches back to the mudroom and deposit them on the floor. The fragrance of still-green willows envelops the room.

We sit side by side and take turns sketching drawings, until we agree on our general approach. Three dogs watch from their beds as we gauge the lantern's anticipated size and select our first stems for further trimming. Braver now about showing affection, I remove pruning shears from Harrison's hands. His eyes question me as my fingers explore his upturned palms. They are callused—rough and hard, like leather. I've never seen hands so large and powerful. And they're always so warm.

"And you," he speaks quietly, shifting to hold and turn my hands in his, ". . . your palms are so incredibly soft. These hands have never seen *one day* of hard labor."

His caress makes me tingle. He's right: I've lived a life of the mind.

The only ways I am physically active are hiking, swimming, biking, yoga. And making love. When we choose our wands of willow to begin bending them, the energy of arms brushing against one another feels exciting. We struggle a bit with our pile, giggling at the awkwardness of so many intertwining stems and arms. Soon we settle into working with the innate elasticity of these green, still-living branches. Instead of forcing anything we had in mind, we allow willows to show us *their* preferred ways of moving, like dowsing rods finding water—like Harrison's body, steering and guiding mine when we danced.

When the time is right, we take turns. One of us cradles the emerging unwieldy shape, while the other reaches for long strips of fabric, then reaches back across the other's body and, stretching arms through stretching branches, carefully lays strips of material to tie and hold perpendicular stems in place. We are like two birds building a nest.

At one point, while my busy fingers are focused on wrapping fabric around intersecting willows, Harrison lets go. His warm palms find the insides of my elbows. The tips of his fingers caress the skin of my lower arms. I gasp at his tickle, as our nearly four-foot-high form wobbles and contracts. He kisses me. But we persevere until the organic shape of our large willow framework becomes durable and strong.

The material we'll use to cover this framework is a delicate translucent weave. Ancient mantras, sutras, and prayers are printed everywhere in small characters and symbols of Tibetan script. Images of horses floating within this script remind me of images from children's books when, as a young girl, I would hope to meet them in my dreams. We try stretching this fine material carefully over our giant egg-shaped form, one section at a time. We can't figure out how to keep it all together. I call an artist friend. She suggests using matte acrylic. Eventually we adhere each piece of fabric to the next, and then to the underlying framework using a paintbrush and plenty of the clear stiffening liquid, until the entire form appears.

We can hardly wait to take our new work of art upstairs for installation. We hang it from the ceiling of Harrison's largest room over the
middle of a long wood-plank table and its twelve chairs. With an over-
sized bulb hanging inside, we flip the switch. It is elegant. Alive. Our
Chinese lantern form resembles a giant seedpod or cocoon, suspended
in space. The prayers and horses on its fragile shell glow warm, soft
amber. I am amazed. We've created a radiant container of golden light.

We sit down together on the couch. Harrison finds my hand and
squeezes it. I rest my head on his shoulder.

The fragrance of green willows is still with us. We listen for a long
while to the sound of heavy rain as it falls on the metal roof. When at
last we stand to leave the orange glow of our lantern, the rest of the
house is in darkness. My arm wrapped in his, we make our way down
Harrison's long hallway. We walk toward his bedroom without a word.
I imagine our lantern—like some tender expression of compassion,
greater than either of us—lighting the path forward.

Stepping into his bedroom, Harrison turns on a bed lamp. I stand
facing him and lift my hands, placing them on his cheeks. I cradle his
face in my palms, the scent of willow on my fingertips. His eyes close.
The tightness in his jaw releases. He draws me into his embrace.

DOGS

Driving down the gravel road to Harrison's valley feels different now. Less frivolous. A veil of ambivalence has been shed. Each time I make the final turn onto the ranch, Willow scrambles out from her hiding place under the back seat and lights up. Harrison and I greet each other as new lovers do. As I unload my overnight bag from the car, I feel his smiling eyes. He places one arm around my shoulder as we walk. He takes my bag with his other arm to carry it inside and up the stairs.

Harrison's house dogs, Oscar and Tula, welcome Willow and me with great affection as *their* weekend companions. Nine-year-old Oscar is Harrison's obvious favorite. It doesn't take long to see why this Airedale's companionable happy innocence lifts the spirits of someone so uncomfortable in being alone. Five-year-old Tula, by comparison, is deep and internal. As with Dollar, I find her intriguing.

When I ask Harrison over tea one day about this all-black dog, half poodle and half Airedale, I almost regret it.

"Tula was born here not long before Moira died. Neighbors kept our two new puppies while we were at the hospital in Seattle. When I came home alone, the neighbors kept the male and returned Tula. I barely remember anything about those days. I suppose Tula was pretty much left on her own. She learned how to fend for herself."

"And she was still less than a year old. No wonder she seems so self-sufficient."

"I could hardly stand or speak during that first year. I remember going to visit my mother, unable to form any words. I couldn't do anything, for anyone."

I'm left to assume it was his wife who was the primary caretaker of dogs, horses, Harrison, and their three boys. All of them suffering her loss. My presence triggered anger from Harrison's second son recently on an infrequent visit. I accidentally broke a bowl and was sternly admonished. "That was my mother's." I apologized, imagining it had been a special bowl. His response: "*Everything* here was my mother's." Harrison's reticence, even around Tula, is clear now. Tula's presence stirs memories and anguish.

Tula and Oscar are excited to join Willow and me for weekend walks. At two years old, Willow sets off to chase everything that runs— even an antelope, who takes her halfway across the next valley. Oscar has an older dog's rocking-chair gait, and Tula is powerful. Her body is dense and athletic. She is an expert huntress and seems eager to teach Willow through example. On a walk just two weeks ago, we watched Tula toss a live muskrat straight up into the air and heard the loud crunch of its bones between her teeth as she caught it on the way down. It's not long before Willow is gnawing on her own quarry. Back in my tiny yard in Great Falls during the workweek, she quickly grows bored. She digs large holes around my fence line. She hunts and kills a favorite squirrel named Chester that my next-door neighbor has loved and fed for years. I bury the dead squirrel, hoping my dear neighbor doesn't notice.

Willow and Tula spend hours together the following weekend, mousing on the hillside outside Harrison's kitchen window. I see Willow bolt straight up into the air like a coyote to the sound of tiny squeaks, then pounce and dig as fast as she can. She joins Tula and Oscar in their daily routines and series of familiar stops: the large woodpile by the stream, sniffing for rabbits, then racing wildly across the creek to the favorite hollowed-out log on the pond, where scent of muskrat draws insatiable desire.

"Look at you, so proud of her!" Harrison teases. "You love watching your adolescent daughter finally learning how to be a real dog."

Traveling farther still in this open country with Tula, Willow has experiences I will never know. I watch her catch whiffs of wild scent and track them. The hairs along her spine stand straight up. Spinning this way and that, she discerns enemies with frantic passion. Lion, coyote, bear? She learns to follow the cues of birds, as well as her own nose, to find the remains of a kill: a deer jaw or elk leg to snack on; something dead to roll in—the smellier the better.

Willow is my first dog and only child. At just eight weeks old, she became the star of misguided training classes in Great Falls. I have subjected an innately shy and wary puppy to all sorts of ridiculous expectations, with mixed results, maybe like my mother did with me. Harrison needles me each time I call and evasive Willow slinks away. "What have you done to your poor dog?"

He insists I've committed the same sin humans always do with their dogs: demanding far too much obedience with very little recognition for individual personality.

"You two are very serious together. Do you *ever* encourage this dog to just play and be herself? Do you know who she really is?"

Harrison is a self-proclaimed expert on many things, including dogs. He takes it upon himself to rehabilitate both Willow and her owner. I will come to believe he does, in fact, know a lot about dogs. The minute he saw Willow, he recognized her.

"Do you know your dog is a potcake?"

Potcake? I'd never heard the expression. He told me my small-framed, yellow dog is exactly what you get whenever dogs have been crossbreeding for a long time.

"They all boil down to this same look. She's what you see all over the world; just look down every street in the old Bahamas, in African villages. She's everywhere."

"I bet you don't know how dogs say hello to one another!" he says, as we sit together on his couch. "Here, let me do it for you." He leans over, puts his nose to my ear, and emits a series of loud short staccato sniffs, followed by a final outbreath, and some slurping. I pull back immediately.

"Yeah," he says, "a woman slapped me once for doing that at a party, but it's true. Try it out!" He drops down to the ground; starts snarling and roughhousing with his two dogs, grabbing at their legs and ears, just the way I've seen them play with each other. As if he, too, is a dog. He invites Willow to join in the fun. She keeps her distance.

Walking back to his house from the barn that same day, he spots the dogs and gets me involved. "Quick! Before they see us, get behind me and hold your arms out so it looks like I have four arms."

We stomp our way along the road and make growly noises until the heads of our three dogs pop up on the hill near the mudroom. On high alert, they begin to bark. Their voices grow louder and more insistent. Oscar jumps up and down and howls. Suddenly I leap to the side; one figure becomes two, and we call their names, laughing. With eyes smiling, tails wagging, they bound toward us to share the joke.

Over time, we notice odd behavior from Willow around cattle. Whenever cows are being worked in the corrals, she starts to quiver and yelp. She expresses a feverish attraction but has no idea what to do with it.

"There's a great example of genetics revealing themselves," Harrison says. "She goes crazy whenever she's around cows. She's showing you what she's supposed to be. She suggests that she might like to *become* the cow dog that she actually *is*. See! This could be flowing through all of us in just the same way, like a phone message, and we're responding to things and we don't know why . . . *this* is your ancestors you don't even know about, speaking to you."

Harrison takes my part-heeler potcake under his tutelage. He invites her to engage when cattle are being worked and quietly suggests how she might be helpful. She learns. Years later, I will be able to point Willow toward a particular cow in a nearby pasture and watch her dash out, rally around its heels until it is back with the group. Like a bird dog with birds, I will watch my companion feel immense pleasure doing what she was born to do—becoming what she already is.

Willow, Tula, and Oscar follow along when Harrison and I begin heading out on horses this year. He suggests I ride my favorite calm old bay gelding, Andre, whom he rode for many years with his wife. Having taken a few riding classes as a girl, I am thrilled to climb on a horse again. Harrison rides T, the elegant dark gelding.

We ride out and up into the hills. T moves forward with such beauty under saddle. With bloodlines that include a famous racehorse, he has breeding that has made him both gentle and anxious, especially if there is any hint of competition. These two geldings are old friends. Even so, I observe Harrison consistently using half-halts to keep T geared down in a contained gait. Neither horse is bothered in the least by our canine gang of three.

On the ground, I have come to know Andre as intelligent, gentle, kind. I appreciate these qualities as we ride. Some days, moving on the backs of horses through hidden ravines, granite outcroppings, rolling hillsides, and open meadows, I close my eyes to feel the soft leather of reins, the step of my horse beneath me. A strong and honest creature is carrying me, taking care of me. I find I am also caring for him, appreciating him more and more as we travel. Like Willow, we are partners, confident on our journeys.

Sitting heavy in my saddle this late summer afternoon, I try not to worry that I am also coming to care for Harrison, a dispirited man who does not feel whole without a woman's love. I've always considered dependency a tragic flaw, a dangerous weakness to be avoided at all costs. Yet striding out beside Harrison today, my heart swings open. Perhaps his ingrained ruggedness is as natural as the rugged wilderness of this valley I love. Perhaps the two of us are like our dogs and these horses carrying us, creatures who simply take comfort in each other's company, differences and all.

As we approach foothills on the valley's western side, I'm reminded of that day the monk said a blessing. Perhaps this place, Harrison and I, our horses and dogs are somehow all enriched by the grace of these collective experiences. Whenever we spend time in nature like this, I no longer feel adrift. Harrison's spirit lightens. I watch T's long brown tail blow with the breeze, moving like a pendulum with the rhythm of his stride, with the beating of my heart. The dogs travel far ahead as we climb the next hill.

AMADOU

S ummer, 2006. This is my second summer floating the river with Harrison. I still don't care much about catching fish. But learning to fly-cast interests me. Standing in waders with water up to my hips one horribly windy day, I try and try and try. Harrison fishes quietly downriver, each cast perfect. Upriver, I'm exasperated, cursing yet another rosary of gnarled wind knots.

Harrison notices and inquires kindly, "Do you need some help?"

"No!" I snap back, beginning to weep. He casts again and leaves me with my difficulties until I explode. The sound of an ancient desperation inside me echoes from the riverbanks. "I just can't *do this*!"

Harrison wades upriver and stands in front of me. "Will you hand your line to me? I bet I can help." He starts to unravel the line, one knot at a time. "It's miserable, I know," he says. "Men don't do anything unless it's miserable."

"I don't understand. *Why?*"

He shrugs his shoulders. "We have to tame misery . . . I've lived this misery myself so many times . . . this is just part of it." He smiles. His blue eyes are gentle. Knots loosen. "Everybody comes unglued on fishing," he assures me.

We stand side by side, the river's current pushes against my legs, wraps itself around my waders until they squeeze tight against the flesh of my thighs like skin.

"I remember being sent to a neighbor's house to ask if I might learn how to fish as a boy. I was handed a bamboo rod and put to work casting a leader into a wash bucket. A gentleman named Murray Dyer took me under his wing. He was my father's best friend. I think he wrote a book called *The Weapon on the Wall: Rethinking Psychological Warfare*, or something like that. Anyway, he was a son of missionaries in China and a self-created Englishman. He always wore a necktie whenever he was hunting or fishing."

"Really?"

"That was how it was done in the thirties. I practiced casting to that bucket for hours and hours. As a graduation gift, Mr. Dyer gave me what could have easily been a 1910 setup for any fisherman in England: a bamboo Hardy fly rod, a silk fly line, a box to keep natural gut leaders wet, a Wheatley dry fly box, and a piece of amadou."

"Amadou? What's that?"

"A piece of fungus that fly fishermen used to dry their flies." Harrison cranks the reel and shortens my line a bit. "Okay, you're all set. Here you go." He hands the rod back to me as he reaches up with his other hand to wipe a tear from my cheek. "Feel better?"

I nod, rolling my eyes.

"Want to try another cast or two, before we head home?"

I like the word *amadou*. The sound of it keeps pulling at my mind like a splendid puzzle, a strange melody I cannot forget. I discover that the species of bracket or shelf fungi found on birch trees generally used to harvest amadou is called *Fomes fomentarius*; in English it is also known as horse's hoof fungus or tinder fungus. The amadou layer is the fibrous section found on top of the fungus, just below the outer skin and above the pores. I find curious recipes for its processing. One suggests soaking the amadou layer in washing soda for a week, beating it gently from time to time. Then it has to be dried and pounded with a blunt object to soften and flatten it. The finished product is said to have great tactile appeal: a fluffy, felt-like material, pleasant to the touch like soft buckskin.

Back at home, I learn this spongy substance was historically used as an absorbent in medicine to stanch bleeding and served as a wound dressing; hence, there's another name for it: "wound sponge." But the origins of the name *amadou*, found in late-eighteenth-century French, lead me to perhaps its most important role as a precious resource. Coming from the Latin *amator* meaning "lover," amadou easily ignites. I find out that early peoples around the world carried and used this substance for at least five thousand years, precisely because it allowed them to start a fire easily, catching sparks from flint with this light-weight fuel. I imagine Indigenous North Americans appreciating the properties of this fungus.

"What a wild thing amadou is," I say to Harrison, over lunch in town a few days later. "A tree fungus that combines the properties of fire and water. *Something in nature that burns, absorbs, and heals?* And its name means love." I am too embarrassed to say *lover*.

"I know." He nods. "It's like the connections of Spirit that twist and braid."

I gaze into his eyes. "That's *so* lovely."

"It's that fire that lights everything."

THE WASHCLOTH TRICK

P hyllis arrives at the end of June with a moving van to her new residence in Great Falls. We share a long hug. She is wearing her customary Southwestern jewelry and hat with long pheasant feathers. On this happy reunion, she wears eyeglass frames spotted with bright orange polka dots. When I admire them, she exclaims, "I painted these myself!" She looks magnificent. She and her husband, Jimmy, quickly settle into their new condominium perched on the banks of the Missouri, where she will be much closer to her Lonetree Ranch during summer months. She christens her new home "The River House." She creates a Southwestern interior with many of her large colorful Western-themed paintings, most of which I have never seen.

She wastes no time setting up a painting studio in a separate building. New gray carpet is installed in the old garage space, immediately after which, Phyllis intentionally splatters paint all over it, "like Jackson Pollock!" She puts in new windows for light. Paints walls. Buys furniture at local antique/junk stores, paints what is old and makes it new again. She accomplishes all of this in a matter of months. Meanwhile, my walls remain bare. After three years of living in my little house in Great Falls, stacks of unopened boxes still sit in my basement.

Today when I visit, she has painted brightly colored doilies onto the fabric of an old couch and chairs. Four old metal school lockers placed near the door, for anyone to fill with their own paintbrushes and smocks, are painted with Matisse-like images. When I visit one week later, she has just finished a large mural on the inside of the garage door. I stand in awe. I recognize portraits of her; she points out her sisters Connie and Mitzi. One figure looks like her mother, Mary Tanner, standing next to Square Butte. There are also references from famous paintings: figures with umbrellas from "Le Déjeuner sur l'herbe," a creature resembling a Minotaur.

"Look at that, how great! You've tipped your hat to Manet, Picasso, Matisse—this is incredible, Phyllis."

"Do you like it? I didn't want anyone to feel left out," she says with a chuckle. "I thought it might make a good backdrop for my new studio. I've got some champagne in the fridge. Let's have a toast: I've decided to call this place the Painting Factory, just like our old buddy, Andy Warhol. What do you think? I kind of like it." Her eyes dance as we clink glasses.

Each time I visit, things have changed. Easels appear, extra smocks hang on hooks. There are tubs and buckets on large tables, filled with paints of every color. There are brushes of every size. One painted shelf holds favorite art books: Matisse, T. C. Cannon, Maynard Dixon, Bonnard. I find a large portrait of Marilyn Monroe hanging in the studio's small bathroom.

"I bet you recognize that," she says. "I made her skirt and the street vent below a bright purple. Just so Marilyn could get even more attention!"

"I can't wait for Harrison to see all this. And he'll love Marilyn," I say, raising my eyebrows.

"How is Harrison? I bet you two have been having a grand time together," she says.

I tell her about our weekends of bird hunting and fishing. She loves hearing about the lantern we created with willow branches. While we talk, I help her fill shelves along one wall of the Factory with cups and paper plates, plastic silverware, cans of soup, crackers and cookies, and boxes of wine, next to a microwave and small refrigerator. A boom box is always playing music in the background, lots of Frank Sinatra and Puccini operas. The Statler Brothers sing "Flowers on the Wall." Michael Bublé sings "The Best Is Yet to Come."

Everything about Phyllis feels good. Her company reminds me of other dear women friends I love and miss, scattered across the country in all the places I've lived. Her vision of life is inspiring, like so many self-taught artists I've known. She never ruffles my feathers. We just soar. Willow and I visit as often as possible. Phyllis paints at her easel while Willow watches me play with Phyllis's two studio kittens, Picasso and Matty. When I show up tired after a long day at work, she always has a can of soup to offer and a glass of wine. We sit on her painted couch together many an evening, telling stories and laughing until dark. It doesn't take long for word to spread among Phyllis's condominium neighbors. The Factory starts to buzz with activity as a favorite gathering place, a salon of lively comings and goings. Phyllis is always there, sparkling at the center of everything.

Like a colorful garden, her studio is soon full of exotic flowers. Friends from all walks of life appear unannounced to have a drink; some pick up a brush and begin their own paintings. Visitors from Norway and Italy join the party and feel right at home. I meet Phyllis's two younger sisters, Mitzi and Connie, when they come to visit from their homes in Denver. All the Tanner sisters wear hats. Mitzi tells me that their oldest fourth sister, Doris, who lives in Hawaii, is still dancing at eighty-five years old. Before Mitzi finishes her sentence, the three sisters spontaneously gather—all in their hats, all in their seventies—to put their arms around each other, form a dance line, and, lifting their legs, do a few low kicks. Visitors clap and cheer. Phyllis is that rare kind of person who treats everyone like a treasure. Everyone she spends time with leaves happier.

This September, she begins to paint portraits. The first one she does is of me. "It's easy!" she says. Phyllis creates a simple likeness from a photo in a matter of hours. She hangs it up in the center of one long wall of her studio above the propane stove. She gets busy painting more bold portraits of family members, friends, and regular guests to the Factory.

One by one, Phyllis hangs them in her studio on what she calls her
"wall of fame." In time, every bit of wall space is filled. Lively paintings
of friends and family hang next to portraits of movie stars like Paul
Newman and Robert Redford; opera stars like Pavarotti; bright scenes
of Lugano, the old country in Italy where she and her sisters still have
family; and lyrical paintings of Lonetree Ranch, her favorite place in
the world.

When it's just the two of us in her studio, Phyllis encourages me to
paint. "Lynne, you know all about art. And you used to paint, right?
You need to start again!"

I tell her I loved painting in college. But I decided I'd never be any
good and stopped. Instead, I became a curator to help talented artists
find success. She urges me on.

"If you love to paint, don't worry about what it's going to look like.
Just let yourself enjoy it."

"Maybe you're right."

"Life is about having fun. You better pick up a brush and get busy,"
she says one day. "This locker can be yours, and here's an easel. Get
some paint and brushes at the craft shop. And next time you come after
work, bring an old shirt. If you forget, I've got plenty of everything!"

I *have* always wanted to get back to painting but felt paralyzed by
self-judgment and fear. No more holding back. Following Phyllis's
lead, I look for a painting to use as my inspiration. I discover a lovely
portrait of Madame Bonnard painted by her husband, one of my favorite painters. Madame wears a red-and-white-striped blouse and
long bright red skirt. She is walking in the countryside with two dogs
and carries a basket under her arm.

Phyllis supports me at every turn.

"You can learn so much by looking at artists you really like. I learned so many things from my old friend Maynard Dixon over the years. Now don't forget what Matisse taught me: If you outline your two dogs and the woman's figure, you can really make them pop right off the canvas. Give it a try."

I drag my feet. One day after work at her studio, while Phyllis paints, I recall when my love of art began.

"In third grade, 'the picture lady' would come once a month from the local museum. I stared into strange figurative landscapes—fourteenth- and fifteenth-century paintings from Italy and the Netherlands—as she told stories about different people in different times and places. I was desperate for a place, *any place*, where I could feel I belonged. I stared into those paintings, listened to her stories, and my imagination stepped right into those images. I felt free."

While Phyllis finishes another portrait, this one of a friend from her nursing years, I picture my favorite scene in the film *Mary Poppins*, when Julie Andrews takes the children's hands and they all jump into paintings on the sidewalk made by Dick Van Dyke's chimney sweep.

"If I am going to do this," I say, building courage, "I want to work on a giant canvas. I want to create an image that feels big enough to step right into it."

The following Saturday, she helps me build a frame and stretch pre-gessoed canvas for a six-foot painting.

It feels delicious to dip new brushes into wet juicy mounds of color. I come to the studio every day after work. Eventually I have painted everything except Madame Bonnard's face.

"Hey, this is looking great!" she says. "I think maybe you should make this a self-portrait. Wouldn't it be fun to put your face in there instead? Here, I'll show you how."

This sudden prospect of a giant self-portrait is horrifying, in-stantly intimidating. Phyllis helps with the mixing of colors for teeth; she shows me tricks for painting eyes. At last, I agree. But as hard as I try, I cannot manage to catch my own likeness. One day, while another informal student, Tanara, is at work at her easel, I put down my brush.

"I just can't do it. Look at this mess. What a failure!"

Phyllis leaves her painting to stand by my side. Tanara listens.

"Now look," Phyllis says. "You have a marvelous painting here. You've been working on this face for way too long, that's all. Why don't we just take it off so you can start over?"

She heads to the bathroom sink beneath Marilyn Monroe and waltzes back with a wet washcloth. Her mischievous smile flashes beneath a brown felt hat.

"You can take a damp washcloth and clean it right off, just like this!"

The countenance I have strained so hard to make perfect suddenly disappears before my eyes. I gasp, nearly jump straight out of my skin. All my desperate attempts at getting it exactly right, wiped out in an instant. Several seconds pass before I notice Phyllis and Tanara are both roaring with laughter.

"It's just a painting, after all!"

The following Wednesday evening, I sink back into a painted chair at Phyllis's studio with a glass of wine. Tonight, she wears the glasses with orange polka dots. She is painting a portrait of her husband, Jimmy, from a photo taken twenty-five years ago.

"Harrison is a wonderful man," I tell her, "but I worry for him. He seems to live in a general state of dread and anxiety."

Large silver earrings dangle and flash from Phyllis's ears beneath a tan leather hat. She is a wonderful listener, always devoting as much eagerness to hearing my stories as she does to telling her own.

"But you two are having so much fun being together, aren't you?" she says, mixing a new color for Jimmy's coat.

"I *love* the ways we spend time together out in nature. But I'm start-

ing to wonder if he might have some kind of clinical depression." I take
another sip of wine, waiting for turkey soup to warm in the microwave.

"Maybe," Phyllis agrees. "When my son, Scottie, first met Harrison, he recognized the same eyes as those of his father. Right after dinner that night, Scottie said to me 'Mother, I think Harrison suffers from depression.' That was *before* Harrison's wife died. So next time you're at the drugstore, you get him some ginkgo and you have him take some every day! That's really helped my Jimmy."

Phyllis lives with a husband who struggles. Working as a nurse, she learned a lot about natural remedies. She loves to tell a story about the time she and her mother, Mary, went to a small workshop with Dr. Andrew Weil at the Feathered Pipe Ranch near Helena, Montana. Dr. Weil was absolutely fascinated with her mother and asked Mary many questions about her home remedies.

"Harrison is just stuck. It's been five years, and he's still thinking about what he doesn't have," Phyllis says, washing her brushes. "But you sure are brightening up his life. He's lucky to have you. He's been living out there by himself for too long now. You just keep having fun. He needs to step back into life. Mother always used to say, 'Life is for the living.' And next time you're up at Harrison's, don't you forget to look for wild asparagus. We used to love collecting it when we were kids. I know you'd both enjoy that."

A few days later, Harrison and I sit together in his kitchen. I place a bottle of ginkgo on the table. "Have you ever seen wild asparagus around here?" I ask. He tells me he might have accidentally wiped out any asparagus a few years ago with weed killer.

"Did I ever tell you that the only three men who have lived on this ranch all lost their wives?" Harrison turns his eyes to look out the window. Last night I asked him about depression. He told me it runs in his family. This statement about dead wives creeps me out. A red-tailed hawk soars over the lower hayfield as he continues. "An indoctrination into the inevitable: we all have to face it alone."

Deep breath. Here we go again.

"A *string* of lost wives?"

"J.Y.'s wife left him in June of 1904. Both wives who lived here after that, Max's and my own, died in that same month, almost on the same day: the day when the first red peony blossoms open in that flowerbed by the bunkhouse that was planted by Max's wife."

I tell Harrison how much fun I'm having with Phyllis painting and suggest *he* take up painting to help with his depression. When we visit Phyllis together at her studio, she gets on board and tells Harrison to "get going!" Pretty quickly, he comes up with an original idea.

"You're an art historian," he says to me one day late in October. "Tell me, has anyone you know of ever painted a portrait of a woman lighting her pubic hair on fire?"

"I believe you would be a first in that undertaking."

"Well then, I'd like to do a portrait of Tawi. But I'd need a nude model."

"I'll be your model," I offer. It's worth it just to watch his jaw drop.

"Okay!" he cheers, as he hurries out of the kitchen. He returns with new paintbrushes, tubes of watercolor, paper, and an easel.

Beautiful chunky snowflakes fall outside that afternoon. I insist he make a fire in the wood stove by the kitchen couch before I strip down. Harrison is amazed at the thought of being an artist with his muse and is a perfect gentleman. While I lie still on the couch, pretending to hold a match to my crotch. I'm so happy Phyllis is back for good. And Harrison appears to be taking this assignment seriously. He ends up creating a fine and truly original watercolor. A pillow at the feet of his reclining Tawi features a gnome-like figure who seems to observe her performance aghast. A hidden self-portrait within a portrait. Harrison proudly titles it "Burning Bush."

DOLLAR

Fall, 2006. Tricolor Drum explodes from the kennel door. Outside, he pees in excitement, then leaps onto the truck's tailgate and scurries into one of two compartments in a large dog box. Nell is already in the cab with Willow, jumping from one seat to the next, tail snapping, owning the space. GPS and electric collars are charged and loaded. Harrison dumps his unloaded gun, a dog whistle, a cooler with lunch, and a box of extra shells into the back seat before attending to Dollar.

Gently, he bends to lift his heavy-coated white setter onto the bed of the truck, where we sit on either side. I wrap my arm around Dollar's still body while Harrison speaks. Dollar lifts his head to meet our eyes, tail wagging. "Good boy, Dollar. What a good, sweet boy," we tell him, as Harrison eases him into the second compartment and latches the door.

We have made a point to sit often with Dollar over the past year, showing him tenderness in hopes of coaxing a lost spirit back into its body. Slowly, the real Dollar is emerging. Today will be his first hunt.

Five miles down the county road, we turn into Leroy Strand's neighboring ranch. Winds are howling. Harrison drives along a dirt ranch road that takes us around a bend up and through wide-open grasslands for another four miles. Rumbling over cattle guards, Willow hides. Nell is whining like a falcon, hunting from her front-seat perch. We stop to park at our favorite spot: right between Round and Square buttes. They rise on either side of us like two massive ships in a moving sea of dried grass. This place feels unspeakably powerful. Just this one pasture is nine thousand acres. Composed of some thirty thousand acres in all, the wild grasslands of this ranch are rich with natural springs and creeks, wildlife and birds. Not so long ago, all this country was a home to Indigenous Northern Plains people—Blackfoot and Crow, Assiniboine, Atsina, and Plains Cree—and millions of roaming bison.

Nell bolts from the truck the second a door opens. She takes off like lightning. Nell is even more dominant now than that self-confident tricolor puppy I first met last year. If she had her way, she'd hunt hard for hours until she collapsed. Harrison yells, demands his little diva come back. "Stay put," he growls, putting on two collars. Drummy barks with excitement from his dog box. Even Dollar joins in. But they'll have to wait their turns. Willow stands calm, she knows the drill. She'll heel for hours of walking today while we follow one bird dog at a time. Harrison and Nell are still arguing. Two alphas. She squirms to be cut loose; insists he must hurry. She was *born* ready.

Harrison taps Nell on the back. "Okay!"

She is off! Silky black ears flap like wings as she swings around to read the wind. Harrison blows a whistle as we step out to follow, leaving Drum and Dollar complaining back at the truck. When she is too far to hear or the wind is too loud, he uses the sound-only mode on the collar to encourage her return. When nothing else works, when Nell is too headstrong to even *pretend* she is listening, Harrison employs the lowest setting on the electric collar. This delivers the irritating buzz she's been trained to turn off by changing her course.

"Look at her go!"

She disappears in tall grasses. We follow her using GPS through bunch grass, timothy, wild buffalo grass, blue grama, crested wheatgrass, green needlegrass, needle-and-thread.

"She's eight hundred yards away now and coming back. Without the collar, she'd be gone in a heartbeat."

I've seen Nell run full speed toward a cliff drop-off she didn't anticipate until Harrison buzzed her, just in time, to stop and turn. Drummy and Nell have both run into porcupines and been covered with needles, out of sight and in need of help. Drum was once drawn away from us by coyotes to the point of danger. In this wild expanse, dogs can easily become disoriented and lost or too exhausted to move. In a fast-approaching blizzard, we have used collars to get two dogs back to us safely before a total whiteout.

Harrison's receiver beeps.

"She's on point! Four hundred yards in that direction."

Our pace doubles up a knoll, Willow by our side. When at last we spot her diminutive body, she's frozen in place with a powerful point, tail erect. I stay back with Willow as Harrison walks in. Using her eyes as her head shifts, Nell shows Harrison where birds will flush. He steps in slowly now, shotgun at the ready. A covey of seven Hungarian partridges rises in a flash of red tail feathers. Bang! Before the shot bird even reaches the ground, Nell has taken off to find her next covey. Harrison retrieves the bird and we move on.

We begin traipsing now around the very place where Phyllis's grandparents and mother, the Fontana family, once lived. I recall Phyllis's written description of her grandparents' homestead and those of thirty-two other families that "popped up like mushrooms" at the foot of Round Butte in the early 1900s.

"During summer months, everyone went for picnics by Cottonwood Creek, and youngsters, eager to help, struggled manfully with baskets loaded down with good things to eat. Often there were taffy pulls. There was hunting too, for deer and elk, and for pheasants, grouse and prairie chickens. And there was good fishing in the streams and rivers. In winter, everyone would bundle up and gather at someone's home, traveling on horse drawn buggies or sleds. Heated and wrapped bricks placed on the floor of the buggy would keep their feet warm against bitter cold. After sharing a feast, later in the evenings, a rug would be rolled up in the largest room for music and dancing until daylight, with one bedroom for card games, another for children to sleep."

Nell keeps us traveling. She points two more coveys of huns and three groups of sharpies until her breathing becomes labored. We call her in and head toward the truck. Passing down along the southern edge of Round Butte, we discover a string of irrigation ditches and a couple of stone foundations. Christopher Fontana, Phyllis's grandfather, had built a four-room home, a bunkhouse, and spring house somewhere around here. This empty place was once filled with *vida Italiana*.

After a picnic lunch, Harrison brings out Drummy, who hunts closer and checks in more often. We head off to follow this gentleman's setter around the far side of Round Butte to a group of hills known by locals as the Libby's. Harrison's long legs carry him efficiently. I run with Willow to catch up.

"We can see this hillside from your kitchen window. Did you know it is called Amelia's Butte?" I ask. "Last week Phyllis told me the story. Amelia was a young girl—an early relative of Phyllis's—who got pregnant out of wedlock. She was shuttled off somewhere to give birth, then brought home without her baby. She was told never to tell a soul. Traumatized by postpartum separation and grief, the poor girl killed herself. Drank sheep dip and poisoned herself right here." A young girl sworn to silence against her will. Like my mother. Like so many girls and women.

"What an awful way to go," Harrison says, just before the beeper sounds. "Drum's on point!"

The setter's strangely sunken body and rigid tail are barely visible in high grass. Compared to his standing point when birds are far, this stealthy positioning, low and conspiratorial, is how Drummy uses his body to tell us: "I know they're really close." Harrison holds his shotgun ready and moves in. I crouch with Willow at a distance. Fifteen sharp-tailed grouse burst into flight. Harrison's shotgun fires once, twice as the throaty cluck, cluck, cluck, cluck of sharpies fills the air. Birds flutter in all directions. When one falls, Drum rushes in to show us the spot. Harrison swings the lifeless body in front of him and pets his dog's head, before Drummy takes leave.

"Look at *this*!" Harrison says.

Willow is at his feet now, jumping and snapping at the grouse. She gets a few feathers in her mouth.

"She wants to be a bird dog! This will be fun. Put your hands over her eyes for a second," he says.

Harrison hides the dead bird in the grass while I squat next to Willow.

"Dead bird, dead bird, Willow. Find the dead bird!"

I let her go. Harrison and I talk with great excitement as we walk around the area, encouraging her interest. She begins to run in circles and quickly traces fresh scent to the exact spot. In no time, she has scooped the bird into her mouth and is trotting away. I call. She brings the bird, reluctantly, and drops it right into my hands.

"Good girl, Willow!" Harrison praises.

I begin to hand the bird off quickly to Harrison. But something about this body's warmth in my hands makes me pause. I think back to the museum. Bustles of bird feathers. Regalia worn for a dance that honors prairie fowl. All the birds and animals that have provided *everything* for Indigenous people. How deeply the spiritual nature of those relationships is interwoven in the act of hunting. I take a moment to appreciate this generous bird.

When I hand the grouse to Harrison, Willow jumps to grab it again.

"Your Willow might turn out to be an excellent retriever in the field," he observes, placing the sharpie in the back pocket of his orange hunting vest.

"Good girl," I say to Willow.

All I knew of grass until these days of walking miles with Harrison was mowed lawns in cities, sprayed with chemicals, kept neat and trim. Now I see how cattle, the wild elk and deer in this valley depend on grasslands for shelter and food. As do migratory waterbirds, songbirds, and raptors in different seasons. As wild bison once did. Their grazing, in turn, encourages the continued growth and health of habitat. Within the dense understories of this expansive landscape grow silver sagebrush, yarrow, wild roses and rose hips, snowberries, wild currants, arrowleaf balsamroot. It's ideal cover for the upland birds we seek.

This land begins signaling to me where everything lives, the preferences of each of its inhabitants. I have seen sharpies affect brilliant evasions from predators, scurrying through tall grasses and bushes where they are so well camouflaged. To avoid aerial attacks by raptors, I've seen these large, mottled brown and gray prairie grouse dodge, fly, and perch in trees, using branches as protection. During a harsh winter, I discover both sharptails and huns burrow into snow for insulation and the safety of concealment. I see how grasses and shrubs in warmer months provide perfect nesting grounds.

Like the English setters, I come to understand that sharptails travel and feed at much higher ranges. They cover more ground, whereas huns typically live their entire life along coulees. Hungarian (gray) partridge ("huns") are smaller birds with cinnamon-colored heads, gray sides with vertical chestnut-colored bar patterns, and grayish to brownish backs. Their outer tail feathers are a distinctive rusty-red, visible as they fly away. Huns often prefer the margins, the edges of deep coulees, where fields and native shrubs meet. They find comfort along the edges of hilltops and ridges. Moving around Leroy's dramatic chasms of the Arrow Creek breaks, I begin to feel the likelihood of huns in my body. Traipsing through an interior area of grasslands, I feel the nearness of sharpies. The softness of cheatgrass underfoot is what huns prefer. Coarser grasses that crunch as we walk are more likely to hold sharpies.

Drum has done well today and is ready for a rest. It is Dollar's turn at last.

We'll use only sound beeps on his collar to keep track. Harrison opens the box and gently brings him out. His relative stupor remains; legs tight, eyes shy, seeking approval. We stroke him, speak reassuringly. The fragrance of this open space is enlivening. His feathered tail lifts to wag, his head rises, eyes smile. Dollar's response reminds me of Harrison: the way he responds to nature; the way he responds to seeing me.

I marvel at how dramatically all this effort on Dollar's behalf is beginning to pay off. As his innate sweetness and tenderness gradually surface, Harrison's tenderness surfaces too. From the very beginning, Harrison knew what an abused creature needed most. Kindness. Patience. No pressure. Love. At his best, this is also what Harrison affords me.

Dollar stretches out as he leaves us to run through open country, free at last. What a pleasure to witness him rediscover what it is to be alive! Through sensibilities he has inherited, he discerns the subtle scents of distinct feathers on a breeze. He turns to follow the arousing sounds of a meadowlark, and now, a covey of sharptails clucking quietly in tall grasses. He is dancing. He doesn't end up pointing any upland birds today, but this doesn't seem to trouble him in the least.

By the time I get home to Great Falls after a Sunday of bird hunting, it's nine o'clock in the evening. I stroke Willow lying next to me and feel the goodness of our day. I flash to another special day, years ago, spent sitting in tall grasses on the rez around this same time of year with an elder. I wanted to learn about sweetgrass. We spoke at length about the qualities of what grows from the earth—the ways in which prayers, like blades of grass, can be braided together to become stronger than any individual strand.

Closing my eyes tonight, I can still see Dollar traveling out into that vast world, exploring without fear. His running back "home" to both of us with such excitement, and the joy we felt. I can still sense those feelings—encouraging his suppleness, helping Dollar to reestablish his place in the world. Most of all, I remember *his joy*.

ARCHERY

I enter Harrison's living room the following Saturday afternoon to find him down on the floor, rolling around with Oscar. As they wrestle, Harrison growls. He jokes with snorts and fake sneezes. He pretends to bite, grabs at the skin above Oscar's stifle and keeps ramping it up, until his companion has finally had enough. Jovial and tired, his Airedale lies quiet next to Harrison, stub tail wagging. The two of them do this often. It always makes me smile. When I notice Harrison's ear is bleeding, he doesn't care.

Over tea, Tula sits on the hill outside, just beyond the kitchen porch.

"She wants to stare into the surrounding valley, dreaming," Harrison says. "So do I. That's a great state of mind."

I understand. This place pulls at me now. As if this valley's nature—like that of an emerging friendship—keeps opening itself so that I might know it better.

"Oscar likes that spot too."

"Dogs have sat like she is now—in the same spot on that same hill, since we first bought the ranch. It's always been a dog's favorite place to enjoy the mental state of watchfulness. It's why we built the house right here."

In the two largest rooms on the main floor of Harrison's house, taxidermied elk heads hang over elegant stone fireplaces made of lichen-covered rocks gathered from nearby cliffs. Each fireplace mantle, a thick gray slab of granite, originally cut to be a grave marker, was quarried from the shonkinite cliffs of Phyllis's family ranch. On one mantel, six clay Chinese figures are placed as an altar. Each woman is kneeling in contemplation, some have instruments. I recall Harrison telling me Moira's memorial gathering took place here when this new house was only a foundation. An elk's long neck overhead stretches into the room. The antlers barely clear the high wood ceiling.

"It's hard to believe now," Harrison says, gazing at high mountains from where we sit. "When I first arrived, I'd run up East Peak twice in one day, a two-thousand-foot climb. I must have put up fifty tree stands."

"Tell me the story of how you got this elk?"

"I was up and out by daybreak one fall morning. Around nine o'clock in the morning, I heard an elk bugling in an aspen patch where I knew there were springs, wallows, and mud seeping down and through—all things elk adore. I moved onto a cow trail and followed it to where I knew the bull was bedded down, just on the other side of a rise in the land. When I peeked over, I saw he was bedded within shooting range. While thinking about what to do, I noticed a yellow flower lit by sunlight. I imagined that if I aimed steadily at that flower, the flight of my arrow would drop over the rise perfectly into the elk. And it did. A moment after I shot, this elk exploded forward into the trees, falling dead as it ran. The arrow landed right behind his shoulders."

In his youth, Harrison devoured literary accounts of hunting around the world. *The Rifle and Hound in Ceylon* by Sir Samuel White Baker, *Man-Eaters of Kumaon* by Jim Corbett about tiger hunting in India, and *A Hunter's Sketches* by the Russian writer Ivan Turgenev. He has traveled to places as far-flung as Bhutan and New Zealand to follow his passions, and archery is one of them. Harrison uses a traditional bow, similar to those used by Indigenous people around the world.

He tells me about Saxton Pope, who, working as an attending doctor, learned about short distance archery from the Native American man known as Ishi, the last Yahi. After Ishi's death in 1916, Pope continued to research longbow archery with a man named Arthur Young. Together, they became pioneers of modern bowhunting.

"But killing is the same, whether it's a bow and arrow or a gun," I say.

"Once, after shooting an elk, I ran up, grabbed the arrow sticking out of the dying animal, and jerked it in and out to expedite its death."

"That's horrible! Please don't tell me stories like that. It's disturbing, so many hunters with guns everywhere, trucks pulled off along the gravel road I drive. Seems like they sit there all day looking for something to kill."

"More often than not, they shoot right *from* their trucks. They shoot, and that's it. The gun solves the problem, and it's over. Too fast and too easily. No chance to learn." He pauses. "That experience you've had with me—of being in nature for hours, in all sorts of weather, the discomfort of enduring—is part of what brings you into what's meaningful. Experiencing what animals experience. The other is just drive-by shooting."

One crisp autumn afternoon, with clouds building over the mountains and a blizzard in the forecast, Harrison and I walk through crunchy leaves over to the Red Nose cabin to set up a 3D target (a deer sculpture) he bought in town. I've asked for archery lessons. He tutors me in how to hold the bow, where to place the arrow, how to position my body, how to stand ready before pulling back on the string. He teaches me to keep my elbow high, how to pull through my back, open my chest until my shoulder blades meet. The importance of finding my anchor. Counting one-two-three, before I let go for the release.

Then he has me walk up to within five feet of the deer target and close my eyes.

"This is how the real masters in Japan teach their students. Forget about the target. Position your body. Lift your bow. As you draw back the arrow, feel the bow settle into the bones of your hand without gripping. Concentrate on the muscles at the top of your right shoulder blade. Feel your fingers accurately find the anchor. Steady yourself. You don't have to release the arrow. Just keep your eyes closed. Position yourself and pull back a few times. Notice what it feels like in your body."

I hold the tension of the string, feeling the space across my chest open.

"Japanese master archers can extinguish the flame of a candle in the darkness," he says.

I open my eyes.

"Now I want you to continue to notice what you felt before. Lock your arrow into position. Try to draw an imaginary line with your eyes, right through your arrow to a single spot on the target. As you count and hold at your anchor, everything becomes one line, before the release."

Archery feels great in my body. Feet planted, chest wide open. It reminds me of yoga. "Ah," he cheers, "that's good aiming! You've got nice form, and a good vertical line in those last three shots. Shooting at a pole was an Englishman's test. In warfare, you can hit a man in the head or anywhere below."

We've been watching clouds of white snow moving in high, first over the mountains around us at seven thousand feet. The temperature drops fast when big snowflakes reach us. We decide to each take a few last shots as the first September storm settles into the valley. While Harrison aims and draws back his bow, a group of black heifers inches closer and closer to investigate. Oscar, his gray-and-tan Airedale, decides to play a favorite game. He sits in the snow, not far behind us, perfectly still, as more and more curious heifers gather around him. Eventually, one brave heifer steps in close enough to touch noses with Oscar for a sniff. "Ruff!" He fake-snaps at her nose and sends them scurrying away. Oscar skips around, delighted, before sitting quietly in the snow to begin his game all over again.

Thanks to the distraction of our target practice, the heifers never discover the two bales of hay loaded in the bed of the truck. Before heading back to the house for tea, we drive up the hill to the mare band—eight mares who live in this Red Nose Pasture year-round. Harrison feels sure that all animals in this valley sense the coming of a storm; he wants to put eyes on these girls before the full-on blizzard expected tonight.

Sure enough, the mares are at the top of the hill; they have been waiting for us. We climb out and toss separate piles of hay, a couple flakes each. I zip up my coat and stand at a distance. Sinuous bodies maneuver around our piles, some asserting their status and pushing others away, before settling down to eat. White snow blankets their backs. Flakes swirl around us. Cold winds pick up force.

"These mares are so incredibly beautiful."

"If you love horses, spend as much time as you'd like with them," Harrison offers.

He stares out at the familiar group, most of whom he has known since they were born.

"These girls were used to constant attention, until five years ago. Since Moira died, I've done very little for them. I'm sure they'd appreciate your wanting to know them," he says, motioning for me to follow.

I'm startled by this invitation into such a sacred space.

We step closer to the group, now eating and quiet. He takes my arm as we walk in snowfall. Moving from one mare to the next, he tells me about how to stay safe. I should watch the placement of my feet in relation to theirs and maintain enough space so if one suddenly swings around, or they all bolt, I won't get hurt.

"Either stand more than arm-distance away, or place your hand on their hind end, like this."

I place my hand next to his on the back end of a large beautiful brown horse named Wicken, now covered with snow.

"You don't want them to step on you or get kicked if you can help it. Horses have blind spots and don't like being surprised by anything coming from behind. They can bolt fast, so be ready."

On the way back to his house, we pull up to the gate; I jump out to open it. As I step back in the truck, Harrison continues.

"Always be especially careful around gates or any other small enclosures with large horses. Train yourself to be thinking ahead. Learn to anticipate what might happen before it happens. You don't want to get penned in or pushed up against a fence. Gates are a place where bad things can happen."

Over hot tea in the kitchen, I am back to target practicing in my mind. Snow falls everywhere around us.

"Where did you learn about closing your eyes?"

"*Zen in the Art of Archery*," Harrison says, before finding a paperback copy in his library upstairs and handing it to me.

I read a beautiful line aloud: "A bowstring leaves the fingers the way snow slips from a branch."

According to the author (a German man named Eugen Herrigel who studied Japanese archery in 1948), what stands in the archery pupil's way is that he is too willful. He thinks that what he does not do himself does not happen. I instantly recognize myself. "The right art," cries the Master, "is purposeless and aimless!" The way to learn is "by letting go of yourself, leaving yourself and everything yours behind, so nothing more is left of you but a purposeless tension."

I recognize descriptions of archery in this book that could describe what I value about my time with Harrison: The practice of discouraging false knowledge and cleverness. Staying open and curious. Freeing the mind through *not knowing*. I think back to my fishing meltdown on the river that windy day with all the knots. My strange panic when Phyllis used a washcloth to remind me that my contorted self image was no different than a sand mandala: poof, gone!

I read one last page this evening before packing my bag, as I do most weekends, reluctantly leaving Harrison and his valley to return to my house in Great Falls.

"You know already that you should not grieve over bad shots; learn now not to rejoice over the good ones. You must free yourself from the buffetings of pleasure and pain, and learn to rise above them in easy equanimity, to rejoice as though not you but another had shot well. It shoots. It hits. The artless art."

STALKING

E scaping town on fall weekends, Harrison and I go stalking. We follow our instincts. We engage our intuition. We feel into the energy of things. I learn to notice the direction of the wind, to follow game trails, to identify tracks and notice scat. We find elk rubs—places on trees where bark has been sheared off by a bull, a tree's exposed skin where an elk feels his power. While in the woods, we hear a bull elk bugling 150 yards away. We stop. To stalk is to listen. We remain still until we hear a branch snap at a hundred yards. Only then do we move forward twenty-five yards, to stop and listen again.

As we walk slowly in full awareness on these exploratory outings, I feel more aware of Harrison's presence. Entering one place after the next, each feels thrillingly wild, especially because I'm here with him walking next to me.

A marshy spot with many tracks sets us to imagining visitors to this favorite wallow departing with mud-covered bodies, large and black as night. A tree well-hidden along an active animal trail makes Harrison ask: "Is this a good place for a tree stand?" We come upon a hidden grove imbued with the spirit of a buck's secret pathway. We find a pond where tracks large and small speak of all those who come here to drink. Each place within the landscape reveals itself as alive, vibrant, sentient. I realize how much more alive I feel since that first night we made love. Each place begs us to wonder how its distinct secrets are interconnected.

Dogs left at home, we travel around the base of a mountain one afternoon and spy a large lone bull elk. He is perched far away near the mountain's peak on a rocky outcropping. In warm late afternoon sunlight, his coat flashes red against the green of the surrounding forest, as if spotlighted on a majestic stage. He remains perfectly still, head high with enormous antlers; a king gazing out over the lower valleys and open plains of his vast kingdom. He is still inhabiting this dramatic perch when we leave some twenty minutes later. He waits for the safety of night.

I become aware of each twig and branch beneath my feet. A deer is nearby; we drop to hide. Wait. Check the wind. Finally step out again with excruciating care. We are alert to the faintest shifts of air, shadow, light. We find a spot on the mountainside to sit and settle in. Hidden near an animal trail marked by dozens of elk rubs, we lean our bodies into one another and relax.

One day through the cover of trees, we spot in the distance a large flock of maybe two hundred crows. They appear first as black dots on the far side of the valley. The group follows a straight line, coming our way. The mass of dark bodies approaches and floats directly over our heads. Hundreds of crows, some speaking with great animation. They sail across the tops of the forest trees under whose branches we hide. They pass without knowing of our presence. We fall silent into the powerful sound of their wings. Awareness returns to the pain in my hips from sitting still for so long. The cold air bites my cheeks and nose.

Sometimes, while waiting in the grass or trees, before the hour when animals begin to move, Harrison speaks softly and tells funny stories. This evening as we sit, he tells me about hunting in British Columbia.

"We were well into our horseback hunt. I'd missed a very easy shot at a moose. The guide found a bedded-down caribou bull. He said, 'The hunt is getting past us; you should really think about getting this caribou.' I began to crawl, moving between stunted pine trees, going from one to the next. Got to the last one and couldn't improve on my distance. It started to snow. I waited and waited there."

As he speaks, Harrison picks at detritus. He begins placing small piles of pine needles, juniper fronds, bark, a pinecone, stems, and soil all along the camo-green surface of my folded legs. My lower body is gradually disappearing, decorated with elements of the forest floor. The ultimate camouflage. In the distant background, a bull elk bugles. Harrison continues.

"After a while I felt a rumbling in my stomach. Had to go to the bathroom. I squatted down in front of my little tree with my pants down, holding onto the tree, and went about my business. Unbeknownst to me, my guide had decided it was time for action. Far behind, he decided to lead the horses slightly in view of where the caribou might notice them, with the assumption that the caribou might think the horses were other caribou and would rise to meet them. I wasn't paying attention until I heard running hoof beats. I looked up, pants still down, to see the caribou blazing by, and grabbed an arrow. It made a staccato sound as I tried to nock it on the string. There was no more time. I came to full draw. The arrow spit right through the caribou, rose into the sky, and disappeared. I couldn't see what happened. I had to pull my pants up first. But my amused guide told me I'd made the shot perfectly. The caribou had tumbled dead."

In the last ten minutes of light, one large cow elk, then another and another, emerge from the forest. Harrison and I sit in silence, side by side. He places his bow and quiver on the ground—hunting is impossible now. As the contours of his face grow dim in fading light, the warmth of his thigh against mine is reassuring. More elk descend the mountainside trail and pass right beside us in single file, traveling on the edge of darkness. I have learned that cows always come before a bull. Female elk are highly intelligent sentries—suspicious of everything. We listen to their soft squeals, the sound of hooves. Their forms disappear as they pass through dark trees down the trail. By the time the bull who has been bugling finally approaches, we can no longer see. In the chill of complete darkness, his energy is bellicose—nothing like the cows before him. Whatever it is that is charging past us—only three yards away—bellows and growls like a wild behemoth full of his own power. It's a thrilling, albeit invisible, finale.

To walk down out of a mountainous wilderness in the dark is exhilarating and unnerving. Grasses crunch beneath my boots; shrubs catch on my shoelace hooks. I ask Harrison to wait. I wish he was more comfortable holding hands. Only the sound of his long stride and my own instinct to keep up lead me from one step to the next. On nights with no moon like tonight, we walk briskly through pitch-black wilderness. I stop for a moment, in awe, standing under a million stars. Walking again, I try not to think about mountain lions. We hear the piercing yip-yip-yip of coyotes, just above us, not far away. I jerk backward when a covey of huns underfoot explodes past my right ear, wings stirring the air. A star streaks across the night sky as we hike up the gravel driveway toward the mudroom and our sleeping dogs. I can hardly wait to be in Harrison's arms tonight.

BEST FRIENDS

Phyllis is putting the finishing touches on a fabulous portrait of her sisters Mitzi and Connie when I visit her studio tonight. Their gray-haired heads are tipped together, one is laughing. I tell her about Harrison's latest painting: a small self-portrait.

"He caught himself perfectly. The blue eyes, the crazy morning-rooster-head chestnut hair, crooked teeth, a bandanna around his neck. It looks exactly like the preppy-gone-wild rancher he is."

A familiar book by Donna Lucey, *Photographing Montana, 1894–1928: The Life and Work of Evelyn Cameron*, sits on Phyllis's painted coffee table next to the couch. I leaf through its black-and-white photographs and diary entries with nostalgia. Back when I was contemplating my big move to Montana, I spent a lot of time staring at these photos.

"It's a wonderful book, isn't it?" Phyllis says. "Donna called me a few years ago, asking if she could come and visit Lonetree."

"Really?"

Phyllis stops painting to open a scrapbook dated 2003—the same year I arrived to live in Great Falls. We look at snapshots of Phyllis, Donna, and a local historian/friend sitting on the front porch of the Meriwether. Donna Lucey, self-proclaimed "author and scholar of badass women of the Gilded Age," introduced Evelyn Cameron to the world as an important photographer of early life in the American West.

"She loved the ranch." Phyllis beams. "We walked her around to all the spots where Evelyn took photos of Lonetree, the old quarry, and shonkinite cliffs."

"Wait . . . Evelyn Cameron photographed your Lonetree Ranch?!"

"Yes!" Phyllis gets up and returns with a smaller book I've never seen with more photographs taken by Cameron. One by one, I recognize local places I've been introduced to by Phyllis and Harrison, but as Cameron saw them one hundred years ago.

"She arrived for a short visit in November 1912, when the ranch was still a stage stop and post office. She traveled from their home in eastern Montana on a bird-watching trip with her husband. They took the stagecoach between Fort Benton and our Lonetree stop. In her diaries, she writes about checking for mail at the post office she photographed. Here it is! She photographed the same building where we grew up."

In that split second, I understood we were all connected. Three women, spirits interwoven, beyond time, through a shared love for one place.

Having immigrated to Montana from faraway England with her Scottish husband in 1891, Evelyn Cameron first photographed the details of her daily life: baking bread, milking cows, working in the garden to grow what they would eat and sell for income. Like me, I imagine the culture shock and excitement she must have experienced. Soon she began traveling with her camera—often alone and on horseback—to photograph the landscapes, people, and wildlife of their new American home. She took hunting photos. Photos of new log cabins being built. The strength of her early photographic portraits reminds me of Phyllis's painted portraits. During my ten years living in New York City (later Atlanta) and spending summers in Montana, I studied Cameron's images and imagined this independent woman's early life in Montana as my own.

Evelyn Cameron's black-and-white photographs are among the first ever to be taken of Western North American birds in their natural habitat. I turn the page to one of my favorites, a close-up of a great blue heron on its nest. It reminds me now of the heron rookery I pass on the road between Harrison's ranch and Great Falls. In 1907, Cameron found a rare friend in young Janet (Jennie) Williams when Jennie's family moved from Minneapolis to live nearby. Cameron often wrote about her husband's struggle with depression. Her diaries suggest she was as relieved and grateful then, as I am now, to have found a female friend in her isolated new life. She mentored Jennie—as the daughter she never had—in baking, canning, farming, and other survival skills. Many years after Cameron's death, Donna Lucey would unearth her dusty glass negatives and diaries in this best friend's basement.

I stop at a portrait taken of these two women in March of 1910, sitting side by side in a doorway of a log cabin. Both women wear blouses and long riding skirts. Their hair is swept back and up. Evelyn Cameron would have been forty-two; Jennie, twenty-six. They lean together with eyes full of love, hands gathered at the center.

ELK LOVE

T oday at work I focus on a girl's elk-tooth dress. Made of red-and-blue trade wool, the dress is adorned with many rows of special elk teeth. Each mature elk has only two ivory eye teeth. These are elk canine teeth, left over from their ancient ancestors who had tusks where two ivory teeth are today. On this side of the Rocky Mountains, the Crow, Cheyenne, and Lakota consider the elk-tooth dress a signifier of family wealth and status; its rows of ivory teeth illustrate hunting prowess and deep love. A Lakota consultant tells me that women have created traditional elk-tooth dresses with pride and used them for many kinds of occasions, including weddings and gatherings to celebrate newborns and young girls. They could wear them to those celebrations or make gifts of them.

A story recorded in the early 1900s about a Teton Dakota Elk Dreamer named Shooter provides further details. When a man killed his first elk, the two ivories were saved for a necklace for his bride or for his daughter. To procure enough teeth for an entire dress, a father or husband had to be an excellent hunter over many years or have enough wealth in horses or other belongings to obtain teeth through trade. These ivories were considered especially prestigious when elk were hunted with bow and arrow. [3]

I've shared with Harrison what I'm learning about the significance of elk among Northern Plains tribes. He is always interested, especially during hunting season. When Max calls him in late September to ask about hunting, Harrison encourages him to come out and make himself at home any time.

Max loves the valley. He calls each year to come visit and to hunt elk. Harrison bought his place from Max and speaks of him as the one man who has most changed his life. After Max's thirty-some years of living there, Max knows exactly the right time to hunt. He feels it.

When we arrive at the ranch one Friday evening, someone's truck is in the driveway. Bull elk are screaming at a feverish pitch in every part of the valley. Bugles begin with a low bellow, then crescendo to ecstatic high-pitched trumpeting. "Max is right on the money. Listen to that!" Harrison says. We walk down the long dark hallway to the kitchen and find Max asleep on the couch. The last log of a wood fire still burns warm in the stove next to him. At the sound of our arrival, he awakes.

Max is a small red-cheeked, gray-haired man, maybe eighty years old. I discover he is mannered and easy going, a gentleman like others I've met of his generation. We sit by the stove while he tells us about his day of hunting. He shares a few good stories about his uncle J.Y. There is a playfulness in this elderly rancher's spirit.

The next morning, the three of us rise early to prepare for the day's hunt. The morning is cold and snowy. We make coffee. Max builds another fire. With full knowledge that a Montanan would want only eggs and sausage, Harrison and I fix a big Virginia breakfast anyway: fried tomatoes, sausage patties, fried eggs, and grits with lots of butter and parmesan cheese. Over more coffee, Max and Harrison spend time looking through the spotting scope at several groups of elk. Finally, it's time to head out. Harrison intends to help his friend.

The first place he drives us, we see elk far off with no way to get closer. Before Harrison can drive on, Max gets out politely and takes a shot with his rifle. Max's eyes are not what they used to be. He has a hard time walking now. Harrison says he will do his best to get us much closer. From this one far side of the ranch, he gets a notion that if we race to a spot on the other side of the valley, there will be a convergence of several smaller groups. We can meet the herd there. While

Harrison drives, Max laughs easily at himself. He jokes with me. "Lynne, do you shoot? You must be better than this old man!"

Harrison edges up the last hill and around the bend. "Okay, this is your chance . . . so *be ready!*" Max rolls down the truck window in the front seat and sticks his rifle out. Harrison stops the truck. I note this gesture. He is sublimating his disgust for roadside hunting; his love for this friend is his single priority. I recall him telling me about an old gentleman fisherman named George, whom he met years ago, when George was about the same age as Max is now. Harrison befriended the older man, finding him stuck in the middle of a river with a fish on the line. Harrison waded out and took hold of him, helping George to move downstream safely and follow the largest salmon he'd ever hooked.

Suddenly, a single cow elk steps out from the willows and stops not more than fifty yards away from the truck on Max's side. He aims, shoots once. She drops stone dead, right in front of the truck.

"Nice shooting! Shot straight through the head!" Harrison pats Max on the back warmly before we all get out. A perfect shot.

This is my first time witnessing the shooting and killing of an elk with a rifle. I'm shocked. She appeared like an apparition. It happened so quickly. I step out slowly and stand in the cold, looking at the body that two minutes earlier was alive. Max and Harrison are relaxed. Max pulls out a knife, a hatchet. I remain separate. I walk off to escape. But I cannot stay away. This is something I want to know, to experience. I brace myself and turn back.

Max has already begun the process of dressing the elk, opening it up from its anus to the bottom of its rib cage without perforating any intestines, then using a hatchet to hammer a big hunting knife and break the pelvis. Reaching up through the ribcage where the diaphragm separates lungs and heart, he slides the steaming intestines onto the grass. It is bloody. In discomfort, I step farther back from the oozing pile of steaming organs.

Max is meticulous and casual. There is good humor about what he has done many times throughout his life. I tell him this is my first time seeing an elk gutted. Kneeling down in the snow, I touch the hair of the cow elk's head and feel her waning warmth. Her eyes are open. Wet. Was she stepping out to assess danger for others? I say a silent blessing. Max asks me if I would like her two eye teeth. I nod slowly. He places them in the palm of my hand. "Maybe you can make some nice earrings with those," he suggests.

I examine the two small teeth in my hand while Max finishes his work. They are beautiful indeed. I pick one up, hold it between my fingers to feel its hard, smooth surface. I nestle this pair in my palm and say another prayer.

When Max returns with his truck, he sets up a come-along at its front end. Then he releases the cable over the cab of the truck, hooks it to the elk on the ground, and lifts her neatly into the truck bed. It's impressive.

Such ease this aging rancher has in moving what must weigh five hundred pounds. These are the practical details of managing death. I appreciate the fact that Max is happy. Something elemental in him has been reignited once more. He gives Harrison the tenderloin. Max will enjoy the rest of this meat all winter with his family. He tries to joke again as he says out loud that this might be his last elk.

We take pictures of each other outside the mudroom before Max heads to town. I take one of Max and Harrison. Max takes the first photograph of Harrison and me together. We are leaning against a truck next to each other in our winter coats and muck boots. In the photo, I am smiling brightly. Harrison gives a puzzled look with one eyebrow raised. Oscar and Tula are jumping up on me.

As Max drives off, Harrison pats me on the back. "Well, that was something new for you. Congratulations. You got to see the whole thing. He's quite a man. I'm glad we could do that for him."

We head upstairs, Harrison carrying the raw tenderloin. He cooks a beautiful dinner to celebrate the success of the hunt. "Here's to Max's happiness and your first real elk-hunting experience," he says, raising a glass to toast over a spicy elk stir-fry with cabbage, red chili, ginger, and garlic.

"I read about Elk Dreamers at work this past week," I tell him. "Men who saw elk in their dreams or in a vision and obtained the power of elk medicine. Members of an Elk Dreamer's Society were known for their mysterious powers to win women's hearts. If a young man had trouble finding a mate or if spouses were fighting, an Elk Dreamer could employ his power and influence, particularly when it involved courting couples."

"Did they do this?" Harrison leans over his plate toward me and flashes a fast flickering of his tongue.

"What's *that*?" I say, recoiling.

"A bull is a bull is a bull—whether it's my Angus or these elk. We *all* want to smell for readiness."

He curls an upper lip in my direction. I roll my eyes.

Then I remember my favorite red stone pipe bowl in the museum's collection: the incised image of the bull elk with his nose lifted; the huge snake he wears like a necklace; the snake's tongue extended. It's hard not to blush while I describe it to Harrison.

"Once you start looking," I note, "there are references everywhere to the importance of elk in relation to issues of the heart. Elk medicine was considered one of the most potent. Which makes perfect sense to me, now that I'm learning all about them here with you."

From the dinner table, we listen to two bulls bugling from across the valley. I take a sip of water and recall the many strange new sounds I've heard this fall over weekends, right outside Harrison's bedroom windows.

"Their voices are such amazing instruments, aren't they? Ecstatic bugling. A melodic cadence so plaintive, like a flute. Staccato squeaks and squeals. The drone of guttural roars, and chuckling into the night. Nobody could deny their power!"

Harrison nods and smiles, eyes bright. I regale him with the stories I've read about Native Elk Dreamer societies and their relationships to matters of the heart. He appreciates hearing more about the deep significance of an elk-tooth dress. We reflect on the blessing of this dinner and this day.

Later that evening, walking down the hallway toward the bedroom, Harrison suddenly turns to me and makes an unusual demand. "Take off all your clothes and go lie down!"

"What?"

"Just do it! This is important!" he insists, as he disappears into the bathroom.

A few moments later, he reappears before me transformed, as an elk with antlers made of sticks. I burst out laughing. He's naked and has painted himself with washable paint his grandchildren use in the bathtub, camouflage green stripes and orange arrows pointing toward his penis, a blanket from the bed thrown over his back. He lifts his head to let out a loud bull-like squeal, makes chuckling noises while rocking his shoulders and hips in front of me. Now I'm laughing so hard my eyes water. He drops his stick antlers to rock me in his arms.

"Well," he says, lying next to me in bed, ". . . it is consummated. The initiation is now complete. This was your first time experiencing an elk being killed. I'm glad it was quick; she didn't suffer. Then you got to see it gutted out expertly and loaded onto a truck by a real gentleman elder and seasoned hunter who has spent much of his life in this valley. You felt his deep appreciation of elk and that entire experience. Then I cooked a delicious elk dinner for you . . . "

He waits for me to finish his sentence.

"... And then a crazy bull mates me!"

He smiles. Turning to lie on his right side, facing me, he settles his head into his pillow and draws the pad of his left index finger along a faint line of orange paint on my belly.

Laying here next to my lover in rut, I am ready for stillness. We close our eyes and allow sleepiness to come. Screaming winds and the whistles of bull elk fill the darkness of night. Hunting season gives way to winter's cold and a new year.

THIN ICE

Winter, 2007. January in Montana can bring deep snow, raging blizzards, arctic winds. The unexpected often demands one's full attention.

On a walk high along the upper banks of the Missouri River one cold afternoon, I'm talking with Harrison on my phone while Willow explores below me off leash.

"We were walking here early yesterday morning, and I got to see those spectacular white ice crystals—hoar frost. It shimmered all along one section of the river's edge, then melted and disappeared. The same thing we saw last weekend on your creek, remember?" I look far below. "Willow is down there on the river right now, having a grand time."

"Well, the one thing you *don't* want is for a dog to walk out on ice—"

"She's out there right now."

And in that one breathless instant, I watch Willow drop right through the ice.

"Oh my God, *she's in the river!* What do I do?" I yell, running down the path toward her, clutching the phone to my ear.

"*Do not* go out on the ice yourself. You can call to her, encourage her. Hopefully, she can make it out on her own, but don't you step out onto the ice."

"*Willow!*" All I can see as I run is her gold head, her nose pointing upward, her front feet rising, then slipping back into the icy river. Again, she tries. And again. But it is too slippery. *All I can do is watch.* Six tries. Now seven. I am closer. I can see she's getting tired. *Please* don't drown, Willow. *Keep trying!* I clap my hands from the bank. "*Willow! Come on! You can do it! Come on, Willow!*"

Standing at the edge of the icy river now, my heavy breath becomes clouds of vapor. Finally, Willow gets one front leg planted, then both, just far enough to pull herself up. She is out! With a feeble attempt to shake herself dry, she slips again. I call for her to come toward me, until she gains footing and begins to travel. Gingerly, at last, she steps off the icy river and onto the snowy bank. I shudder as I drop the phone to sweep my cold wet friend up into my arms.

The following weekend, when snow in his valley has a heavy layer of frost on top, Harrison and I head to the Red Nose Pasture in the afternoon with hay for the mares. We spot all eight, standing tall and still, staring at us from the opposite bank of the creek: Haiti, Hess, Halcyon, Ibis, Wicken, Maruka, Sassy, and young Burna. Their backs are covered with snow. Icicles hang from their manes. This looks especially beautiful on Sassy, who is dark like Black Beauty. Halcyon is equally striking, her coat a gorgeous gray white. These girls have been waiting for us. They lick their lips, smelling the hay. But they know well what Willow and I had not. They will not step out onto ice.

"If a horse's legs are compromised, they're finished. They're way too smart to risk it. Hold on," Harrison says, plowing the truck right over the creek. The sounds of ice chunks crunch, break, and clatter beneath the tires. The horses move around one other. We park and spread flakes of hay in separate piles so that each horse has plenty of space. Dominant mares—sisters Haiti, Halcyon, and Hess—push to make their claim, others move off and away. Like Haiti, the lead mare, Halcyon is alive with tension. Harrison tells me the entire "H" family genetics carry an emotional strain. But today they settle quickly. They are cold and hungry. Anyone living in nature—including these mares —must carry deep practical knowledge about how best to look out for themselves if they are to survive.

One particularly cold morning, Harrison and I head down to the barn to check on animals after a punishing blizzard. As we approach the pond, he stops the truck. We both gasp. Blood, a lot of blood, is smeared across the pond's frozen surface, a broad long red skid mark on a canvas of white.

"Oh my God! What happened?!"

Leaving dogs in the truck, we climb out for a closer look.

The gruesome trail ends in the center of the pond, where a mangled deer lies partially frozen. Tempering my shock, we inspect the scene more carefully.

"Look at that," Harrison says, pointing to the far end of the pond. "The violence must have begun there, where the blood begins, just below that high bank." We walk down, find tufts of deer hair, and what look like scratch marks in the ice. This is not the first kill we've encountered together on the ranch.

"During last night's storm, a lion must have waited or stalked a doe until it traveled right here, stepping out to cross the ice."

We walk up and around to investigate the high bank above. Blowing winds have erased any tracks. Clues are often all one will ever know of lions. They are brilliant at remaining invisible. The most dangerous predator in Harrison's valley knows everything about how to use the contours of the land, dense woods, low visibility, cold, wind, the difficulties of deep snow, and darkness, all to its advantage.

We imagine this wilderness 'murder mystery' as it unfolded. At the perfect moment, the lion must have burst out to attack its prey below. It acted with full knowledge of its advantage, digging dagger-like claws into the ice for traction. The deer could not have run on ice with cloven hooves. It never had a chance. In the blistering cold of last night's attack, its neck would have been broken quickly, its bleeding body slammed across slippery ice without mercy. Its organs must have been devoured while they were still warm, before the sated lion slipped away into the invisible white of the night storm, carrying the stains and scent of its victim with it. We stand on the bank in silence. I think about the mares. I am sure they know about lions.

On our way to the barn, a doe and young twins are pawing at snow to eat the grass beneath. I feel acute concern for their safety.

"Aren't you worried for your cows?" I ask.

"Lions have plenty of feed here with all these deer. Some ranchers around Montana lose calves to lions every year. We don't seem to have that problem. I suppose they're like all animals: they prefer to expend the least amount of energy possible to get what they want. But everything in this valley knows about lions."

Lions often kill deer near the house, all along the corridor of trees that line the creek and pond. Last year Leroy's ranch manager showed us a mountain lion's cache near Cottonwood Creek, where a cat had dragged a deer kill and covered it with grasses and brush to store for later. That same year, Harrison and I were walking in the snow one morning after a heavy snow when we discovered the tracks of more than one lion, one large and several small, around a fresh deer kill in the woods beside the creek, just a three-minute walk from his house. It appeared we were looking at the tracks of a female feeding and training her cubs.

That was the first time I had seen how lions will sometimes surgically remove their favorite organs, then walk away. In a place like this, mountain lions can afford to take only what they prefer. All meat eaters know organs provide the most power. We've watched the remains of a lion kill feed hungry eagles, coyotes, crows, and magpies for days. Even our dogs.

"Twice a year," Harrison tells me one evening, "I'm snowbound here for several days. I can't really go anywhere. I don't mind. But it's hard on animals."

The next weekend, a power outage (and a generator that never switches on) leaves us without heat, lights, or phone service in the middle of a two-day snowstorm. On other occasions, pipes have burst. Cars won't start. Brakes freeze after driving through the icy creek to and from his house. Last winter, the heater in Harrison's dog kennel shut down. Everything must work harder, and often gives out. While none of this seems to faze Harrison, it all (still) triggers low levels of panic for me. I try to help out as best I can. Mostly, I feel relief that these considerable responsibilities of keeping everything going on an isolated ranch aren't mine to carry. I keep a sharp eye out for sick animals, for frozen watering tanks. I assume a constant concern that creatures have enough to eat and drink. I remind myself that Harrison is doing everything he can to keep them all safe.

One brisk winter's evening after a week of below-zero temperatures, a white feral cat suddenly appears, like a ghost, outside Harrison's kitchen window. We have caught a glimpse of him only once or twice down at the barn. He is desperate enough tonight to show himself and beg for food. Again, I feel alarmed—and grateful for the chance to help. A plate of warmed leftover elk meat set outside disappears within moments. Harrison puts cracked corn out for deer but then discovers in doing so that he has gathered bait for a hungry lion. Wild creatures must largely be left to fend for themselves.

Sitting across from me over dinner at a restaurant back in town, Harrison is flaunting what he refers to as his "superior Virginian heritage," a family lineage that includes Richard Henry Lee, a signer of the Declaration of Independence. I don't know Harrison to be a racist. But suddenly everything my parents—and later, Black and Brown artists, scholars, friends—have taught me about racism sounds the bell. He seizes on my dislike of the word "superior."

"Isn't part of your job to make judgments about why some works of art are *superior* to others?"

"Harrison, 'superior' is the language of *oppression*—the habit of placing a higher value on some people over others."

He pauses. "I suppose you're right. That wasn't my intention. I've never really thought about it that way."

I sit with his words. They ring true, albeit shocking, like the plumber admitting he had never met anyone with black skin.

"Where I come from, white privilege has a long and complicated history. And you're quite right when it comes to men. We're hopeless. Women are *always* more interesting." He takes a sip of wine. "We need more powerful women in leadership positions. I don't understand why women don't all just pull together to form some sort of global radio network to educate and organize the masses. Does something like that exist? It's so obvious."

"If only it were that easy. You really don't get it, do you, Harrison?"

"As far as I can see," he says, "your gender taking the reins is the only hope we've got."

I told him about the man exposing himself when I was a girl and my mother's story of incest. He seemed both flummoxed and horrified. I love that he appreciates women. And, on a regular basis, I am jolted by what I discover he has never stopped to consider.

Sitting by the kitchen's wood stove surrounded by windows on the ranch, we watch a rough-legged hawk soar over snow-covered fields and ridges scouting for mice, rabbits, partridge. At night, we listen to coyotes barking nearby. I imagine them talking about a fresh kill. Mice move into Harrison's house and cabins to stay warm. A rabbit holes up under the hood of an old truck. Industrious pack rats get busy.

A week after finding that dead deer on the frozen pond and just before we set off on a short road trip, the "check engine" light leads Harrison to look under the hood of a new truck he hasn't used much yet. Where is the engine? It's completely hidden! In its place, from one end to the other, we find an elaborate nest of tightly packed thistle leaves, embedded with all manner of shiny contraband. We laugh to discover Harrison's missing bird dog whistle, bottle caps, a spare key. He rolls up his sleeves to begin digging out this impressive claim by pack rat squatters, only to find new filters, hoses, and wiring destroyed.

Toward the end of the month, I'm visiting Phyllis at her studio. I relax on her couch with a cup of hot cocoa, admiring her seemingly effortless elegance at seventy-six years old. I love the way she refers to her favorite artists as intimate friends. "My good friend Matisse always said . . . "

Phyllis recounts animated stories about Picasso's love life—and about her own in the same breath. She describes the fun she had dancing the can-can at Yellowstone National Park, when she worked there as a young woman. I smile to remember the dancing stick figure at the entrance to the Meriwether at Lonetree, and recall that her older sister, Doris, is still dancing into her eighties. This is something they've come by honestly: their mother and father, Mary Fontana and John Tanner, used to give dancing lessons to anyone who was interested when Phyllis and her sisters were growing up.

"I love to dance. Harrison is a good dancer, too," I tell her.

"I bet he is," she says with a smile.

When I mention juggling endless headaches at work, she muses, "You just need to remember what Mother always says: 'A lot of people around here have never been two feet from a cow's tail!'"

She is delighted to hear stories of my weekends with Harrison on the ranch.

"My goodness, you're having all sorts of new experiences, aren't you?! People just don't understand that things are *always happening* when you live on a ranch. You just can't know until you live it."

"I couldn't believe the size of that pack rat nest"—I gesture with my hands—"It was this big! It filled the entire hood. Best of all, on one end of it they had placed a little sign they'd stolen from the dog kennel trash can that said in big bold letters: IN CASE OF PEST INFESTATION." We laugh out loud. "They must have really felt excited about their new digs," I reckon. "Kind of a shame they went to all that work, only to be evicted."

"Pack rats love to play. And they're grand collectors. I remember we had some in the house when we were growing up at Lonetree. They would take potatoes from the kitchen all the way up to the top of the stairs, then have a ball rolling them down. We'd listen to the *thud-thud-thud* for quite a little while, until Daddy would get up and shoot them, right there in the house."

"Oh dear. I suppose you can't blame creatures for trying to get comfortable and out of the cold," I say.

"I bet you didn't know anything about mountain lions or pack rats until now, did you? And calving is just around the corner for Harrison, isn't it?"

"It's all new to me and, yes, I might help with calving next month. Harrison told me a story the other day about one of his first winters on the ranch, when wind chills dipped to forty below and three feet of snow blew to create five-foot drifts. He headed out into the cold with his hired man and a tractor to where they last remembered seeing calves and dug down into those five-foot drifts, trying to save the live ones."

It is during these harsh frigid days and nights, when the barometer can drop quickly and dramatically, when every wild creature is keeping watch, looking for shelter, and waiting for advantage, that tiny new calves will be born. Two years ago, Harrison's first cow to calve went off to a hillside by herself in late January, unnoticed, and was attacked by a pack of coyotes. They may well have taken the calf before it even stood up. Its mother likely suffered temporary paralysis in giving birth because they killed her too.

When I show up on the last weekend of January, cold winds are blowing hard. Harrison and Rick are rounding up all the pregnant cows, placing the heavies—those who were bred first and are closest to giving birth—in a separate corral. The rest of the heifers (first-time mothers) are kept together in another corral, and the experienced older cows in a third corral. From these three enclosures, all across the creek from the barn, Harrison and Rick can keep close watch day and night.

It snows all weekend. I notice unusual winter songbirds, perhaps finches, on the stone walls outside Harrison's kitchen. They are cinnamon-colored with rosy wing feathers and a gray head. Next to chickadees, they look large and hardy. Each time I bundle up and step outside to feed these intrepid, cold-weather birds, they seem unafraid. I run to pour more seed for them before leaving on Sunday. At the time of year when daylight is shrinking and nights grow long, this unexpected presence of songbirds brings comfort.

NIGHT CALVING

It's one o'clock in the morning, and a winter storm is raging. The door downstairs to the mudroom slams shut several times. Harrison hasn't yet left. From bed, I imagine he must be filling a bucket with warm water to pour on the windshield so he can see and on truck doors frozen shut. Finally, I hear the sound of the engine starting. The walkie-talkie on my bedside table is turned on. Ten minutes later, under a warm comforter, I picture Harrison down at the barn, trudging around in these frigid winds and blinding snow with his flashlight through paddocks holding a total of a 180 older (experienced) pregnant cows and pregnant (first-time) three-year-old heifers to keep watch.

If he spots a cow lying down who appears to be having contractions, he will note the time. He may bring her into the barn if there's room or sit tight in his truck for a while to see what happens. If she struggles too long with no results, she may need help. If he spots a cow walking around or lying down with a calf that is halfway out and hip-locked, he has to help. While battling tonight's storm, he must check carefully in every dark corner of both paddocks for any newborns, chilled and covered in snow.

This February and March, I help over the weekends as much as possible. My ninety-minute drive often stretches to two hours through ice and snow. During big storms, I'm stuck in Great Falls. Harrison and his ranch hand, Rick, are tethered to the ranch, on constant watch with three-hour shifts. Harrison and I talk a lot by phone, but I'd rather be with him. On weekends when I am there, he leaves bed each night and heads down to the barn. I lie in the dark, waiting. This vigilance continues day and night for two long months.

During his three-hour day shifts, we sit together in his truck by the barn, heater on, and observe. Cows with huge bellies and frozen eyelashes amble in frigid temperatures, tails switching, vulvas swollen, waiting. Lying on cold ground or straw, they roll their heads, the steam of their heavy breathing visible as the pain of contractions rises and subsides.

I get to see an early calf born during this very first weekend in February. It drops like an apple to the ground as it leaves its mother's body, covered in a filmy, slightly bloody fluid. The amniotic sac of a newborn sometimes still covers its head after birth and can create breathing problems. A mother will immediately lick the calf's face and ears. Her licking serves three purposes: clears the calf's nostrils, stimulates the cow's milk production, and helps dry the calf as the pair bonds. Seconds after another calf is born this same weekend, Harrison dashes in and scoops the sack away from its nostrils and mouth when a confused first-time mother doesn't lick. He sticks a small piece of straw up each nostril causing the little one to snort and take its first breath, then dodges quickly out of the way so the young mother cow can take over.

Brutal blizzard conditions are already in full swing by the time I arrive the following weekend. The temperature is thirty-five degrees below zero—with negative 55 degrees windchill—when Harrison rolls out of bed and grabs the flashlight. He sleeps with clothes on, ready to go. I offer to come along. "There's no reason for you to be out in this storm," he says, leaning in to kiss me. As we've rehearsed, I flip my walkie-talkie's button on. He takes his in case he needs help.

I went with him last weekend one night in tough weather like this. He's walking among thirteen-hundred-pound cows on icy ground. Mothers are secretive about when and where they give birth, but when temperatures fall far below freezing, newborns are in immediate danger. With killing windchills like tonight, a mother's licking has adverse results. Her calf's wet ears will freeze and break off. Hypothermia can cause brain damage and even death. A plastic sled is kept near the calving paddock to carry calves born in extreme cold like tonight. Getting between any mother and her newborn is tricky. Once Harrison loads a calf and straps it in, he must cross an icy creek in the dark while pulling a heavy sled with an often writhing, crying, or near-dead sixty-pound calf, and its anxious mother bellowing in close pursuit. A chilled calf is placed inside a giant hot box in the barn—a warming oven for newborns. If all this happens quickly enough, a calf's body temperature usually can return to normal. A life is saved.

Harrison climbs back in under the covers a few hours later.

"Anything happen?" I ask.

"No one was giving birth tonight. Too cold." He presses next to me. His teeth are chattering. His hands feel like ice.

Several weekends later, on a cold clear and starry night, I watch with my own flashlight from a safe distance with Harrison as a bubble begins to protrude from a cow's vulva, followed by two small front feet, one ahead of the other.

The elbows clear, then a nose and eyes. Two slicked-back ears appear. The entire head is out now, followed by one shoulder, then the other as each works its way out of the pelvic opening. Suddenly, the cow stands.

"Why's she walking around?" I ask, alarmed.

Harrison is quiet as we watch the front of her calf hanging and swinging from the cow's back end. He watches for the calf to free itself. It doesn't.

"What's wrong?"

"Sometimes the hips get locked up," he says. He slides his flashlight into his coat pocket while I shine mine into the dark. He sneaks up behind the cow, grabs the suspended calf's front legs, and ratchets the body ninety degrees. It looks violent, but when the hips turn, the rest of the calf slides instantly out in a slippery mess onto the ground.

Harrison jumps away and the cow turns, nose lowered, throat rumbling as she speaks to her newborn.

On weekdays, I dress in a skirt and blouse and drive four minutes or walk to the museum. I spend long days sitting inside, researching and organizing Native American works of art for my bison exhibit. On weekends, I check road conditions and don long underwear, jeans, muck boots, and a Carhartt jacket before setting off with Willow to experience the rawness of winter night calving.

The intellectual part of me is living as a scholar/curator/educator. The heart part now lives as a help-partner and rancher-in-training, a city woman unable to have children of her own helping to deliver two hundred baby calves. This second part is both intimate and less familiar. Standing knee-deep in the flow of life, everything feels so inherently authentic, so bracing and pure. Everything has a life of its own.

I put seed out for chickadees and winter finches before we head down to the barn this morning. As I finish feeding seven barn cats, Harrison has just left a stall where a cow is locked in a chute with her head immobilized. His sleeves are rolled up; he has a tough look on his face.

"What's wrong?"

"This cow has a fetus twisted and turned upside down."

Rick is humped over. Both men have dark circles under their eyes. Harrison was short with me yesterday. They are understandably feeling the wear and tear of being on call 24/7. They are only halfway through eight exhausting weeks of calving.

"It doesn't sound good. What can you do?"

"It's dead inside her. It needs to come out."

Rick calls a vet; he asks him to come quickly. He returns a few minutes later.

"He'll do the best he can to get here in this storm. In the meantime, he wants us to pull out hot water, keep everything clean, and use plenty of lubrication."

In a cold barn, two men move into action. The vet told Rick how to use a broomstick and try to get the calf out. Harrison kneels down on straw and reaches far up into the cow until he gets his hand on the dead calf's feet and tries pulling them out. It's hard work, but he eventually gets one leg out, then a small bit of the other. Rick ties its feet to a broomstick and starts turning clockwise, trying to ratchet its body around so it's right side up and might come out more easily. It doesn't work. I cannot fathom how the cow, still locked in the headstall, is able to bear this torture.

When the vet finally arrives, we're all relieved. "It's bad out there. Can't see a thing from Geyser to here," he says, as he pulls out a knife, and makes a large cut along her left side. The calf is lifeless, gone. He removes the fetus and sutures up the cow. She dies two weeks later.

If a healthy fetus is in the correct position but a mother has been straining with contractions for too long, ranchers may resort to a milder intervention: pulling the calf. The cow is placed in a head catch in a calving stall with metal wings that fold away. The rancher reaches into the birth canal to find the calf's nose and legs and to make sure everything is facing correctly. They half hitch a strap and chain above one pastern joint, then half hitch again over that half hitch to make sure it holds. They do the same with the other leg. I've seen Harrison hook the chain to a come-along and slowly start to crank. The hand-operated winch with a rachet moves in time with the cow's contractions, resting and pulling, until the new calf drops.

"Look at that!" I notice one day, as we lean against the wooden fence, watching another calf drop to the ground. "Before the mother even licks it dry, her baby is struggling to its feet, stands up, and wobbles around in search of warm milk. All in its first five minutes of life."

"That's a good cow," Harrison tells me. "And her mother is a good mother. See how she nuzzles her calf toward her udders. Very different from some of the young heifer mothers. They all figure things out eventually. Or they leave the ranch."

Later that same day, a first-time mother becomes deeply disturbed when a small something suddenly appears on the ground behind her. She backs away as this unfamiliar creature begins moving and stumbling toward her, thrusting its nose between her hind legs. She's inexperienced, but her calf is persistent. Eventually, she relaxes and allows her baby to nurse. Meanwhile, inside the barn, a less-persistent three-hour-old's mother won't stop kicking him off, even when she is put in a head catch.

"This is the crucial time to get him fed," Harrison mumbles as he grabs some hay for the mother to eat. After tying her back leg so he won't get kicked, he milks her himself into a clean blue bucket. Back in the tack room, the yellow liquid is carefully poured into a large plastic bottle for hand feeding. He empties the last few drops onto my finger for a taste.

"It's almost like buttermilk," I say, my nose wrinkles, "with bad vanilla flavoring. And salty." My tongue rubs against the roof of my mouth to wash the taste away.

"You'll like this one better." Harrison grabs a glass jar from the fridge—cold white milk gathered yesterday from another nursing cow. It tastes creamy and sweet.

"Somehow I've lived forty-seven years of life before tasting fresh cow's milk," I marvel, enjoying another sip. "But why is the other so different?"

"If we can get it, we try to keep a jar or two of fresh colostrum on hand. It's the super-duper milk, rich in nutrients and antibodies, that cows start producing before they give birth. Calves need to ingest it within their first few hours. Same with humans. It builds a healthy immune system and boosts growth."

He turns and holds out the baby bottle.

"Offer this to your new friend. See if he'll drink."

I enter the stall quietly and sit on straw next to a tired sixty-five-pound black calf. He doesn't stir. His nose is shiny and wet. His eyes are beautiful, large and round, with long eyelashes. They blink while I scratch his cold head and ears. Everything in me wants to take care of this little fellow. Gently, I suggest the bottle, rubbing its nipple slowly along his lips. I pour a few drops on my fingers. He sniffs them. A pink tongue emerges for a lick. Together, we figure out how this can work. He takes the nipple into his mouth. I tilt the bottle and he begins to suck. He's hungry!

Harrison returns my big grin from just outside the stall. It is impossible to deny the deep wonder of feeding a newborn his very first meal. When the bottle is empty, I stay until his eyes grow sleepy.

"That will take care of him for now," says Harrison, closing the gate behind me. "We'll check later to make sure his mother is being attentive to his needs."

As the month of March comes to a close, groups of mothers and their youngsters are graduated onto clean ground. Older cow-calf pairs are in a large pasture on the northeast side of Harrison's valley along the creek. First-time mothers and their calves are moved to the pasture by the house. This allows Harrison to keep a close eye on them and make sure inexperienced heifers are mothering properly. We drive through the herd each day to check for sickness. I look for the ear tags of special calves I've cared for and know.

"Listen for anyone calling for their mothers wanting to be fed," Harrison says. "Look for mothers with big tight bags who haven't been suckled in a while. Might be a heifer who has forgotten she has a baby. Or a calf gone missing."

Tubs of mineral and protein are put out for these three-year-old mothers to get them going quicker into their next heat for the new year's breeding. Occasional winter storms can last into May. Grass won't be good until June, so in the months that follow calving and well into branding season, Rick and Harrison still deliver large round bales of hay. Hungry mothers are increasingly taxed from milking. They rush down the hill with their frisky offspring the minute they hear the tractor. Calves watch and imitate their mothers. They will soon eat hay themselves. Others, tired from a day of learning how fast they can run, lie on a fresh bed of hay to rest.

Harrison is exhausted. Steady vigilance still shapes each day, with almost two hundred new youngsters now also in his care. But I am ready to retire walkie-talkies. He is grateful for full nights of sleep.

III.

WIND

(2007–2008)

BRANDING WITH COWBOYS

Spring, 2007. I spot Harrison by the barn, saddling his gelding T when I pull up. He's got Andre tied up for me. We're gathering 180 cow-calf pairs today.

"Good morning," he says, leaning in to kiss my cheek. "I'm glad you're here. Busy morning. Rick's already up and out."

I grab a brush to clean off Andre before Harrison lifts the saddle onto his back.

"We'll bring everyone into corrals. No need to separate the pairs until early tomorrow before the branding crew gets here. You ready?"

"Sure," I say, though I'm not sure at all. I step up and into the saddle. "I'll give it a try."

We ride out into mountain pastures with Willow on our heels. Harrison holds back T with half-halts while I follow on Andre. Collecting the herd includes flushing cattle from ravines and stands of aspen. Approaching a grove, I study the angles Harrison assumes with T to make things happen. He leaves plenty of space around and behind a group, then drives from behind to move them forward. Groups of two, ten, and single cows with offspring pour out of hiding places bawling. Most funnel down hillsides to join others already gathered. For those who would rather not cooperate, Harrison positions T's body to put pressure on a cow's front shoulder and yips until she turns or stops. I join in on Andre, trying out my cowgirl yips and yaws to push one stubborn pair. Willow is fascinated.

Riding behind the gathered herd, we push them slowly toward the barn. I notice a few stray pairs wandering off toward the aspens to the right. Turning with Andre, I wave to Harrison and shout confidently,

"I've got this! Come on, Willow!" Before he can yell, "*No, wait!*" Andre and I gallop away to save the day. Willow keys off me and begins chasing the pair. We end up bringing them back at full speed and split the entire herd, sending calm mothers running, their calves scurrying in all directions like wild kittens.

Real herding, I learn quickly, is not what you see in the movies. Deliberate, calm cattle work is always more efficient. Better to encourage or invite gently than to frighten with too much pressure.

We walk our horses, side by side, behind regathered cattle toward the corrals.

"Brandings across Montana happen in April and May. I had to lock in tomorrow's date months ago," Harrison explains. "I've got six guys lined up, and I think they're working at two other brandings this weekend besides mine."

I settle into my saddle as Andre walks on. "This will be my first branding."

"You're about to see *the* big social event of the year."

We rise at the crack of dawn. After eggs and sausage, we leave the dogs at the house and go meet Rick. Harrison's corral system includes a series of metal chutes that aren't necessary today. He shows me where to stand. Gates leading to narrow alleyways are opened, some gates leading into corrals are shut.

"These passageways have curved corners instead of sharp right angles to help reduce stress," he explains, just moments before things get rolling. "They're based on Temple Grandin's understanding of how animals respond to space, shadows, and light. Once we get our sorting done, we'll put these mothers out to pasture."

We use long flexible rods with flags on one end—as well as our arms and body positioning—to move and separate calves from their mothers while keeping a safe distance. Cows bellow. Calves bawl. Metal gates slam shut and swing open. I try not to slip on cow manure or get run over as we move quickly to cut and sort.

"This is sad, taking babies from their mothers." I project my voice to be heard over the din. "They're not happy with us."

"I've done what I can," Harrison shouts, slamming another metal gate closed before a quick cow can follow her calf.

It's still early when we hear pickup trucks with horse trailers in tow rumbling along the gravel road toward the barn. Each man steps out of his truck in boots, chaps, cowboy hat, and fancy silk scarf. Some have big shiny belt buckles. Working dogs leap out behind them, border collies and heelers eager for the day. The cowboys stroll back to open their trailers and bring out their horses and tack—well-worn saddles, maybe a new one with leather that creaks and stirrups still stiff. Dogs sniff other dogs. Old friends exchange smiles and quiet jokes. The professionals have arrived.

Some of the best cowboys for miles around are here for Harrison's branding, a credit to Rick. All six are in their late forties and fifties. In their youth, these men rode saddle broncs, bucking bulls, rangy horses too ornery for the owners. Now their aging bodies carry the aches and pains of too many broken bones. But everyone seems relaxed. Friends helping friends, doing what they love.

A large round pen has been set up outside the corrals where we've gathered all the calves. Off to one side, a small propane portable stove is heating up Harrison's three different branding irons—O, C, and a crescent-moon "eyebrow" over the initials. Two large plastic barrels turned on their ends are used as tables. One station has vaccines, needles, and syringes. Another has rubber gloves, paper towels, plastic bags, notebooks, and clipboards; potato chips, candy bars, fruit, Bud Lite, and Coke for breaks. Rick's wife has prepared a meal for everyone at the end of today's work: a big batch of elk chili, cornbread, salad, and a chocolate cake.

Jim and Cody, two of the cowboys, joke around as they mount their horses, ropes at the ready. Some mother cows have already wandered off to graze. Many stand right outside the round pen, reassuring bawling calves.

"How can I help?" I ask.

Harrison hands me a clipboard and a pen. "Your job is to keep track of each calf as they're worked. Someone will shout out a calf's ear-tag number, and as they're inoculated and branded, you'll check them off." He flashes a smile. "I feel quite smart having a Ph.D. to keep my records."

Two cowboys ride into the large corral among a hundred and eighty calves and swing their lariats in the air until they rope the back legs of the first two. They walk their horses into the adjoining round pen, dragging the heeled eight-week-old calves, each weighing about two hundred pounds, behind them. Four wrestlers come forward, two swing each calf to the ground with the branding side facing up. One kneels on the calf's neck and holds a front hoof. The other grabs the top back leg, pulling it toward his chest while his boot pushes the calf's under leg away. Once each calf is restrained, more people rush in. Those with large syringes give shots. Cody stands by the hot stove, removes red-hot branding irons from the fire and hands them to Jim, who arrives to place each of three individual irons directly onto the flank of a wailing calf. It screams out in pain, tongue extended, eyes rolled back, choking on smoke that smells of its own burning hair and skin. After this traumatizing ordeal, which thankfully lasts only three to four minutes, each calf is released to find its mother. Mothers who stay close will talk to their offspring all through this rite of passage. Once released, those same good mothers are right there to reunite with their bewildered babies, offering milk and comfort.

Someone roping off horseback misses three times and gets teased by his buddies. These cowboys play while getting the job done. They work fast—calves are up and out as quickly as possible. I appreciate their comradery, horsemanship, and roping skills. Yet cowboy life in the American West is shockingly violent. Babies being dragged and burned is hard to stomach.

Behind sunglasses and a straw hat, I repeat ear-tag numbers as they're called out. I train my focus on a mindless job. It's been four years since I left an intellectually rich and creatively stimulating city life back East. Juxtapositions like this are not unfamiliar. One fall, I stayed in Montana and worked as a waitress at a tiny bar on the Blackfeet Reservation to make extra money, biding my time before returning back East to teach at Harvard. I'm grateful for the novelty of today, a chance to see more of what happens on this ranch.

Now Harrison takes his turn, grabs hot irons out of the fire and places them on hair and flesh. Calves scream out in pain as I watch him disappear in clouds of smoke. Who is this man? Maybe I am insane to think that in some mysterious way, this landscape was calling me *home*.

After fifty animals have been worked and released, ropers dismount for a break.

I put down my clipboard and step away from the group. Harrison approaches with a smile and places his hand on my back. He stinks of burned hair.

"These guys are pretty damn efficient, aren't they? They could do this in their sleep."

"It's quite a show."

"We're not needed here. Why don't you and I head back to the house and check on the dogs? Would you like that?"

After polite goodbyes we set off down the road, arm in arm. It occurs to me that ranchers usually don't leave in the middle of their own brandings. Harrison is being kind.

"Do you *have* to do this?" I ask. "Isn't there another way to identify them that isn't so painful?"

"Montana law . . . they have to be hot branded. Has to do with establishing ownership, travel, sales, possible theft. I thought this might be hard for you. We'll let them get their work done, then wander down later."

"But you built this up as lots of fun, *the* big social event of the year—"

"It is. But not mine."

The distant sound of calves and mothers calling for one other and cowboys laughing carries on spring mountain air.

"This is *my* museum," he explains. "The only thing that interests me is another chance to appreciate the aesthetics of each cow and her offspring. I study hair texture, the shape of heads and faces. Can I spot a calf's breeding in its conformation? It's strange. To know and admire these cattle brings such pleasure. Like a child with marbles. Like you might feel about a group of horses, or paintings."

"But you're picking up hot irons and *burning bodies?!*"

"And I send them to market to be killed."

In front of the house, I stop and face him.

Harrison looks into my eyes. "I don't like branding either." He pauses, still gazing at me. "This work of ranching doesn't seem to be about the ultimate destiny of cattle. It's about doing the best you can to care for animals for as long as you've got them."

Years later, I would appreciate more about the imperatives and significance of caring for cattle. I would learn about Allan Savory and holistic management practices that employ livestock to heal the environment. I would discover that cattle are some of the only herd animals today that can be used deliberately to do—in small ways—what tens of millions of wild bison once accomplished—fertilizing the land with their manure, composting it with their movements. Their grazing improves soil health, sequesters carbon, accelerates photosynthesis, stimulates plant growth, boosts biodiversity, providing a spectrum of necessary benefits to grasslands. All this helps protect and conserve the threatened ecosystems of old-growth grasslands like Harrison's. There are multiple points of view about all this. Eventually, I would

understand more about one side of the argument: Some people—
including the Audubon society—believe cattle and good practices
can help to sustain this fast-disappearing habitat that a wide diversity
of bird species, other creatures, and plants all depend on for their
survival.

By the time we walk down to the barn, branding is over. Cows and
calves have been turned out onto clean grass. Pairs have reunited. Some
calves are nursing, others are grazing. A few are playing, releasing the
stress of the day. Mother cows graze in the mid-afternoon sun. A few
dozen lie beside a large group of sleeping calves.

CHORES

J ust days after branding, flood season arrives. Harrison meets me in the rain on a Saturday morning late in May, motions for me to park at the dog kennel. I climb out in my raincoat and muck boots. Willow jumps out into mud. Harrison is drenched. Three geldings, Spoon, Sonny, and T, stand knee-deep in water in front of the barn.

"Half their paddock is underwater. Shouldn't we move these guys?" I ask, wiping rain off my glasses.

Harrison leans in to give me a slow wet kiss. "Come on, let's get to the tack room first." He motions for me to follow.

We slosh through swollen waters of Cottonwood Creek, past the horses, and into the barn. In the tack room, we gather up everything off the ground. We move saddles to higher racks and grab buckets and pitchforks before they float away. I pour cat food into dishes and climb up on stacked bales of hay to feed marooned barn cats. Next, we head back out into pouring rain with three halters to gather wet geldings and lead them to higher ground, careful not to slip and fall in slick sticky gumbo on the way up the hill. When we have done all we can, we cross a high rickety footbridge behind the old barn, then trek a quarter mile up the back way to Harrison's house in the rain.

After shaking off in the mudroom, we head upstairs.

"Makes you wonder why old Max built his barn so close to the creek," Harrison says, pouring hot tea into cups.

"This is ridiculous. You need a bridge over that last ford, closer to your house, Harrison."

"All right. This fall. When the creek is low again, you and I will build a footbridge."

Come rain or shine, I begin to help Harrison over weekends with the daily feeding of animals. Chores are done in the morning, after coffee, and again around four o'clock in the afternoon. Daily rounds are opportunities to put eyes on everyone. When we find difficulties, we attend to them. A young mare is lame; a sliver of wood is lodged in her hoof, and she needs help. Driving around, we discover a bloated cow. She is clawing at the ground, digging her own grave. I have seen this twice before—watched Harrison use a pointed object to puncture the cow's stomach; like popping a balloon, the gaseous toxins leave her belly and, this time, it saves her life. It's a good feeling to have accounted for every creature by the end of each day.

Mares, geldings, older horses, bulls, cows, and heifers are all kept in different places in the valley. Depending on the season and availability of grass, they must be fed. Harrison sometimes spells Rick in the tractor. He gives me a hand up, and while he delivers fifteen-hundred-pound round bales to older cows and bulls, I ride snug up next to him in the cab. When we drive out past Moira's gravesite in the winter pasture, where a large boulder and stone bench sit on top of the hill, is he feeling her presence?

One spring day, we travel by truck and find all the horses content in their respective pastures chasing green shoots of grass. No need for hay. The cows and their young calves graze on new grass too. Branding burns have healed. Harrison loads fifty-pound sacks of cake (protein supplement) into the back of the truck, and we head off for the daily feeding of heifers and yearling bulls. Heifers are fed cake to encourage their cycling; young bulls are confined to smaller paddocks. Some have not yet been delivered to customers. Others will soon be put out on grass with cows to breed.

We pass through the gate and into the hilly pasture that holds sixty young heifers. Harrison lowers the window and begins calling as we drive along: "C'mon, *c'mon!*"

"Each rancher has his or her own style of doing this," he tells me. "I like the old Virginia way of calling to 'em."

As compared to winter months, when heifers stand at the gate waiting for hay, spring grass is intoxicating. They're out of sight, so we drive to the top of a high hill. Stepping out, Harrison calls until black forms emerge from the aspens. When one or two start to move in our direction, we know the rest will follow. He calls until we see the whole group in motion. Girlfriends travel together. All except a few stragglers pick up into a lively run. No one wants to miss out. Mischief is writ large in these sixty pairs of big, young, brown eyes and swinging tails as they approach.

At five miles an hour, Harrison leans out his open window, pounding his hand on the side of the truck. "C'mon!" Inquisitive girls follow. This is a familiar game. They know he'll soon be pouring cake. "Right now, we're just one of the heifers," he says. "But in a few moments, they're gonna all take off ahead of us, and then . . . look! I think we've already got a yippie-yi-yay!"

As if someone had shot a pistol signaling the beginning of a race, heifers take off for the lower feed troughs, bucking and scampering through mud and grass, kicking their heels high in the air as they run beside the truck. They frolic galloping past us, chasing each other, swishing tails, veering from one side to another. Racing down the muddy hill, they slip and slide all the way. Cyndi Lauper pops into my head whenever we feed heifers.

Next, we visit the younger bulls. When we arrive outside their paddock near the Red Nose cabin, Harrison steps out, reaches into the back of the truck, and tears open two heavy bags of cake. "There's a fine line between trust and being careful here. These guys weigh upward of a thousand pounds. Always remember that!" He pours cake into troughs positioned outside the dirt paddock as fifteen hungry bulls stick their large heads and snouts through the fence rails to eat. Last week, Harrison's ninety-two-year-old neighbor, Leroy, got trampled by a bull when he stepped into a tight passageway in a bullpen.

"He survived. But I hear his entire body is still one big black bruise."

Bulls amble along like hippopotamuses. But they can move quick as lightning.

"I once saw a full-grown bull charge another bull and toss his two-thousand-pound rival into the air and over a fence." On another occasion, Harrison watched one of his bulls bolt thirty yards and instantly crush the hind end of the most expensive bull he had ever purchased. Nothing else makes deep moaning sounds like these boys. A friend of Harrison's son arrived from Los Angeles to the ranch during the night a few months ago and, stepping out of his car, became terrified. He couldn't see anything but heard monstrous noises in the dark. He dropped his luggage and ran inside the Red Nose cabin. Everyone had a good laugh the next morning.

Feeding bird dogs their dinner is our last chore of the day.

"Have you ever seen puppies born?" Harrison asks tonight, stirring canned dog food with water at the kennel sink.

"Nope."

"Would you like to? I just bred Dollar to Nell. I'm hoping you'll help me take care of her litter. We'll have puppies in two months."

I can hardly wait.

Stepping in among male dogs, Dollar is always first to run and jump on us, his butt and tail wagging wildly. Since that first hunt on Strand Ranch last fall, he has continued to blossom. Still, he carries a certain tightness. But he bubbles now with happiness.

I squat to pet the two boys after they've eaten. Dollar almost jumps into my lap. His glistening eyes look directly into mine. Harrison decided to use Dollar instead of Drummy, hoping some of his exceptional sweetness will show up in his offspring.

Trees are fully leafed out when Nellie's pups arrive eight weeks later. I'm not there for the big event, but Harrison is downstairs with Nell. He calls me at work the next day.

"What an idiot I am. I walked down to check on Nell before going to bed and discovered a first puppy had been born. So I sat next to her bed in the laundry room and proceeded to watch three more being born. I got to see the whole thing happen. Everything seemed fine, and Nell was taking care of her four little puppies when I finally went up to bed around eleven. This morning I went down to sit with her and enjoy the puppies. I found three more than when I'd left."

I head to the ranch right after work on Friday, excited to admire Nell's good work. She is, of course, excellent in this new role as mother. Vigilant and growly, she won't allow anyone except the two of us near her litter. Her puppies look more like little rats at this early stage. I pick up one at a time, cradling each tiny white body in the palm of my hand. When I bring one of the little girls up to my face, the uncanny accuracy of her tiny pink tongue finding its way straight into my mouth surprises me.

"Have you decided on names yet?"

"I was thinking of Bec for the little girl you're holding now. And I like Bastion for this little guy here," he says. He picks up another squealing body.

We head back downstairs the next morning, coffee mugs in hand. Chores can wait. I find little Bec to hold.

"Didn't you say you had an aunt named Rebecca who was important to you?"

"Aunt Rebecca was a librarian with white hair, a tremendous lower puffy throat, and big blue eyes. She worried about me and took me under her wing when I was a small boy. I'd been carted around the world, could barely speak English, and was afraid of everything."

Harrison takes a sip of coffee and strokes a puppy.

"She would leave the library each day to meet me as I walked home from elementary school. I would lie on Bec's lap on the sofa, and she would tell me stories about George Washington and the significance of not telling a lie."

Nell watches with soft eyes as I place Bec at one of her teats.

"I suppose she was telling me, 'Character is important because of the treacheries of life. Hold up your end of things, with honor and truth.' She was at the very top of what a human being can be. Someone of true substance."

"You've been lucky."

"Aunt Rebecca displayed the qualities of any great leader: steady, sound, strong. Unflappable. Someone of exceptional moral character. When called upon, they will always do the right thing. She gave me an experience of comfort and love that I sorely needed."

He reaches down to help a puppy moving in the wrong direction in search of milk. It's decided: Bec and Bastion are the two we will keep.

Chores in my family meant doing jobs around the house to earn an allowance. The importance of assuming responsibilities was a serious matter. I learned—especially from my mother—that to uphold my end of things required a meticulous and constant striving, not only to achieve but to right every wrong. My own life, like hers, would require a wicked perfectionism at any cost. In a recurring nightmare, I would see myself walking alone on a sandy beach, turning after each step to erase my tracks. *Never good enough.* Some part of me always felt defective.

Preparing our dinner tonight, I am aware that chores here with Harrison are not about expectations. No deadening requirements for perfection or self-promotion; only the honest pleasure and freedom of caring for living creatures. Caring for Harrison too. A sense of purpose. The joy that comes from *just that.*

After dinner, I say goodbye to Nell and her puppies. I kiss Harrison after loading Willow.

"I wish you didn't have to go," he whispers in my ear.

"I wish tomorrow wasn't Monday."

I gaze in the rearview mirror as I drive slowly away. A strange thought arises. What if the raw substance of my early discomfort in life, instead of continually unraveling me over time, is now weaving me back together?

I stop at the kennel to say goodbye to Dollar. His thick-coated bottom and feathered white tail wag wildly. I have tried not to invest too much in Harrison's dogs. Yet here I am, scratching and loving again on Dollar before I leave for home. Wishing these kenneled dogs had more freedom. I've already let them into my heart, just like Harrison.

INDIRECTION

Gradually, I allow myself the pleasure of coming to know all eighteen horses. Three older horses graze in a paddock next to the dog kennel. Other mares and geldings live on opposite sides of the valley where open hillsides rise to meet hidden wilderness of higher forested mountains. To open gates when hiking out to visit them on my own, I must use Moira's birthdate on combination locks. I note the strange coincidence that she and my father were born on the same day: February second. Both died rather suddenly, around the same young age.

When Harrison and I step out of the truck one fresh spring day to halter horses who need worming, he hands me the halter and points to Teaspoon, his youngest son's gelding. "Go ahead. Give it a shot."

But Spoon won't let me near him.

"Okay, show me how this is done," I say, handing the halter back to Harrison.

"This is the best way I know to approach a horse when they would rather avoid you."

Still at a distance, he moves in front of Spoon and stares straight into the gelding's eyes. Harrison begins to approach. With a halter in one hand and a tube of worming medicine in the other, he takes one step at a time. The minute Spoon begins to tense up, Harrison stops. When Spoon turns his head to one side, Harrison moves in that same direction to reestablish his front-facing position. Again, he locks eyes on Spoon's. He stretches arms and hands to either side, as I've seen him do when moving cattle, to block off space. His arms become imaginary fencing. At last, Spoon's eyes become soft. His ears tip forward. He drops his head, licks his lips, allows Harrison to approach.

Harrison places the halter over Spoon's neck and nose. He speaks softly as he inserts two fingers inside the gap in Spoon's mouth where there are no teeth, and squirts in wormer. Then he quietly removes the halter. Teaspoon returns to his buddies.

My turn. I try the same thing on Sonny, another gelding in this pasture. I talk quietly to him as I step forward, my eyes locked on his. It works!

"*Why* does it work?" I ask, rubbing Sonny's forehead while Harrison squirts wormer into his mouth. Sonny throws his head up, spits some of it out.

"It's a lot about mind control. I'm telling him: *You're mine.* My intention becomes a lariat he can't escape."

It felt more like a conversation with a horse to me: an invitation and a response. I want to know everything. I begin with the older horses. One bright day in early June, Harrison brushes Brise while I brush Andre. The bird dogs bark wildly from their kennel when a cock pheasant flushes from the willows. Setters light up with desire. These calm old horses aren't bothered.

"Brise is the most impressive horse I've ever known," Harrison says, running his hand over her back gently. "She feels things deeply. She has the softest back I've ever sat on. Her son Andre too."

"I know; Andre is incredibly comfortable to ride."

As Harrison strokes Brise, his mind and body seem to relax. He drops into a tender place.

"Brise is the spirit of a horse Bedouins wrote poetry about. She was royalty from the beginning. When Brise and her foals went to drink from a trough, they were always first. Each one of them, when they matured, was supremely confident."

Harrison's habitual platitudes about his former life are exhausting. Descriptions of horses invariably feel like descriptions of how he still feels about his dead wife.

Yet I can attest to Brise's special spirit. I remember the first time I stood next to her on my own. It felt as if I were standing near an old-growth tree. Her body emanates gravitas. At nearly thirty years old, she has lost some of her vision. She has become uneasy in her vulnerability. I am a stranger. Rocky's eyes are soft and kind, even as her arthritic knees are knotted with pain. We feel grateful all three have made it through another winter, able now to enjoy new spring grass.

I make a point to bring them treats: grain, carrots, apples. I discover Rocky is wild for carrots and will eat as many as I will allow. Andre gets pushy with his head wanting access to every bit of grain. Every so often, Brise permits me to get close enough to give her an apple. Both she and her gelding son Andre love to roll an apple around in their mouths for a long time, sucking on it, savoring it as they must have when they were foals. Harrison guesses Brise may also suck on apples because her teeth are mostly gone. While Andre and Rocky enjoy treats, I touch wet noses and rub the soft tips of furry ears.

On one morning walk, I spy Andre lying down in grass at the top of the hill. I approach quietly. He is sound asleep. Brise and Rocky are grazing nearby. Thinking I might safely lie down with my friend, I position my body near his back and head, away from his legs. As the sun rises, my body sinks into the cool ground. I listen to Brise and Rocky graze. Meadowlarks are singing. Andre snores heavily next to me. We lie on the earth for a while. He stirs. I whisper, and he allows me to stroke his head and still-closed eyes. I kneel to continue stroking my sleepy companion, who wishes to remain in his grassy bed for a bit longer. What a lovely—and completely unexpected—start to a day.

Another afternoon, while Harrison works cattle, I wander away for a hike, seeking the company of younger mares. The band of eight are grazing low, right outside the Red Nose cabin.

Haiti is seven years old, an Anglo-Trakehner. The first to come right up to me, she introduces herself, wants me to know her. She is a beautiful bay with a white mark on her forehead. The squared shape of her face is different from the others, easy to spot. Her dished brow is a mark of Arab blood on her Trakehner side. Haiti is willing to hang around for as long as she is being stroked—until, in the blink of an eye, she lifts her head. Her body spins, electrified with energy, and she gallops away. Rolling her head in the air, she acts bossy and pushy with the other mares. She drives them off, up the hill, and they are gone.

This first day alone with younger horses, Haiti taught me about her position as lead mare. Like cows and bulls, a horse can be soft and docile one minute and powerfully explosive the next. Being with a horse has a lot to do with energy: yours, theirs, and everything around you. Horses have no interest in spending time with someone who is distracted or hurried. They have little tolerance for an agitated mind. To approach a horse—to speak to them and to be with them—one must be calm and gathered, more focused and gentler than normal. Present.

On future visits, I pay attention to my energy. I take deep long breaths and practice shifting my internal gears from head to heart—before approaching. I allow for space between my thoughts and actions. The horses respond favorably. I experiment with different gestures, notice their responses, begin to discern secret manners of communication. Puzzling interactions between individuals suggest relational status within the band.

A bay named Hess is huge at 17.1 hands high. I take a special shine to her sister, Halcyon, also a Trakehner. Halcyon is the elegant twelve-year-old gray who is spirited and highly responsive. Like Hess, Halcyon stands tall at 16.3 hands. I find her thoroughly endearing.

All these mares are half sisters except one. Harrison waxes poetic about another of Brise's offspring named Montana, who no longer lives here. Another half thoroughbred, half Trakehner, Montana was his wife's special eventing horse and won lots of ribbons. When Moira died, Harrison loaned Montana to someone who wanted to use her as a therapy horse. Years later, she is still with them.

I disappear on my own to spend hours at a time with this mare band. While they graze, I stand with them. When they walk, I walk with them. I go wherever they go, except when Haiti gets an urge to rile everyone up and whisks them away. Approaching me from a distance, they rarely follow a direct line. When I slow my gait, even turn away, I see that this *indirection* makes them comfortable, bold, willing to approach.

I discover that if a mare coming toward me stops or if I sense she is about to stop and I step backward, she immediately feels relief. Another day, I bend at the hips to position my body more like a horse's. They respond with interest to my horizontal form. They approach to sniff my hair mane.

Eventually, I become a citizen of their world. Haiti still insists that she always is first to greet me. Behind her, Halcyon is passionate in her desire to connect. Burna, the youngest, a three-year-old bay filly with a white blaze, becomes comfortable enough in my company to let her nose drop to the ground, close her eyes, and fall asleep while I sit next to her, rubbing her forehead.

Brimming with pleasure, I return to the house and tell Harrison about my afternoon. He has just come back from fishing the creek.

Over a dinner of fresh trout lightly breaded and cooked in a cast-iron pan, he reflects on what I'm doing. "That's really interesting. Just spending time with horses, without asking anything from them. You submerge yourself in their band for hours at a time, *simply to belong with them.*"

He finds great joy in my joy. Yet something in his eyes is also sorrowful. My love for horses recalls *her* love for horses. Just yesterday, we were bickering about how, often, it feels we speak two different languages—a common experience between any man and woman. But he compared our fledgling relationship to "something superior and unimaginable," something that "few other people will ever know in their lives." *Six years* since Moira's death now, and *still*, he has one foot in the land of the dead. The grieving lover's memory of a flawless perfection leaves limited room for the living.

But a day spent with horses, then sharing a dinner of fresh trout tonight with this man I care for is more than enough. I know that Harrison far prefers my company to being alone, as I prefer his. Our approach to one another involves indirection. I reason: *If he has loved one exceptional woman this much, he must have whatever it takes to recognize and feel that kind of love again.*

Harrison and his horses remind me to be present and patient. To keep my heart wide open, free of expectations. To allow them to teach me who they are. Does he have the patience and desire to learn about me in this same way—without words, without fear?

On a walk with dogs the following weekend, I spot Rick driving the tractor down the road by the barn. A stiff dead cow is in the tractor's bucket, her four legs straight up in the air. I turn back to tell Harrison. He's sitting at his easel, painting, and doesn't look up as I give him the news.

"It's 542. She died this morning." He dips his brush in a glass jar full of dirty water.

"What happened?"

"Rick just found her in the registered pasture."

The disturbing image has burned itself into my heart. "How do you deal with all this? That was *awful* to see."

He stares at his easel, quiet and composed.

I take a breath. "I guess if you grow up on a farm like you did, you see death, violence, loss on a regular basis?"

Harrison mixes a dark granite gray on his palette. Finally, he looks me straight in the eyes. "You really care," he says. "All you have to do is care. And accept. That's it."

Last week he finished a painting using several of the photos I took of the Sip 'n Dip's interior during our short-lived bar experiences two years ago. He placed the two of us in his foreground—me in my glasses, him in a cowboy hat with a five-dollar bill in his hand—standing at the bar of the lounge on a very crowded night. Mysterious mermaids swim on the other side of the glass wall in front of us. Down to the thatched ceiling, pink lights glowing upward through stacked cocktail glasses, and ghoulish-looking customers, he conveys its bizarre carnival-like atmosphere to a T.

Today, I linger next to him to examine a more somber painting of horses.

He moves his chair back from his easel and puts down his brush.

"Do you recognize anybody?"

Leaning in closer, I think I recognize four of the eight horses: Sassy, Ibis, and Maruka. A small little filly with a white blaze peeks out from under one of the other horses' manes: Burna. Harrison confirms my guesses.

"At the beginning of a long, dark time, I would go to Moira's grave and kneel down and kiss the dirt where her face should be. Then I would sit beside the grave and look out at the prairie. Once, as I was sitting there so still, the horses came. With their heads lowered, questioning, they stepped forward, slowly gathering around me, breathing in their lost mistress. Sharing with me her greatness. This one is called *Horses at the Grave.*"

I stare at this new courageous painting. Harrison is nowhere in the image, but he permits his heart's hidden grief to be seen. Eight inquisitive mares tell the story, their expressions puzzled, suggesting sorrow or longing. Their lowered eyes stare straight into the eyes of the viewer.

All you can do is care.

A GOOD SHOT

Summer, 2007. I've just spoken with the taxidermist who will recreate the body of a bison bull using the hide of an animal donated by an area rancher. The bull is one of many being raised for meat and, after he is "harvested," his indomitable likeness will be the centerpiece of our bison exhibit. When visitors enter the final gallery, they will encounter a full-scale replica of a young Indigenous Northern Plains hunter on horseback, riding a sculpted horse at full gallop alongside the massive bull, bow raised and arrow drawn.

The taxidermist is at the bison ranch this morning to choose the specific animal to be immortalized in our permanent exhibition. It will die in full flesh, with a thick winter coat. When I hang up the phone, I feel uneasy. I now bear some of the responsibility for this bull's imminent death.

When Harrison shows up one afternoon to visit me at work, I invite him to peruse the museum's extensive historic gun collection. They don't interest me at all, but I need to learn about early guns in the context of my bison project. His knowledge and passion might help.

I show him three Sharps buffalo guns (large-bore rifles) slated to be in my exhibit.

"*Tens of millions* of wild bison roamed the Great Plains . . . " I say. "The largest mammal on the North American continent. The heart and soul of Indigenous Plains culture. A magnificent beast, here for at least five hundred thousand years. Once this gun came along, during the second half of the nineteenth century, the four great herds of this country were decimated. In just twenty years, the *entire species* was nearly wiped out."

"A formidable killing machine. Perfectly suited for its purpose," he notes. "It must have been something, seeing those huge herds as they moved across the country."

Harrison is wearing a periwinkle shirt. He brushes up against me as we stare into glass display cases. The electricity between us is a pleasant distraction.

"A lot of thought goes into designing guns," he says. "For you, they are dangerous. For a gunmaker or handler, it has to become an element of your will. Early designers understood that if you have a charging lion, the balance, the caliber, the form of a gun needs to be a highly efficient part of your body at a dangerous moment."

I insist he wear the requisite white gloves before we look at more guns in storage.

"Now here are some real works of art," he says, as I open a fancy gun case. "See this Holland and Holland and that Purdy? Both were great English guns used for elephant hunting and other big game hunting."

Just the thought of it turns my stomach.

"The Rolls Royce of guns. Elegant, used by royalty and famous explorers." He drifts on, "If you look long enough, you'll begin to notice that the best guns have exquisitely clean, simple lines. They appear less valuable than they really are, kind of like a Stradivarius."

Back at his ranch on Saturday afternoon, Harrison is anxious to build upon my perceived interest. He removes one of his own guns from a cabinet in the mudroom.

"With this shotgun, as opposed to a rifle, your eyes are open, and the gun is not consciously aimed. It's more about an instinctive swing. Shot size depends on the bird you are hunting. The higher the number of the shot size, the more shot pellets there are in a shell. The lower the number, the heavier and larger the shot." He extends the shotgun as an offering. "At least learn how to hold one."

I'm reluctant. *Holding a gun is not a sin*, I tell myself, *any more than holding a bow and arrow. I want to learn about this object.*

Harrison places the shotgun in my hands. Fear rises in me, measuring its weight. I examine the details of its form while he explains the importance of a gun's balance.

"Feel for it."

Its steely nature feels repulsive.

"In mounting a shotgun, it should come up consistently under the cheekbone and be ready for instinctive action."

The last thing I want is to bring it closer, inviting a dangerous stranger to touch my cheekbone like a perverse lover. "Are you sure it can't shoot out at me from behind?"

"You've got to bring it closer to your body like this." He puts his hands over mine and moves the gun into my chest, up to my jaw. "You can't keep away from a gun. It only works when you are completely one with it. Hesitancy and fear will only make you miss."

Learning archery hadn't been a problem. Guns feel entirely different. A barrage of troubling associations will not leave my mind: mass killings at malls, schools, and places of worship. Individuals shot to death by police for no reason other than the color of their skin. The brutal carnage of military warfare. It is impossible to not be aware of this country's off-the-charts gun violence. From the moment I moved West, these latent feelings have been triggered by Malmstrom Air Force Base, buried missiles, a culture centered on guns and hunting wild animals. Only recently did I learn Montana is the number one state per capita for hate groups. Warily, I cradle Harrison's weapon in my arms, unable to separate the experience from acts of cruelty. For this moment, however, I will suspend judgment. My immediate concern remains: Could a bullet or shot come right out the back of the barrel?

"Nothing is going to happen as long as you have this safety switch on. See how it works?" He shows me how to put shells in and take them out. And then, how to place my index finger just so, squarely on the trigger, and pull.

I am determined to conquer fear.

"The gun shoots a spray of shot that the bird will fly into, if the shot has been delivered in a swinging form. You don't shoot at the bird. Instead, you swing the gun through the bird and beyond it, pulling the trigger at the instinctive moment where you believe the bird and shot will come together. When you commit yourself to the fullness of that instinct, it is remarkably capable."

He suggests we move outside for a subsequent lesson. The weather is hot and sunny. We wear snake gaiters to protect our lower legs from rattlers. Standing in high grass, I would rather enjoy birdsong or go for a hike. But I listen to his instructions.

"Imagine that you have a water hose in your hand. Pass through the bird's trajectory with the spray. I start from where the bird started and follow the imaginary curve of its flight, swinging and sweeping it past the bird, when the trigger will fire, and the gun will keep sweeping."

Harrison demonstrates.

"Any doubt is like Morse code: the gun swing will have a series of distinct dashes as opposed to a fluid straight line. When the gun is completely invisible, when you forget about it as if it were a part of your body and a part of your desire to get the bird, it handles best."

"I'd be up for trying," I say, squinting one eye and swinging the gun across the sky. "But I have no desire to 'get a bird.'"

Harrison disappears and returns with five tin cans. "This will be fun," he promises, placing each can along a fence line on top of posts. "Let's see how you do with these!"

I'm obsessed with making sure the safety button is always where it needs to be. He helps me get into position and steps back. I take aim, pull the trigger. My shoulder registers the nudge of a slight kickback. The cans eventually have a few holes in them, and one flies off into the air.

Before fall hunting season arrives, Harrison introduces me to something more challenging. In a large meadow, he loads a series of round ceramic disks or "clay pigeons" into a small green machine he's borrowed from a friend, then jettisons one disk at a time into the air. He gets me into position with a shotgun, then takes his seat at the machine.

"Tell me when you're ready," he says.

"Ready."

He sends a disk flying, I swing to pull the trigger—and miss. Each time I say "Pull!" another clay pigeon sails through the sky, unbothered. After several misses and suggestions from Harrison, I try closing my left eye instead of my right.

"Okay, pull!"

The clay disk explodes in midair like fireworks.

"You did it!"

One by one, Harrison sends more clay disks flying in every direction. Sighting with my right eye, I hit four in a row.

Over dinner, Harrison returns to my practice.

"You're a good shot. A real natural. But there's a special experience that becomes available *only* when you cross that line and become a predator. It affords a certain perspective."

"Murderers on death row have a certain perspective. Veterans of war too."

"Don't do it if you're not comfortable. We can shoot clay pigeons whenever you want."

The next day we hike out across open country with Willow and the setters. I observe Harrison and his gun with new awareness. I watch the bird dogs as they lift their noses to hunt the hillside just ahead of us. I try to imagine myself as a hunter. I grapple with the discomfort of coming face to face with my own inner predator.

"Don't worry about shooting," Harrison repeats, stopping to kiss my furrowed brow. "My biggest joy in hunting is being with my dogs, giving them the pleasure of doing what they do. Hunting is already giving you experiences of intimacy—with the land, with the dogs. Just remember that if you ever do become a hunter, you'll feel something different. And you may not like it."

It's Monday night after work. Willow explores patches of sagebrush and chases scent along the river. We wear our orange vests. A hawk flies overhead. Last week Harrison's friend John took us out with his pointer and a prairie falcon named Gretchen. We got to experience the stunning intensity of a falcon's hunting stoop, her high-speed attack dive to catch a hen pheasant as it burst from cover in front of his bird dog's point. Following the trail this evening, contemplating the skills and patience a mountain lion must have to hunt deer, I pick up my pace. Never did I imagine I would be spending this much time with a man who has hunted his entire life.

"For me," Harrison has said, "fishing and hunting are about endurance more than catching a fish or shooting an elk. *Vincit qui patitur.* He conquers who endures."

I wouldn't believe it if I hadn't experienced it firsthand: Harrison can stand in a river casting for *twelve hours* until he falls forward asleep into the water. He will sit for five hours in a tree stand in below-zero temperatures, returning to the house in the dark, white as a ghost and hypothermic. He reminds me of the way hawks hunt: waiting in a high tree branch for hours, flying low over hillsides like this one along the river, back and forth, until it succeeds in feeding itself. Some part of Harrison always seems hungry.

Willow returns to me on the trail with a brittle, dried snakeskin. She is proud. Removing it from her mouth, I recognize how I've been feeling lately: *so ready* to shed a worn-out skin that has become too tight. Two great horned owls sit in a large cottonwood tree. I know this pair. This is where they live. One of their striped feathers lies at my feet. Farther along the trail, I find a small orange flicker feather, and one that is long and iridescent—a magpie's tail feather? A great one for my hat next time I visit Phyllis.

A feather feels like a talisman. I keep a collection in a carved box at home. If I picked up every feather I ever found, I'd have enough to create a whole cloak: Like the winged bird-man regalia worn by Indigenous warriors of the Mississippian cultures; men who danced to summon the power of peregrine falcons as warrior avatars. Fashioning large wings, I might conjure the spirit of Thunderbird, recognized by many Native people for its supernatural qualities and indomitable strength.

Twilight comes early now. I slide these three feathers inside my pocket before loading Willow into the car. We travel the familiar ten minutes home. I have no appetite, but Willow gobbles up her dinner before joining me on the couch. She's like Harrison, always ready for more. Three new feathers sit on the coffee table in front of us. I choose the rounded, tan-and-brown-striped owl feather to tickle Willow's ears, then trace her spine. My dog and I are content in each other's company, but Willow really comes alive when she is out hunting with Tula. I feel the same way with Harrison.

THE BIRDHOUSE AND
DR. DELOSS

It's early September when I arrive at Phyllis's studio in Great Falls and find her finishing up a dramatic portrait in oranges and purples of Luciano Pavarotti, who died today. She has written the names of his many favorite operas in the background and, along the bottom of her tribute, the words "Farewell, dear friend." We chat together and listen to Pavarotti in the love duet of *Madame Butterfly* while drinking green tea and nibbling on blueberry scones. Somehow, we discover we've both lived in France.

"Did you ever meet any gypsies while you were there?" Phyllis asks.

I shake my head no.

"They were very shy, but when Jimmy and I lived there, I noticed they would come by and rummage through the trash for food. I began making picnic lunches for them. I'd wrap everything up and leave it in the trash. I think they really enjoyed finding something nice."

Like yellow warblers I see along my daily river walks, Phyllis elicits a joy beyond herself. I don't tell her, but I feel a bit like one of those gypsies. I never invite anyone to my house and never want to talk about where I live. But she's curious.

"I bet your house is wonderful. You must have collected all sorts of fun artwork in your years of curating, haven't you?"

"I do have some small pieces I love. But it's all in boxes in my basement. There just isn't room in my tiny house." And then I change the subject. I am embarrassed at how little my own life has reaped. Her studio is my great escape in town. My imagined life.

In Atlanta nine years ago, I had pored through magazines about the West and cut out photos of my dream house in the wilderness. At thirty-eight years old, I became intentional about the future I wanted to create. I actively envisioned in written descriptions what my life would look like in five-year increments: forty to forty-five, forty-five to fifty, fifty to fifty-five. This exercise, I believed, would help attract what I most ached for: a place of belonging in nature and in love. In my early forties when a boyfriend moved on, I refined my vision. But something has gotten lost along the way.

Growing up in Kansas City, I spent summer days outside, mostly alone in quiet neighborhood parks. Or I would disappear down old wooden stairs into our storm shelter: the dark, musty basement of our house. The washer and dryer were in one corner. There were piles of stacked storage boxes and a small separate cellar room with shelves of canned goods, where the family would squeeze in with flashlights and dinner plates when tornado sirens sounded.

In the middle of our cement basement, next to a heating vent, there was an old cobweb-covered workbench where I kept my art supplies. This was my place of magic, of creation, the one place in the house where I could find a measure of comfort in colors and forms, where I could be alone and disappear into the imaginative process of making things. Yet I never turned the bench itself into a work of art, as Phyllis surely would have done.

One day, Phyllis insists on visiting my house. When she steps inside, I feel the sting of still-unrealized dreams—my tiny home's complete lack of soul and beauty, even as she raves on. "I love it! This place is adorable. It's got all sorts of possibilities. Why don't you let me help you fix it up?"

I admire everything about Lonetree Ranch, her River House, and her painting studio in Great Falls. I am thrilled by her offer, and we make a date. My phone rings the evening before. I recognize her cheery voice.

"Now I just want to make sure you're still up for this. If you say yes, you really have to let me do my thing! Don't get scared, but are you ready?" She laughs.

I smile to myself.

I pick her up early the next morning at her River House. She is wearing her brown felt hat with a band of porcupine quills, flashy turquoise jewelry, and bright red lipstick. "Let's go to a furniture store first, then maybe an antique shop or two. Do you have any favorites?"

We purchase a few lamps we like, a nice old table and chairs. We take the chairs to her studio and paint them cornflower blue. Phyllis pulls out a hairdryer to speed things up so we can head back to my house with our goodies and start rearranging. This high-energy process consists of Phyllis chirping directions while I try to keep up. Each time we create an opportunity for something on a wall, I get excited.

"Oh, I have just the thing for that spot."

I dash downstairs to rip open boxes that have been here for the four years since I moved, until I find a favorite piece, then fly back upstairs, eager to show Phyllis. She cheers with delight. We give the item a place of honor and keep going.

The more I bring up from the basement, the better my home becomes.

"Phyllis, I feel like old friends are here with me again. I thought less was more. I never imagined there was room for all this."

"Oh no," she says, full of glee. "You've got to bring in all sorts of colorful things. The more you fill a small space, the better the feeling. See how cozy and happy this place is now? Don't you love it?!"

We sit down on my new blue chairs to admire our work.

"You've got so many wonderful paintings and sculptures of birds in your collection. And look how darling your bird feeders are outside your window now that we've painted them. Don't you think it would be nice to call your house 'The Birdhouse?'"

And from that day on, we do.

The next evening while I am walking with Willow along the river's edge trail, six pelicans soar overhead with their enormous wingspan. Soon they will be leaving. When they first arrive each spring, these unlikely visitors gather on the edges of small islands along the river below, their white-and-black-tipped feathers flashing as they stand in rushing waters to feed on fish. Theirs is but one of many comings and goings I track each time Willow and I walk here.

In my four years in Great Falls, I have come to know the yearly cycles of marmots and foxes, coyotes and weasels, beavers and owls, pelicans and goldfinches along these river paths. I have come to depend on this place for my daily access to nature, for proximity to these wild and free seasonal habits. I anticipate the arrival of tiny yellow warblers that dart across the path. I gasp each spring when sighting a male scarlet tanager. Swallows flying just over my head, flocking to hundreds of small mud nests in cliffs along the trail. Canada geese leading their large groups of olive-gold goslings to waddle down the hillside of the park along the same path and swim into the steaming spring waters of Giant Springs.

A few weeks after Phyllis helps me jazz up my Birdhouse, I pick her up at her River House and we take the hour drive, past Fort Benton, past Geraldine, and on to Lonetree for a slumber party on her sleeping porch at the Meriwether. We stroll over from the old granary to revisit the house where she grew up, the old stagecoach inn now transformed into a private museum full of childhood memories. Inside the front door, I notice a black doctor's leather bag sitting on top of a piano in the foyer. Upon touching it, I discover it's made of clay. Written on the front of the bag is the name of her great-grandmother: SARAH TANNER DELOSS, MD 1842–1906, CHICAGO, IL.

"I made that bag years ago in honor of my daddy's grandmother. She was such an interesting doctor, and she was a famous psychic too. There she is," Phyllis says, pointing to that large black-and-white image, the portrait of Dr. DeLoss hanging above the piano.

This time, I study it. The woman wears an elegant high neckline with a stitched collar that flares out to either side beneath her ears. Her hair is swept up into a bun. Her presence is commanding. Her eyes are eerie and otherworldly.

Phyllis and I sit together on the porch back at the Meriwether, happy as two meadowlarks to be sharing a bottle of wine and pasta, on our own, in this special place. But we are not alone. Phyllis points to her little buddy perched on the edge of the porch: a wren, who last week was kind enough to scold and chirp a warning to her about a rattlesnake under the porch stairs. She recites names for each of the deer that come to feed while we eat our dinner. Soft evening light of late summer changes from orange to pink on the white Chalk Cliffs of Antelope Butte.

"Tell me more about your great-grandmother," I ask.

"Just a minute, you'll really be interested in this," she says, disappearing inside the old granary. She returns with a framed letter and a black-and-white photograph. "That's great-grandmother Sarah, sitting in her new Model T with friends. And this is a letter I received two years ago from a medical doctor doing research on her."

She reads it aloud in the cool of the evening like a wonderful bedtime story. After establishing her own medical practice, Sarah had listed herself around 1893 in the city's directory as a 'psychometric physician.' According to a magazine of the period, that meant she used her sixth sense in diagnosing patients.

"That's fascinating," I say. "Sounds like she was a medical intuitive?"

"Well, that's right. And in 1890, Sarah had over one thousand patients all over the United States. She was kind of famous." She pauses before reading the last two sentences of the letter. "She seems to be what we would term a 'psychic.' I am curious if any of her descendants have also made that claim." Phyllis stops reading, puts the letter down. "Now isn't that interesting?" she says. "I've always been psychic myself. And I know you are too."

Phyllis and I talk often about this strange quality of knowing things, which she considers at once delightful and straightforward. Before retiring to the sleeping porch tonight, we imagine how difficult it must have been for a woman like Sarah DeLoss, working as unconventionally as she did, in a male-dominated profession during the nineteenth century. In still earlier times, a similar woman might have been burned at the stake. Even today, mysterious sensibilities are commonly dismissed. Nearly always.

Both Phyllis and I have seen things before they happened, known things without knowing how. During summers on the reservation, this sort of thing didn't seem odd at all. In nature with Harrison, he encourages me to follow and trust my own intuition more. For most of my life, sensing the secret energy of things remained a private experience I barely admitted, even to myself. Yet for Harrison, intuition is the only thing he *can* trust. For Phyllis, it is something glorious to be treasured—as natural as breathing in this sweet night air before falling asleep under the stars.

TREE STANDS

Harrison returns after dark one Saturday evening and changes out of camo before sitting down next to me. I tell him I've been comfortably reading here on his living room couch, wondering why anyone would want to sit high up in a tree for hours on a small uncomfortable metal platform in the chilling cold.

"To be in a tree is to be alive in the forest," he explains. "It becomes the best of all vibrations about a sense of 'this is where I should be.' You move with the wind, rock back and forth. In all kinds of weather. You're quiet. Still. I've only killed two bucks in the seventeen years I've lived here. For me, it's all about what I imagine while I'm there."

"And that makes it worth all the discomfort?"

"I've seen a buck and rattled him in from far away. He'll march in hissing mad. Ready for a fight, stomping stiff-legged with his ears pinned back. Once I saw an owl land nearby. I wiggled my little finger, just slightly, next to my chest. The owl swooped down from his perch right at me, thinking it was a mouse, until I waved him off at the last minute. I've seen bobcats. Squeaked to one and watched it approach my tree until it figured out something wasn't quite right and sulked away."

I lean against a pillow, stretching my legs to rest them on Harrison's lap. He rubs his palm along the length of my calves. Our lantern of willow branches and Bhutanese prayer flags glows like a warm fire. Harrison's elk head extends its neck above us from the stone fireplace.

"And one time, a mountain lion tracked me to my stand."

He brushes the sensitive underside of my arch where I'm most ticklish.

"I could hear its footsteps below me. Still too dark to see. I knew it was no deer. It sat down right at the base of my tree for a long time. There were branches between us, so I figured I was safe. But I sat very still, knowing it was there with me. Minutes later, in the first light of day, I caught my only glimpse of it, when it finally walked off into the woods, long tail trailing."

On an especially cold night with a full moon, Harrison returns with a new story. Again, we snuggle on the living room couch, our lantern glowing saffron orange. He almost whispers, as if it were all still happening.

"I sat in my stand tonight and watched a whole migration of elk in the dark. They traveled like a secret caravan, hundreds of them, one after the other after the other, passing right beneath me. This went on for a very long time. I could hear them quietly speaking to each other as they moved through the woods single file."

Harrison thinks a lot about which tree stands he might want to move. One day I hike out with him to take down an old one. "Here we are," he says, dropping his backpack to the ground. I scan the clearing until I locate his secret perch. He screws a few removable "steps" into the aspen's white trunk, then begins to climb up, adding one step at a time. When he has placed enough to reach the stand, he climbs back down.

"Care to experience what it's like up there?"

I make myself climb and don't look down. At last, I grab the stand, carefully pulling myself up onto a small wobbly platform wedged and strapped between limbs. For a few short moments, I am a child in her tree house with a soaring view of the world. I'm surrounded by the comfort of aspens. There are yellow leaves everywhere. I'm hidden high within a cathedral of flickering light. The height is too terrifying to stay for long. But I am glad to know the feeling of it.

Harrison heads back up the tree to tinker with his stand. Relieved to sit upon fall leaves and solid ground, I examine the details of what is around me: the way the creek runs beside the tree, a drinking spot for animals. I close my eyes, train my ears to the trickling sound water makes as it passes by here. I notice logs on the ground, how they create a path right in front of the tree where Harrison placed this stand so many years ago. His doing or nature's? In a corner of the clearing is a tiny bird I've never seen before. I remain perfectly still, admiring its ruby-red crown and its great busyness. I rehearse the notes of its beautiful song, jumbled and loud.

By the time Harrison jimmies the old stand loose and begins the scary climb downward, I have been still for thirty minutes.

The spell breaks. Harrison is back on the ground, doing something odd. He leans far back with knees bent, one end of a rope in his hands, the other stretched upward. Using all his body weight, he pulls, trying to force the last part of the stand down from the tree.

Wood moans. Then I hear a cracking sound. A huge limb at the other end of his rope breaks from the trunk, flies through the air, and whacks him in the head.

He falls to the ground.

I run over. "Are you okay?!"

There is a one-inch gash in the middle of his forehead. He lies still for another minute. He sits up and blinks. Tries to laugh at himself. Blood trickles down his face.

"You're bleeding," I tell him.

"This happens all the time. I just get so excited about what I'm doing—"

I shake my head as I lean down to help him up. "Sometimes I wonder how on earth you've made it this far in life."

This is something we have begun to say often to one another. I collect his tools, toss them in his backpack. We hike home for some first aid.

I DON'T CARE

Harrison objects one evening when I drop a dirty pot I've been washing into his trash can.

"There's nothing wrong with that pot, asshole."

I've gotten used to his unconventional terms of endearment. I lift the pot out of the trash and march over to show him. "Look: All the nonstick coating on it is chipping off and going right into your food!"

"*Maybe*. I've been eating things cooked in that wok for a long time. It's probably looked like that for years, and nothing's happened."

He doesn't seem worried at all about accidentally ingesting lead birdshot in the grouse he's just shot and is serving for dinner. He reveals a slight concern one day when he realizes that for years, he has paid no attention at all to applying animal meds with his bare hands. I'm down at the barn with him when he habitually dips his hand into a container of bright blue goop to dress a horse's wound.

"That is horrible looking! What is that?" I ask.

"I have no idea. Go ahead. Read the label and tell me."

I read aloud. "Caution, always wear gloves. This has been proven to cause breast cancer in humans."

Harrison has a strong constitution. He eats moldy rolls, serves up scary three-week leftovers from his refrigerator and canned foods from his pantry that are ten years past their expiration dates. "Once," Harrison tells me, "I finished off an entire instant dinner before realizing I'd microwaved the plastic top right into it."

I'm not surprised.

I was nervous but excited by an invitation to spend Christmas this year with him and his family. Only after the fact do I find out his three boys and their wives—while kind—were all perplexed during the holiday gathering, uncertain as to who I was and why I was there. Harrison never built a bridge, left all of us out on our own. I looked at him, confused.

He's someone who is so intelligent and aware when moving through wilderness, yet also, there's this poor communication, this habit of inattentiveness and insensitivity. His absence of mind can be dangerous. One time after using a pitchfork to spread straw in a horse stall, he threw it down without looking, nearly spearing my foot. I still forget sometimes and follow too closely behind him when hiking in woods, only to have branches he clears for himself swing back and whack me in the face.

One Saturday afternoon, Harrison is sitting at his desk. I stand next to him in a familiar state of frustration. The topic is unimportant. We both know we're right.

"You and I are so different," he replies. "You'll never understand and that's okay. How could you? The kind of understanding I know can exist between two people is something you have no idea about because you haven't lived it."

"Oh dear. I'm so tired of all this, Harrison. No matter how well we get along, no matter what amazing experiences we share, you *always* circle back. We've had more than three years of getting to know one another. Why are you even *with me* if this constant refrain about who and what I'm *not* is what you feel? Maybe you need someone else."

"No! I like being with you."

"I grew up buried alive by judgments about who I should be and who I wasn't. I've spent a hell of a time exorcising those punishing voices in my head, just to get to a point where I can be kinder to myself and to others, so I can accept and love exactly who I am. I'm not willing to give up what I've worked so hard for . . . not for *anybody*, including you."

I step past him into the bedroom, heart beating.

I can do this.

He sits silent at his desk. I gather my overnight bag, then dart past him toward the top of the mudroom stairs.

"Wait," he says.

We stand face to face at the top of the stairs.

"I don't want you to give up anything, sweetie. I admire you tremendously—and everything you've accomplished. You must know that by now. You're in a whole different league than me. I know nothing at all about what you describe as an experience of self-love and acceptance."

"Then take the time! Do the work! Deal with some of your own shit and stop dumping it on me. You literally grew up"—*or didn't?*—"with Moira. You met when you were children. It's been six years since she died. It's just not fair—or healthy—for you constantly to be comparing what we might or might not have to what you had with her."

"I know."

I look down the stairs, then back at Harrison. "I'm forty-seven. You're sixty. Time is rolling on. We've lived two different lives. We've both loved deeply. Both suffered loss. We each have our own baggage to carry. There's plenty *I* understand about life that *you've* never experienced or imagined, Harrison."

"I'm quite sure of that."

A tear makes its way down my cheek. "Moira was your refuge—your single source of unconditional love in life. I get that. It seemed like my father was the same for me. But your unresolved grief keeps shutting me out. I will *not* be shoved into some box. I've survived this long on my own. I'll be fine. I've had it with this third-wheel status."

I pick up my bag and turn, ready to walk.

"Wait! Please stop." Harrison touches my shoulder.

I turn around. His eyes are moist.

"Please. Please, Lynne. Give me another chance. Don't leave. I need you."

"Where is all this going, anyway? Do you ever think about that at all?"

"Yes. I do."

"And?"

"I care about you a lot. It's just taking me a long time." He offers a sad brave smile. "Anything of real quality takes a long time. But . . . I believe we have everything it takes for that to happen."

I exhale and put down my bag, exhausted. He folds me into his arms.

Later over tea, I can't resist. "Sometimes, Harrison, you remind me of a children's storybook called *Pierre: A Cautionary Tale*. It's about a boy named Pierre who always says, 'I don't care,' even to a lion who is about to eat him."

"I know. I'm rarely listening or paying attention to anything. You have a steering wheel in your brain. I'm more like the hitchhiker in the back seat, worrying about whoever is at the wheel. My mother never had an idea of how to care for her children. All I learned from her was how to duck and hide."

Snippets of what I've repeatedly heard—about his childhood and his wife—haunt me as the light fades. Staying most weekends, I have noticed how at the end of every day, Harrison gets anxious and uneasy. He drinks to forget, to feel the relative comfort of numbness. Often, he is twitchy as he tries to relax in bed next to me. On occasion, he screams out in his sleep.

Tonight, I put my arm around him and suggest the perfect therapy for us both. "Let's go downstairs and check on the puppies."

BUNDLES

T he rancher with the bison herd called today to say the meat from our bison bull is already at the butcher's. The bull's pelt will be sent to the taxidermist tomorrow. I've forwarded an image of a painting that shows the exact running position I'd like the taxidermist to sculpt for the mold of the bison's body. I imagine this bull giving its life so it might hopefully inspire and help teach museum visitors about the importance of honoring *all* our relatives. After a long day at work, I arrive with Willow to find Phyllis busy painting in her studio.

"Oh, Lynne! I'm so glad you're here. Hi, Willow!"

I approach her easel, happy to see my friend. Today's portrait is of her daughter, Nicole.

"What do you think? Should I add some more purple? Hey, have you ever noticed how there is a little bit of purple in everything?" She winks, puts her brush down to pet Willow. "Are you hungry? Heat up a can of soup if you like and tell me what you've been up to."

Her cats, Mattie and Picasso, are lying together, cleaning each other on top of her bookshelf. While a bowl of chicken soup heats, we sit together on the couch where I tell Phyllis about the bison bull and recent experiences with Harrison in his valley.

"People who are connected to the land know all about nature, don't they?" she says. "How to find wild animals, how to use roots and leaves, all about trees. I bet you feel more of that, too, now that you're spending weekends on the ranch."

"I do," I say, still admiring her portrait from across the room.

When Phyllis's children, Scott and Nicole, were little, the family spent a summer at Lonetree and lived off the land for an entire month, eating only what the land provided. She had read the 1962 Euell Gibbons classic, *Stalking the Wild Asparagus*.

"Tell me again what you and your kids ate for a whole month?"

"Oh, we had plenty to eat. Dandelions, watercress, wild onions, wild mint, mustard greens, wild asparagus, rock currants, sarvisberries, chokecherries, cattails," she says. She places her brush in a jar of water. "Poor Scottie, he still makes a face about the taste of boiled cattails, even after all these years."

"That bad?"

"Well, I guess *maybe* they might have been *just a little bit* on the tough side." She wrinkles her nose and smiles. The pheasant feathers on her hat wiggle. "But you know, as Mother always says, 'Life is for the living.' We had a good adventure."

"What did your neighbors think?"

"One day that summer," she says, a twinkle in her eye, "a local friend drove all the way out to see us and brought some chocolate chip cookies. I said 'Oh, no thank you, we're living off the land.' When I sent her back home with her cookies, she promptly told everyone in the town of Square Butte, 'Those poor Dickson kids, their mother is making them live on weeds!'"

We laugh so hard, we can't stop. While Phyllis pours us each a glass of homemade limoncello, I take my bowl of hot soup out of the microwave. I think of my own childhood, so full of seriousness and trepidation. But I'm here now.

"The experiences I've been having on the ranch," I say, "it's all been reminding me of Native American bundles. The whole valley feels like one vast living bundle, an enormous treasure chest full of mysterious information, with its specific pageantry of creatures."

"Bundles?"

Willow moves closer to Phyllis, who rubs on her head while she listens. I take a few sips of soup before speaking.

"Bundles are wrapped collections of sacred items among some

Native people of the Northern Plains. A large animal hide—elk, bear, bison," I tell her, still thinking about my bison bull hide for the exhibition, "is filled with the pelts of interrelated birds and mammals— raven, magpie, muskrat, mink—along with feathers, rattles, bone whistles, bags containing red earth paint, pine needles for incense and tobacco, all wrapped inside the hide. They're opened each year as part of seasonal ceremonies."

"Isn't that wonderful," she says. "Have you ever seen one opened?"

I pause before answering. "Yes. I was surprised—and honored— to be invited once by a bundle keeper. It was a holy experience that I'll never forget."

Mattie the cat stretches and jumps down from the bookcase. Willow lifts her head. Phyllis gets up to turn on the propane stove and then returns to petting Willow. Mattie jumps on my lap, purring.

"Various creatures on the ranch keep presenting themselves to me in unexpected ways, at unexpected times," I tell her. "It makes me want to experience every single plant and animal, so I can learn from them. Horses are teaching me a lot—strong creatures can be incredibly tender and vulnerable. Even Harrison's dog Tula has such deep knowledge of her valley. She knows every animal's scent, calls, daily habits. And taste."

I stroke Mattie's soft gray hair. "Last weekend, I watched Tula eat every single bit of a muskrat. She rolled in the discarded head to cover herself with scent before devouring it whole. According to her, muskrats are an exceptional delicacy. And then, of course, there is Harrison. Time with him always teaches me more about patience. Endurance. And keeping a good sense of humor." I wink at Phyllis.

"Oh, you mean like my washcloth trick when you were *maybe* over-thinking things?! You never imagined how easy it could be to just wipe off your face and start over, did you?"

The two of us begin laughing all over again.

We step outside with our limoncello and take a short walk to the river before the sun sets. As we walk, her arm woven through mine,

Phyllis mentions something about her 104-year-old mother, Mary, being ready to leave. "It seems like she might finally get her wish."

Along the Missouri's bank, chirpy rhapsodies of grasshoppers and crickets fill the air. Wind chimes ring. Kingfishers chitter. Swallows are visibly thrilled by a twilight hatch.

Over the weekend, Harrison and I circle back to the construction project we talked about during last spring's flood. The water in Cottonwood is low now. Even so, each time I go for walks with the dogs, I must wear muck boots to ford the creek. Each springtime in this valley, when mountain snows melt and rain comes, the creek rises with rushing waters too high and fast for any person or vehicle to cross. Today, a warm late autumn Saturday, seems the perfect day to build our footbridge.

Neither of us is handy in the least. I never saw either of my parents build anything and have never built anything like this myself. But after the success of our homemade lantern, Harrison and I are game to try.

Our effort at engineering is primitive. We begin with two heavy wooden telephone poles on the ground. We hammer a long series of short flat wooden planks on top of the poles. Then on both banks, under the cottonwoods, we build high pylons of piled rocks wrapped with chicken wire. Harrison brings the tractor to lift our new bridge and sets it in place. On my next walk down to the barn with dogs, our bridge seems impossibly high. But the two of us feel good about our effort.

The following day, inspired by our bridge, I am ready to create something else. I drive over to the Red Nose cabin by myself with my carved box full of feathers, some canvas, and paints. Not far upstream along Cottonwood Creek, this cabin always feels wilder than Harrison's house. The mares greet me. I inhale the luscious scent of cottonwoods and grasses on their necks, hold strands of their manes to my nose. This cozy spot by the creek, first built by Max, was later expanded by Harrison. The cabin has two wood-burning stoves and a small bedroom. I head inside to put water on for tea. Above its kitchen area, Harrison's taxidermied mountain lion crouches on a platform near the ceiling, ready to attack. In the bedroom hangs an elk shot and mounted by Max.

Last time I was at Lonetree, I admired Phyllis's technique for keeping crows and their mess off her porch. First, I cut, then paint, long thin strips of canvas with bright colors and designs. I use a hairdryer so the paint dries quickly. Next, I light some sage, as I've been taught by Native elders, and say a prayer over what has come to me as gifts. Opening the box, I examine my collection. I attach a single large feather—owl, hawk, crow—to the end of each strip. Outside with hammer and nails, I hang my fetishes, one every two feet, along the outer edges of the porch roof.

Willow and Tula are waiting for me on the newly decorated porch when I step back outside with a cup of licorice tea. The afternoon is pleasant, the sound of the creek soothing. I'm excited about our exhibition at the museum. While up north doing research on the reservation last month, I found this contemporary quote.

"In my body, in my blood runs the spirit of the buffalo."
                    —Arvol Looking Horse, Oglala Lakota, 2000

I draw another sip of tea. As much as I might try, the true depths of these connections—over many generations—is impossible for me to fathom. My wish can only be for *all* human beings, at some point in our lives, to experience at least *some* measure of these relationships. The spirit of this dog is part of me. This cat. A horse. A cow. "Animal" is the single family to which we and all living creatures belong. We all share the breath of life. Listening to the creek, the story of amadou returns:

the spongy fungi used by fishermen for drying flies, a natural substance that easily ignites. *The spark of Spirit that connects everything.*

Tula walks over to lick my hand. I feel her breath on my fingers. A kingfisher flies along the creek through cottonwoods. Tula's ears perk. The mares are grazing across the creek now, far up on the open hillside. My heart is one with the spirit of those mares. In the feel of Tula's warm breath, in the light of Willow's soft brown eyes, the spark of Spirit connects us.

I close my eyes, fingers exploring Tula's ringlets of soft poodle hair. A gentle breeze brushes my skin. When my eyes open, I am astonished. The feathers hanging from colorful strips have come alive, swaying back and forth. Their nature is to dance on the wind. Each feather still carries within it the spirit of a bird.

BOTHERED AND THIRSTY

Dressed in camo, we hike up the hillside at the top of the heifer pasture to sit inside a small hide of hawthorn bushes, not far from a watering tank. I nibble on sarvisberries along the way.

"We'll be here for a while. This would be a good time for you to meditate. I'll just take a little nap." Harrison lies back and closes his eyes.

We often nap together in hiding places during the early hours of an evening elk hunt, lying on the earth and falling asleep to the sounds of birdsong, inhaling fragrances of pine and juniper. Today I cross my legs, get comfortable, and drop into a peaceful period of sitting. When I open my eyes, the light is changing. Harrison tells me he had a good twenty-minute nap.

"I was amazed you were still meditating when I woke up. You do a very good job of being still!"

I grin, refreshed. "I sat like a mountain."

He brings an index finger to his lips. I turn my head slowly to follow his gaze. A large bull elk is traveling down the draw straight toward our watering tank. The bull arrives, bothered and thirsty. We huddle in excitement. The huge animal is so close that we hear him swallowing, gurgling, and snorting as he drinks. When he finishes, the bull lifts his magnificent rack. Mouth still drooling, he extends his long neck toward the sky and a thunderous scream erupts, like lava from a fiery volcano. His call leaves me quivering. None of us stir for several moments. The bull turns and walks away.

Two nights later, at dusk, another giant bull elk explodes out of the forest, a wild beast possessed. He tears down the mountainside, bursting and bristling, striking the expanse of a large open meadow like a bolt of red-hot lightning. His dominance crackles in every direction. The shock of it surges through me.

Harrison gets his annual elk with a rifle two weeks later, while I'm at work. I am relieved not to have been with him. When he picks me up at the museum on a Friday afternoon, he has just come from the butcher. Two coolers full of wrapped elk meat ride with us in the back of his truck. He leans over for a kiss at a stoplight on the east end of town.

"Tonight, we will have elk tenderloin."

Setting the large table beneath our hanging lantern feels like preparation for the sacrament. It's mid-November, a season for giving thanks. I light a candle, bring out wine glasses, and open a bottle of wine. How fascinated I was as a girl by the set of small delicate glasses kept in a purple velvet-lined case my father brought out in his services for church communion. Harrison arrives, carrying two plates of beautiful tenderloin medallions in a sarvisberry sauce, with sweet potatoes, and green beans.

"Bon appétit."

I take a first bite and close my eyes. The taste is exquisite; the meat like sweet juicy butter. I imagine this particular bull with his herd of cow elk, grazing in the same high meadow where we watched that colossal creature explode onto the scene at dusk. I can feel the dappled light along secret trails through woods of lodgepole and limber pines where I, too, have traveled. Where I, too, have slept. Swallowing my first taste, I recall the sounds of that bull elk we watched as he swallowed, smacked his wet lips, then lifted his mighty head to bugle. I think of the cow elk who stepped out in front of us and gave her life that day we spent with Max last year. How she appeared, like a gift, on what was likely Max's last hunt.

The following weekend on a warm day, we sit high on a hidden grassy knoll and appreciate a breathtaking view. On the steep incline of the hillside, we awkwardly attempt to make out, while our horses stand against the rocky cliff. They sense our amorous energy. Leaning in, they begin nuzzling one another and us. We laugh and finally give up. On our backs, we watch high clouds drift over wide-open plains. I listen to the sounds of T and Andre breathing. Warm sunshine and cool moist air caress my skin.

"I've got an idea I've been thinking about," Harrison says. He pauses for dramatic effect. "How would you like to come to Scotland with me?"

I'm stunned with happiness.

Thus begins a plan that will take us to Scotland ten months later.

By December, cattle and horses are in winter pasture. Large groups of elk have moved to snow-blown hills or farther on to the east, down to lower elevations for grazing. Some bulls have separated to form their own bachelor bands while others are still traveling with their cows. A few whitetail deer and mule deer show signs of late rut. Brook trout have completed their spawning.

Migrating birds have all departed except a few who stay: owls, magpies, certain hawks, eagles, ruffed grouse, and Hungarian partridge, still together now in coveys until they begin to pair off. Sharp-tailed grouse tend to come up from the east in December to eat hawthorn berries. Pheasants are poking around near whatever is being fed to cattle.

Each weekend, I put thistle seed out in feeders for chickadees, redpolls, and our growing group of some *ninety* stout winter finches. We discover their official name in our Stokes field guide to Western birds. *Gray-crowned Rosy-Finches.* Except for an occasional blizzard and the push of warm Chinook winds, this is the quiet time in Harrison's valley before calving.

MARY FONTANA TANNER

W inter, 2008. A huge crate arrives from the taxidermist at the museum today. When the magnificent bison bull inside is finally set free, all I can do is stare in wonder at the mighty spirit he still embodies. I burrow my hand and face into his thick coat of coarse brown hair, feeling my way into the complicated relationship between what we revere and what we kill. The inexorable link between life and death.

On a cold second Saturday in January, Phyllis calls Harrison at the ranch to let us know her mother has died. Mary Fontana Tanner, born in 1903, who first arrived in Montana as a young girl on a stagecoach, lived to be 104 years old. When we express our condolences, Phyllis jokes with us, just as she has with her mother for so many years. "Well, *you know*, at one hundred and four, you *really are ready to go*."

I search through oral histories at the Montana Historical Society for an interview with Mary Tanner recorded in 1982. I purchase a copy of the recording as a gift for Phyllis.

"This is wonderful!" she says, greeting me at her studio's entrance with a big hug. "I have lots of interviews Mother did over the years, but I don't think I've heard this one. Hello, Willow," she says, reaching down to touch Willow's head. "Shall we listen to it now?" She takes off her painting apron and hangs it on a hook.

"I was hoping you would say that."

We sit together, her propane stove our campfire. Mattie jumps between us, curls up, and begins to purr. When we hear Mary's first words, I am stunned. Her voice sounds *exactly* like her daughter sitting next to me: the same intonations, same quality of wonderful jokes, a similar way of laughing. Mary is being interviewed on the porch at Lonetree Ranch. The historian is asking her a series of questions about her early life in Montana, about Lonetree Ranch, and about the small Italian community of families who lived between Square Butte and Round Butte in the early 1900s. How different her perspective must have been from the ancestors of Arvol Looking Horse, who by that time, were confined to living in poverty on the Cheyenne River Indian Reservation. How relatively animated and lighthearted those immigrant Italian families might have been. Mary's sonorous voice fills the studio.

"Back in my day, we did everything with horses: farming, haying, traveling in buggies. You had your own chickens and canned goods, your own cream and butter and wild berry jellies. You'd see someone coming and put on the coffee pot."

Her stories communicate many of the same qualities I admire in Phyllis. Both of them foraging for food, baking bread. Neither of them hesitating to deal with a rattler if it presented a danger. I might as well be purring right along with Mattie. The warm spirits of powerful women, mother and daughter, live in that lilting voice, that sharp wit, that matter-of-fact confidence. Hard workers, creatively ingenious. Generations of independent women who were able to appreciate life as a grand adventure.

Mary recalls for the interviewer one summer when members of the Wilson family returned for a visit to see the old Lonetree stage stop home where they had originally lived, before the Tanners bought it. A Wilson granddaughter sat on the steps of the front porch and cried, remembering those in her family who had once loved this place and were now gone.

Mary's voice pauses, then rises, wistful. "Well, I imagine one day my children will be sitting on these same stairs crying after I'm gone. But we all live and then die. That's just the way it is."

I glance over. Phyllis's eyes look moist.

As light snow falls outside the studio, the residue of early estrangement from my own mother and sister and the shock of my father's early death is still with me. How long it can take to see beyond the blinding fog of shame.

Everyone was doing the best they could.

We all live and die. That's just the way it is.

I lift Mattie from my lap as the interview ends, walk over to shut off the CD player.

"Here's a toast to your mother," I say, raising a glass.

Phyllis cheers and raises hers. Willow stands to stretch, sniffs a plate of crackers.

"Come on over," Phyllis says, motioning me to her easel. "I want to show you my latest painting and see what you think."

She has spent today finishing a hilarious portrait of her mother. Mary's wrinkled face grimaces defiantly. She is wearing one of the ridiculous hats Phyllis and her sisters brought during their visits to see her in Fort Benton.

"I love it!" I smile broadly and put my arm around Phyllis. "That's quite a hat."

"When Mother was at the nursing home, we'd arrive with wild hats we'd made for her—I like to add bouquets of plastic flowers, ribbons, leather, whatever I can find. Everybody there loved our visits because we all sang." Big silver Southwestern crosses dangle from Phyllis's ears, flashing in the light. Her smiling lips are painted strawberry red. "Mother would wear our hats for a short while. But she didn't think we were *half* as funny as *we* did."

Phyllis points to one corner of her painting. "Do you think it needs more purple in these flowers? Hey, I might have mentioned it before, but have you ever noticed . . .?"

We finish her sentence together, ". . . there's a little bit of purple in everything?"

"Thank you for your gift, Lynne. I know Mother is relieved to have gotten out of here. She's up there right now on Square Butte, dancing with Daddy."

Before leaving, I tell Phyllis my news. "Harrison and I are going to Scotland together in July!"

She is thrilled, and she knows exactly where we are going. She makes me promise to take my hat along, with some long pheasant feathers for extra fun.

On the fifteen-minute drive home, I enjoy thinking of Phyllis growing up in a family environment that was alive with laughter. Willow pulls her head out from under the seat. She knows home.

My hand rests on her head for a minute before we step down onto the icy sidewalk and into this chilly night.

SQUEEZE BOX

Watching for newborns and for signs of labor with Harrison early one cold February morning, I notice how his dogs (and now Willow) also watch. They are active participants. The milky poop of nursing calves must taste particularly good to them, as must the sticky remains of amniotic sacs and afterbirth lying on snowy ground. Willow is a full-fledged ranch dog now. Her days are spent tracking, moving from one potential snack to the next.

We sit together later that evening by Harrison's fireplace in the living room. Our lantern casts soft light. Passing time until he needs to check cows again, Harrison recalls his first experiences with calving on the ranch, after purchasing this valley from Max.

"I arrived in a blizzard. John Sitzleburger, my first ranch hand, had been bucked off his horse—a blood clot had shifted while he was on a bar stool calling his mother—and he was dead. I came directly from his funeral through the blizzard to take over the ranch. I looked in on his house. There was hair all over the floor; it was clear he'd just given himself a haircut. And I went to work."

I place another log on the fire. Outside, snow keeps falling.

"I'd bought Max's thirty cows with the property so I could meet Forest Service requirements. Only had a little tractor; no way to feed effectively except to take the round bales up a hill with the tractor and push them downhill by hand. No cattle facilities. Everything was held together with baling wire and rotted off at the ground. I came upon this scene—confronted with a calf that wouldn't suckle its mother. I knew how to milk cows, had done that as a boy. I put the cow in a head catch, milked her, and tried to interest the calf in warm milk, but it wouldn't take. The calf seemed not all there."

I remember seeing a calf like that down at the barn yesterday.

"I called up Max, and he said sometimes it just helps to give 'em a kick. So, with Moira and my youngest son, Levin, looking on like two priests saying, 'You *must* accomplish this,' I gave the calf a kick. And sure enough, it worked."

"Sounds terrifying to be suddenly responsible for so much!"

"It was daunting. Twenty below zero. In the dark. Alone. As stark a separation from the world as I could imagine. Out of that same blizzard appeared a cowboy with a black hat, a black mustache, and a bulldogging scar down his cheek. He said, 'I hear you folks need some help.' I hired him on the spot."

"Did it get better once help arrived?"

"Yeah, but even with a hired man, I've always shared the responsibility and taken half the shifts. Having to commit, by myself, at night, was unsettling. Still is. Even when you've watched others do it but are left now to do it yourself, it's extreme loneliness. I was always afraid of calving. During my shifts, it always feels confusing, unfamiliar, cold, lonely—like I was on the moon, and *by the way*, this is your job. You have to be resolute, with nowhere to go and no one to talk to. For someone who has avoided so much in life, this was the perfect trap."

I reach to pour myself a sip of wine. He passes.

"I didn't have very good cows when I started out. That first calving season all on my own, I had a pregnant teenager and sure enough, she's in labor, there's nothing to do but help. I pull the front legs out far enough to get double half hitches with an obstetric chain around the calf's legs, hook it up to the winch, and start cranking. The poor heifer groans, and I'm desperate, so I try to make myself negative to work. I say, 'Damn it, I'm going forward with this winch, and if I kill her, I kill her.' Even as I timed my cranking with the contractions, letting her rest in between, my mind had to steel itself: 'You *will* make this work.'"

"What happened?"

"She falls over on her side groaning. I go down with her, and as the calf comes, warm afterbirth pours all over my head. The calf is out, I put a strand of straw up its nose to make it sniff. I set it upright in the straw. When I release the cow, she immediately turns to mother her calf, and to my amazement, everything is fine."

"Wow!"

Snowfall outside is getting heavier.

"What did you mean, you tried to make yourself negative to work?"

"Perhaps I have to get mad to act. Dive in, grit my teeth. I don't really know what I'm doing, but I have to do it. You've spent your whole life backing away from commitments of any kind, and suddenly you're stuck with a pregnant teenager delivering a baby."

We sit for a minute in the warmth of embers still glowing in the fireplace.

I check my watch. "Time for you to be on duty again."

"Wanna come along and keep me company?"

"Sure."

"I can hardly get myself to go down there again and see that poor calf suffering."

"The same calf you were doctoring two weeks ago?"

"He's still no better. He's got a catheter. We wiped maggots off him last week, put baking soda under his hide with a syringe. He came back a little bit with more electrolytes and antibiotics."

"Jesus. That's awful. Okay," I say, touching his shoulder and changing my mind. "You better get going. He needs you. I'll make dinner. You're doing everything you can."

Willow, Tula, and Oscar sit near my feet while I brown elk meat and grate cheese for elk tacos.

There is no escaping loss on a ranch. I will not forget that dead cow in the bucket of the tractor, all the unlucky calves we aren't able to save. The bright color of this cheese reminds me of marigolds placed on the elaborate Day of the Dead altars I used to exhibit each year. They were created by members of Atlanta's Mexican community. I looked forward to this holiday, when it is believed the border between the spirit world and the world of the living dissolves. For a brief time, families welcome back deceased relatives as honored guests to share laughter, dancing, and feasting. This seems healthy to me. Stirring elk meat recalls the deep honor of what will nourish our bodies tonight.

Harrison's steps are heavy as he climbs the stairs one hour later.

"Well?"

"I just hate doing all this to thar poor fellow. It's not making any difference. And he's having such a tough time. Miserable," he sighs. He heads to the cabinet for a wine glass.

"When do you decide to just let him die?"

"He'll be gone by morning."

One afternoon, between shifts, I finish reading *Animals Make Us Human* by Temple Grandin. I zip up my coat and pull gloves on when we are back on watch again, standing by the corrals. Only a few pregnant cows and heifers remain. The sun is out, but it is forty degrees.

"It's been a while since I read that book," Harrison recalls. "Wonderful how she could see through a cow's eyes to understand how they react—how different angles and noises cause fear."

"I feel the same way. I dread the sounds of your heavy spring-loaded metal gates slamming shut; the noise of chains chinking loudly against metal stalls." Saying this, I recall the revelation of relative quiet when I left NYC after living there ten years. Silence here on the ranch is astonishing.

Every sound is a voice. Each sound arises, then disappears. Everything dissolves back into the silence that remains.

Dogs bark. They hear Scott, a delivery man, driving up the road to drop off a package.

"Dogs aren't generally fearful like cattle and horses because they're hunters," Harrison interjects.

Another woman might label it mansplaining. For the most part, I don't let Harrison's penchant for explaining things, often pointing out the obvious, bother me. It's a benign habit. He does it with men and women alike. It's part of his voice, like a bull's grunting or a bird's song.

I'm coming to see the world more through a horse's eyes. When Harrison and I are out riding, I notice something on a fence line, and it's not right. Sitting deeper in my saddle, Andre and I walk over to investigate. It's a deer skull with antlers that Harrison found a few days ago and placed on a high post. Andre is calm by nature. But something that looks unusual or out of place, especially something flapping in the wind, is noticed by any horse and can potentially cause fear. Hiking with Harrison into mountains on a hunt, we move slowly and deliberately. Quick sudden movements are feared by animals in the wild.

"All of the mares used to be scared of Tula and Willow each time I'd approach on walks," I recall. "Now Burna is just curious."

"But if you were on her back and they ran up behind her, she might bolt. A bird might suddenly flush out of the grass beneath her feet."

These well-intended reminders, while appreciated, can get old. Harrison forgets I've already had both things happen while riding with him and I handled them well. Still, I file them away.

"Make sure you're anticipating what might be scary, *before* the horse reacts."

At the end of our four o'clock calving shift, Harrison opens the truck's tailgate, and our three dogs jump in. We head up the long hill toward the winter pasture. Rising to the top, he cuts the engine. Snow is falling. Dogs don't mind; they're happy to be out. From our high vantage point in the warmth of the cab, we see geldings on one hillside, the mares on the opposite side of the valley. In the Red Nose Pasture, the bulls are in their paddock, and cow–calf pairs near the barn.

Harrison places my hand in his. This is not a gesture I take for granted. He squeezes. I squeeze back. His warm palm—large and rough—rubs against mine. Our fingers lock. He repeats again what he tells me now at least once a week, "Have I told you how comforting and calming your hands are? Your touch always makes me feel better."

BRISE

Andre and Rocky are now nineteen years old, and Brise, grandmother to my favorite four-year-old mare, Burna, is thirty-one. Harrison has described Brise as having the softest back he has ever ridden. Now her sloped spine is that of an ancient horse, hollow and deep. There is an unmistakable stillness and vulnerability about her. Out of concern, Harrison has moved her to the safest barn corral by herself. As we drive past her on our way into town today, I notice she is lying down, her nose to the ground. She is just sleeping. I shudder but dismiss a more ominous feeling as we drive on.

When we arrive home in the dark, a barn light glows white like a strange aura around her slumped grayed form. The memory of my feeling returns. "Oh, God. I wondered if this was happening when we left. I should have said something."

Brise is lying in exactly the same place. She is alive, but she hasn't moved. Her body is ravaged from stress. Her eyes, full of terror.

"What do we do?" I ask, alarmed.

Harrison sinks into the familiar horror of this responsibility and moves out into the night without a word. I go to Brise, kneel down to touch her face and bring comfort. But she is frightened, chilled to the bone, and drenched in sweat. I run to the tack room to get a blanket. Five bird dogs bark from the kennel as Harrison starts up the tractor's engine and drives into the corral. He pulls the huge machine right up next to terrified Brise, jumps out, and leaves the engine running.

"What are you doing? She needs our help! This is insane!"

He throws the blanket aside. "That's what I'm trying to do! Now get out of the way! Here, hold this flashlight and help me!"

I can hardly breathe as he works in the dark to rig a large piece of canvas under her quivering belly so that she is connected to the heavy machinery by a pulley. I want this moment to be sacred. The racket of the tractor makes me tremble. All I can do is watch as he climbs in and attempts to hoist Brise up onto her legs so that the weight of her body doesn't keep restricting blood flow, even damaging her lungs.

In his blinding anguish, perhaps seeing in Brise the memory of his dying wife, Moira, he is going to try everything possible to save her. One last effort. A few months earlier, he and Rick tried this with a cow who had become paralyzed—unable to stand on her own after giving birth. I bottle-fed the calf while they left her mother dangling from the bucket of the tractor holding her weight, her feet just touching the ground. She hung there for four days, lowered only to eat, and eventually, she was able to stand again on her own.

But Brise is finished. Already half gone. The tractor abruptly lowers her, and her decrepit body folds and collapses onto the wet spot of cold ground where she has likely struggled all day. Her eyes tell us everything. I stand back and away, in tears, and watch as Harrison kneels down to say goodbye, then leaves for a minute and returns with a handful of grain. He offers it to her. One last kindness. Suddenly he looks up and begins yelling at me again. "This is horrible. Go away! Go get in the truck!"

I turn my back and bring hands to my ears, as he places the pistol against her skull.

His eyes are dark when he returns to the house over an hour later.

We sit side by side at the kitchen table in silence.

He sighs, staring out the window. "When you put animals down or witness this kind of death over the course of so many years, it piles up. Eventually, you don't just react to the moment, you react to the load."

THE LEK

S pring, 2008. A month later, one Saturday in April, Harrison and I wake extra early. We want to experience the full wonder of a spring morning. I step through the kitchen doorway with coffee into the dark and listen. Water is rushing through the valley. Two pairs of noisy geese talk with animation on the far pond. The air is brisk with glorious fragrance. Down in the mudroom, I pull on muck boots and my black wool jacket, before grabbing the gray hat with furry earflaps. Gloves have disappeared. A blue silk neck scarf will have to do. We leave Willow, Oscar, and Tula still drowsy with their breakfast and hike up the hill to a favorite stretch of open land beyond the house.

Early dawn breaks across this low mountain meadow. As yellow light spills over the horizon, hundreds of meadowlark voices rise from shimmering prairie grasses. We stand still to listen. Their throaty melody is familiar as the voice of one individual singing at a time—each one impressive on its own. This joyous meadowlark chorale is unfamiliar and sublime—one thousand times the power, one thousand times the beauty. We have entered a cathedral. The grace of their hymn pours up and over us, all around us, through us. We look at each other with astonishment.

Still spellbound, we return hand in hand to the house. We climb into the truck and steal down past the barn in silence. Most of our gray-crowned rosy-finches left sometime last week to fly north. The setters are quiet at this hour, slumbering inside their kennel. The two oldest horses are also asleep. I look for a third, still missing Brise. At the top of the hill, Rocky is rolled to one side with head flat on the earth. Her knees rest while bearing no weight. Andre lies upright with eyes closed, wet nose propped firmly against moist fragrant ground.

In the pasture just above, we drive past a dozen whitetail deer lying together. They stand out, still wearing their shock of winter hair against this early green grass. High above the next gate, a familiar kestrel flutters in place, her eyes locked on something below. She folds in her wings and plummets from the sky.

The sharp-shinned hawk we often see is perched high today in a cottonwood tree by the creek. This marshy place, where every sound is soft and muted, must be an excellent hunting beat. A second hawk, perhaps a mate, sometimes perches three trees down along the creek. The truck rumbles across the last metal cattle guard. Man-made noises are so dissonant here, compared to the softness of feet on new grass. As we turn onto the gravel county road, a new flock of robins sweeps past us.

Harrison drives slowly. We stay quiet, watchful. Individual meadowlarks are still belting out their melodies. Rambling along, we pass one perched on a fence post, another on a stretch of barbed wire, still another balancing atop a tassel of tall grass. A lone pronghorn antelope trots out across the road into open grasslands. Harrison slows even more as we pass Corley Canyon, a cold place where rolling prairie drops off into deep dark coulees and hidden passageways. We have traveled this canyon with the bird dogs, and more than once I've felt the strange chill of a silent phantom. Hair rises on the back of Harrison's neck too. Like the bodies of deer or horses, ours tell us of lions who travel this invisible corridor.

We crest the top of the next blind hill and spot a white truck rolling toward us. Harrison eases to a stop, rolls the window all the way down, and gives our neighbor's ranch manager, Jack, a polite greeting.

"Great morning, huh?"

"Yep, sure is. I was just out checking on a bull that's running around."

"Ah, spring fever!"

"Yeah right. Knocked down a fence and now I can't find him. Let me know if you see him, will you? He was over there in the Corley pasture. I'm gonna have to head back there in a little while and look again."

"We'll keep our eyes out."

"Hey, you two might enjoy it up there," Jack says, pointing ahead. "Wyatt and I had fun yesterday. We drove out early—around this time of the morning. There's a bunch of sharp-tailed grouse drumming up at the old corral at the top of the hill. You should check it out."

We wave and continue driving up the road.

"Jack was talking about a lek. Do you know what a lek is?"

I squint my eyes with suspicion. "Hmmm. This must be one of those mysterious words like flehmen, right?"

"A lek is a place where grouse gather to carry on with courtship behavior, where they prance around and display. You'll love this."

We turn off the county road and onto dirt at the top of the hill, then drive past the old gate and head through a mountain pasture to the east of Square Butte toward old corrals. "Stop! Park the truck!" I say, pointing. In the low light of early morning, we count fifteen to sixteen sharpies moving around in the corrals up ahead. "Look at that," says Harrison. "It's a barn dance, and they're already do-si-do-ing!"

We close the truck doors gently. The air is chilly. As we reach the edge of the corral, they all scurry off and hide behind a wall of wood panels. We wait. Strange sounds begin to rise from behind the panels: scuffling in the dirt, lots of rattling, clucking, lurid cooing. "The action is still on back there!" Harrison whispers. We listen into the crisp morning air, giddy with anticipation. We feel like two operagoers when lights flash and voices hush, waiting for the red velvet curtains to rise. A few birds finally decide we aren't a problem—or simply forget about us—and one by one, the entire cast struts back onto the main stage.

Each spring, male sharp-tailed grouse return to the lek to establish boundaries. As they dance out, these cocks appear so consumed with their own importance that little else matters. These are the same birds Harrison hunts with his setters, but something is different. Their plumage is the familiar mottled dark and light browns against white. But at this time each year, courting males display extra bright colors: yellowish-orange combs flash large above their eyes, and shiny violet glands swell like jewels around their necks.

We watch them confront one another and face off. Ruffled and erect tail feathers rattle in the air. Wings extend. Feet stamp the ground rapidly. With loud clucking and gobbling, males squat and shuffle, thrum and dance around one another with mechanical movements like wind-up toys.

Their bodies quiver in a precise and rapid rhythm as they spin around in circles or rush forward. Each cock is displaying his energy, good looks, dancing, and vocal skills to fend off competing males and to win a female's approval. There's a popping that sounds like a cork, and now, a kind of gobbling like a turkey.

Tympanuchus is a small genus of birds in the grouse family, typically referred to as prairie chickens. The genus contains three species, lesser prairie chicken, greater prairie chicken, and sharp-tailed grouse, all of which gather at communal display grounds or leks. *Tympanuchus* comes from ancient Greek roots and means "holding a drum."

Our auspicious peek into this secret world of dancing prairie grouse reminds me of Blackfoot and A'aninin men I've watched dancing at powwows. They strut and sway in spectacular regalia—fancy head roach headdresses, feather bustles with breech cloths moving like fanned tail feathers. They carry mirrors and feather fans, and wear noisy bells around active legs and ankles. They wear the kind of regalia I've examined in the museum's collection.

The Prairie Chicken Dance (or Chicken Dance) is practiced by many Indigenous people living in the same habitats where these birds live. It is said to be a very old dance, referred to by at least one elder as "the granddaddy of all dances." Its origins are with the Blackfoot (Siksika) sacred Kiitokii Prairie Chicken Society. Intended to mimic this springtime mating dance, men preen, strut, and charge at one another to impress the "hens" with intricate body movements and dance steps; tense, strained muscles; precise and rapid rhythms. Blackfoot, Plains Cree, Stoney Assiniboine, Tsuut'ina, and Sioux dancers are among those who have traditionally honored their grouse relative in this way. Today, contemporary dancers continue to compete for prizes in highly competitive Chicken Dance contests.

Enraptured, I lean against the corner of the corral and gaze through a rare window into what was once part of a vast living knowledge. The shared intimacies of belonging to a particular place; the dance of sacred kinships as I'm experiencing them in this moment and this place with Harrison and these grouse.

Harrison taps me on the shoulder and points. A different group of dandy males—cooing, clucking, purring, and whirling, stomping their feet like a rapid-fire drumbeat, and slapping their tails with a clicking sound—are directing their efforts toward females who have just slipped onto the scene. These boys are going for it. In stark contrast, the hens appear calm, quiet, and dignified. They stand on the sidelines and observe with apparent dispassion the flamboyant proceedings performed on their behalf. Hens may visit up to ten different leks before they decide to mate and nest. Noisy males spin around in circles and stomp their feet. Discerning females quietly and calmly assess the situation. Something about all this feels vaguely familiar.

It is hard to leave, but I'm cold. We return to the truck as pink-and-orange sunlight stretches out over this high plateau and trickles down into lower steppes and breaks. Harrison starts the engine. I crank the heat and rub my hands together.

"How wild was *that*?" I whisper.

"Let's pull up closer," Harrison says. "Maybe we can catch one last encore."

We arrive with the truck and, before we know it, delirious grouse come out from hiding and begin running in all directions. This time they leave the perimeter of their dancehall corral. While we sit high up in our heated box seats and watch the show through truck windows, fancy males begin whirling their colorful bodies below and all around us. They're dancing and strutting, heads extended and angled down, wings fully spread and quivering on both sides of our vehicle, busy feet striking hard upon the earth.

We drive back along gravel roads in the early full light of day. As Harrison opens and closes the last metal gate, the English setters bark to greet us. Rocky and Andre are grazing. Four geese quietly explore the far bank of the pond—their secret reconnaissance before nesting. Back at the house, anxious dogs want out. Oscar looks sleepy, but Willow and Tula can hardly wait to say good morning. I lie down in the grass for kisses. In a heavy heap, Tula drops into the cradle of my arm, groans with delight as she snuggles in, then rolls on her back, licking and biting my chin. Willow and Oscar bark at something. Tula jumps up, and the three of them bolt off. A meadowlark sings from the grass above the house.

NANCY

There is mounting anxiety on Harrison's part this spring in anticipation of my meeting his ninety-two-year-old mother for the first time. More than once, he mentions how invasive she can be about a person's privacy. One month before we travel to visit Nancy, she calls and tells Harrison she's been doing some research on his "new Montana girlfriend" with an ex-girlfriend in Virginia. In their plot to come between us, Nancy tells him they've discovered I've been married several times and that I use aliases. He confronts me in the hallway.

"I have something to ask you. Accusations have been made. It's very important to me that you tell me the truth."

When he asks, I laugh out loud. "Wow! That's insane! Are you serious?"

"I suspected as much. But I had to make sure."

I don't know if I am more astounded by his mother's warped ingenuity or by Harrison's need to verify my honesty.

Nancy lives at an assisted-living home in Charlottesville, Virginia. She lived here independently for years with Harrison's father until he died seven years ago. We enter her room and find a small, thin, pale woman with silver hair, bright pink lipstick, and blue eyes. She wears khaki-beige pants and a lime-green cardigan over a white top. I had imagined her wearing one of the bright-colored floral Lilly Pulitzer dresses or "Lillies" she wore in early family pictures taken at their home in the Bahamas. Several 1950s Inuit prints from Cape Dorset hang on the walls of her room. She is seated next to a large window and a long table with twenty-some different potted orchids.

First sight of her dashing son sets Nancy's eyes ablaze. He helps her stand for a hug and kiss. She doesn't take her eyes off us as he pulls up a chair for me, then sits down on the bed next to her chair. The two of them volley back and forth in conversation. Harrison seems slightly cautious, like someone playing with the still-hot embers of a fire. They share an air of cynicism and mockery. She then trains her gaze on me. A toy black poodle comes over to sniff my legs.

"That's Jinn," Harrison says. "This little dog knows how to walk down the hallway and open the automatic doors at the front entrance. She lets herself out, then returns to the room. All on her own."

Nancy holds a keen stare. Her mouth registers a suspicious smile. I think of the devious story she made up about me. She asks me what I think of Harrison.

"He can be a real gentleman, when he *wants* to be," I tease.

"Has he beat you yet?" she asks.

I raise one eyebrow. "He behaves himself *most* of the time," I respond, smiling at Harrison.

"Do you keep him in line? He might need that," she says, returning her scrupulous gaze to Harrison. I try not to picture his stories of her beating his father with a cane and his own hairless legs.

Nancy tells Harrison to get her a favorite protein drink in vanilla; she complains they only give her chocolate, which she hates. She continues to interrogate me with crackling eyes and an inscrutable mouth. At some point, after several questions, a bit of conversation, and more teasing, we're enjoying each other. I am sufficiently sophisticated to not be summarily dismissed.

"I like you," she decrees. Harrison is observing with interest.

"I like you, too, Nancy. Harrison has told me about his memories of Thailand when he was young. Your time living there must have been amazing."

"The best time of my life," she says, the intensity of her eyes softening.

Nancy tells me about befriending a member of the royal family and how they rented their home there from some uncle of the Thai prince. During their five-year stay, she came to know Jim Thompson, the famous silk designer, traveling with him on shopping trips for antiques and art for his museum. He once took her on a private tour of the Angkor Wat temple ruins—still largely hidden within the jungles of Cambodia—during a period of salvage efforts by the French.

"When you came back, you brought me a beautiful traditional crossbow," Harrison recalls.

"Made by a local Cambodian."

I ask about Tawi, without mentioning Harrison's painting of this Thai woman who once lit her pubic hair on fire in front of him. I'm aware that he never told his mother about that odd event.

"She was our number two girl, from Chiang Mai," Nancy confirms. "She was a wild thing. No elegance. Would climb a tree and get fruit for her lunch."

When we say our goodbyes, I bend to give her a hug and kiss. Her eyes smile. She asks when we'll be back. As we leave the building, Harrison puts his arm around me.

"Your mother is tough, but I like her," I say. "I'm glad you prepared me. Did you notice? When she discovered she and I have so much in common—writing and researching, a love of art and culture, *and you, of course*—there was a moment when her eyes turned menacing. She shot a glare at you, as if you were cheating on her. Like a jealous woman who might need to get rid of me. I'll admit: I was relieved when she said she liked me."

"I don't doubt any of that. You're very lucky. She wouldn't say that if she didn't. She doesn't like many people."

Nancy once rifled through her newly married son's intimate private letters and photographs and chopped them all up to create a collage she thought Harrison would like. "That's her modus operandi with family relationships," he told me. "Scissoring her way through affairs that she has no business doing."

We walk across a huge park toward our rental car. The day is pleasant. We find a bench to sit and talk.

"She obviously adores her favorite son. She's *smitten* with you," I say, squeezing his waist. "It's good you're visiting her. Good you've still got each other."

"I barely remember anything about that time. But I remember being with her after Moira died. I'd lost Hal. And my father. We'd both lost our anchors in life. I was so out of it, I just sat for hours with her in silence, eyes closed."

"She's got a great eye for art. And she's quite an orchid lover."

"When we lived in Punta del Este, Uruguay, for a couple of years—which back then was an empty place along the shoreline—she would send me into pine forests to find orchids for her. I was about seven years old."

"I'm guessing all those potent martinis that led her to pick fights were made with gin, hence the dog's name?"

"It's J-i-n-n or D-j-i-n-n. She's had a long line of black poodles over the years, all named Jinn. It's an Arabic noun that means 'hidden spirits.' Beings that are concealed from the senses."

"She loved Thailand. I would too."

"She wrote a short book about her experiences there. It's called *The Spirit House*. I've got a copy back home, if you're interested. Spirit houses are built in Thailand as homes for ghosts, hidden spirits."

"Cool concept. Great title."

"In old Virginia, my mother could trace the family's lineage far back. Growing up, she would always hear, 'Aren't we *lucky*?' And they were. When we arrived in Thailand, while my father was off doing his Secret Service work, she would sit for hours and share stories with her landlord, a relative of the Thai royal family. She loved telling him how his family's position in Thailand reminded her of the same aristocracy and exclusiveness she had always enjoyed in Virginia."

"Such dependence on social standing—"

"Absolutely. She and my father grew up in the era of Fred Astaire and Ginger Rogers. When they were happy, my father would walk around the house singing tunes from *South Pacific*. Everyone was imagining themselves in a caste one step higher. Life for them was a romantic fantasy."

I take a moment. Bite my lip. "And she spent time with Jim Thompson. Remind me of his story?"

"Jim Thompson was a Princeton graduate. I think he moved to live in postwar Bangkok in 1946, two years before we arrived. He was serving as intelligence chief for the OSS, the predecessor of today's CIA. At that time, many people were spies. We lived there from 1948 to '52. We arrived the same year Thompson co-founded his Thai silk company. He would go on, of course, to become an international design legend in the silk industry."

"What kind of art were they shopping for?"

"I don't know what my mother bought. Thompson assembled a compound of traditional Thai structures on the banks of a Bangkok klong and filled his home with an unbelievable collection of Southeast Asian ceramics, sculpture, and artifacts. He was a worldly figure. I'm sure my mother found him very handsome with his slick blond hair and piercing gaze. He would entertain sumptuously, six or seven nights a week, and anybody who aspired to significance—that would be my mother—angled for an invite to his house."

"No wonder those years were so memorable."

"She had a certain attraction to power. Fifteen years after we left Thailand, Jim Thompson mysteriously disappeared without a trace. Never seen again." He pats my thigh. "Shall we walk?"

CROWNING

I knock on my friend Kelly's Forest Service log cabin door in East Glacier with a special gift, hoping to surprise her. But no answer. I met Kelly seventeen years ago during my second summer of research on the Blackfeet Indian Reservation. We hiked a lot over all those summers in Glacier Park, falling in love with its backcountry together. She works here now as a naturalist. I check my phone messages and hear her voice: "My water just broke! Jason and I are heading over to Whitefish to the hospital."

I return to Harrison, burning with urgency. "We have to go to Whitefish."

"Why, what's up?"

"Kelly is having her baby right now! *I want to be there*! We're already halfway. Can we do this?!"

"Okay. Let's go."

Kelly knew me when I was living in Atlanta and bleeding for two years. She knows the struggles I've had with my mother and sister, how much I love children; how hard it was for me to give up any chance back then of ever having my own. When Kelly got pregnant, she promised she would tell me when she was going into labor.

Ninety minutes later, on the other side of the Rockies, we arrive at the tiny hospital. I find her easily; she has just finished a round of intense contractions. She manages to introduce me to the nurse. "Okay, it's time," the nurse says. "Let's all go into the next room. Jason, you'll take one leg, and Lynne, you'll take the other."

Oh boy, I think. *Remember your calving lessons.*

Harrison has disappeared.

Kelly lies down on a white cot in the middle of a sterile room. A stainless-steel sink is on one wall, and at the foot of the bed is a small seat on wheels next to a table with shiny instruments laid out on a silver tray. Kelly is told to bend her knees, and Jason and I are positioned to stand on either side of her, our hands on her knees. Her green eyes and nostrils flair as the next round of contractions begins. She has refused all painkillers; she wants to feel what every other animal feels.

The nurse tells her it's time to push. Holding her leg, I watch the features of her courageous face register the severity of pain. She screams and prays as she wages battle with each round of agony. In between contractions, Jason offers ice at the wrong moment. She yells at him to get away. I offer a cool washcloth for her forehead. After more than an hour, only a tiny part of the baby's head is visible. Jason tries to joke: "He's probably coming slower because he's got big ears like me." We encourage Kelly mightily during each subsequent round of contractions. But nothing changes.

Her nurse finally decides to make a small incision to enlarge the passageway. When the full head pops out, it looks to me like an alien between her legs—five times bigger than I had imagined. There is a sudden scurry of quiet activity by the nurse and midwife as the baby's umbilical cord is unwrapped from around its neck. We reassure Kelly. "Everything is all right." More intensified rounds of excruciating effort. Kelly weeps, pleading: "Please, dear God, help me! I can't do this anymore, please help me!"

At last, the final hurdle is overcome. The shoulders slip out into view, and the entire body comes squirting out. That last part is *exactly* what happens when a calf's hips appear and it drops to the ground. It's a boy! Ellis, with Irish bloodlines coursing through him. He arrives into the world with bright red hair just like his daddy's and Kelly's father.

I give the new parents a beaded leather bag in the shape of a turtle meant for keeping the umbilical cord, made by a Blackfeet artist friend

Jackie Larson Bread. After the cord is cut and placed in the bag, I leave the new family to tell Harrison. I find him sitting alone in the truck in the parking lot with the window down. My adrenaline is still pumping, hormones exploding throughout my body.

"Well?" he asks.

I stand at his window hardly able to speak.

"That's wonderful, sweetie. And you got to see the whole thing?" His hand reaches outside to wipe the tears flowing down my face. "I've seen lots of animals born, but I've never seen an actual baby come into the world. All three of my boys were born by cesarean. I keep telling my daughters-in-law I want to be right there in the room when the action starts. But all they do is roll their eyes."

He shakes his head, then smiles. His calm hand rests on my arm. "How lucky, how very lucky to have been there."

SPROUTS AND SAPLINGS

W e return from up north before the end of a long weekend, so I stay over. Awake with early light, a cock pheasant trumpets the official news of spring. He crows insistently, stretching toward the sky to drum fluttering feathers. This happens each year, right outside Harrison's bedroom window. We face each other in bed, eyes smiling.

I push myself up. Harrison rolls over in bed with a groan.

"I've got to get outside this morning for a hike," I say, pulling on pants and socks. "It's impossible to be inside when everything is so gorgeous."

He rises slowly. I am on a mission and can't dress fast enough.

"Want to come along?" I ask.

"Where are you going?"

"I just want to feel the day."

"I don't do hikes. Hikes are for people who like forced marches for exercise, without any sense of what's around them." He reaches for his jeans.

"Yes, yes. I *know*. I wonder how much you might be missing out on, Harrison, with all your prescribed ideas about what you *don't* like."

I pull on his earlobe and give him a kiss, as we turn to walk toward the kitchen.

"Oh, I'm *quite* sure that's true." He heads straight to the coffee maker, empties out yesterday's grounds, grinds more beans. "I guess I'd go with you, if it's interesting."

Inviting him might have been a mistake. "I think I'll just head out on my own this morning. Do my usual circle around the valley with the dogs. I like exercise."

I grab a few eggs to scramble while Harrison waits for coffee. He sits at the table, staring out the window. My mind is also somewhere else.

The chances that my job as special projects curator will receive permanent funding have been dashed. Once my bison exhibition is up and running eight months from now, I'll need to find new employment. And Great Falls is not somewhere I plan on staying. I haven't told Harrison yet. Our trip to Scotland is only three months away.

Down in the mudroom, three excited dogs convey everything I need to know for now. Wagging tails, spinning bodies, licking tongues—eager for *any* adventure. Oscar, Tula, and Willow inhale their breakfasts while I fill a small backpack and grab a raincoat, gloves, binoculars, and water. The air outside is fresh and moist.

At the place where we must cross our new footbridge or ford the creek, I pause beneath the cover of budding cottonwood trees. While my three companions nose their way through rushing waters toward the pond, I am overjoyed to inhale a first whiff of springtime. I touch a cottonwood bud, sticky with amber-colored sap, and lift my finger to my nose. Its tantalizing perfume is the signature scent of this valley. These medicinal buds will soon become heart-shaped leaves.

What if this is my last spring here? My whole body shudders. I cross the bridge to the other side with a pounding heart. Down wooden stairs and back onto earth, I stop again to look around me.

On the far side of the pond, I spot the goose who nests high in the hollow tree. She is peeking out from her hole. There will be goslings soon. How far must they drop out of that high tree nest when they experience their first flight? Each year, after only a few days of floating on the pond, they mysteriously disappear. Where do they go?

Tula and Willow speed past me. A beaver traveling upstream splashes, settling into the old beaver lodge on the far side of the pond. Maybe I won't mention this new arrival to Harrison. Swallows are back, feeding midair. Time to be on the lookout for flashy bluebirds.

Near another high old budding cottonwood down at the barn, the three dogs and I greet setters at the kennel. Songs of the first red-winged blackbirds fill the air.

We leave the road to ascend steep grassy hillsides painted yellow, purple, pink, red, blue, and white with blooming wildflowers. Early spring is the time of shooting stars and pasque flowers (wild crocus), mountain golden peas and arrowleaf balsamroot, flowering wild currants and cream-colored chokecherry blossoms that smell of sweet almonds. A meadowlark rises from grass. Farther along, at the edge of an aspen grove, a robin sings atop a budding branch. With our winter finches' recent departure, we anticipate the arrival of new songbirds, their cousins—goldfinches and Cassin finches, flocks of juncos, towhees, lazuli buntings. Some hidden brilliance seems to inform these arrivals. The blossoming of yellow wildflowers brings yellow birds. With blue flowers come blue birds.

I mount Rattlesnake Hill today without a caution. It's not yet hot enough for snakes to leave their dens. Even so, when I dial Moira's birthdate into the padlock on a gate, uneasiness returns. Suppose Harrison really *can't* allow himself to love another woman. If that's true, part of me wishes he would just cut me loose now.

Will my heart *ever* know how and when to finally walk away from all this?

Higher still, the air is brisk and clear. The dogs and I rise to the altitude where budding cottonwoods along creeks and groves of aspen give way to forests of pines and firs. I spy a group of forty-some elk. More will follow. They have shifted back into this high valley where they likely were born, grazing intermingled with Harrison's horses and cattle. One crow calls to another. Willow and Tula listen. A pair of golden eagles soar overhead. Migrating raptors like Cooper's hawks will soon return. Red-tailed hawks and kestrels are odd; some migrate, some stay. Bald eagles, prairie falcons, sharp-shinned hawks, and these golden eagles are all permanent residents. Coming to know this valley firsthand keeps showing me how all these things—habitat, grazing, wildlife—are so intimately connected.

On the way down, we pass through the heifer pasture. I stop with the dogs to pick balsamroot, bright yellow flowers reminiscent of sunflowers. Eventually, I find myself on the east side of the valley along what was named "Squaw Creek" by non-Natives, where an elder Native woman supposedly once lived. I told Harrison last weekend when he brought me here about the derogatory meaning of the word *squaw*. "Old Woman Creek might be better," I suggested.

Max showed Harrison this woman's former campsite under the trees, now only a slight depression on the downwind side of cottonwoods facing east. Max had heard the story from his uncle, J. Y. Warren, about a Native woman living on the property sometime in the 1880s before J. Y. arrived. Sitting here with Willow even now, I find protection from wind and the warmth of sunlight. Would she have used animal hides to construct a shelter? The story suggests she dug a hole in the ground to stay warm and safe under these cottonwoods at night. Across the creek, a steep hillside where the bank is shaded always retains snow. Ideal refrigeration. At the base of this hillside, a spring would have provided fresh water. I bend down by the creek, imagining this Indigenous woman in J.Y.'s story who would know everything about how to survive, old and all alone. Picking fresh mint from the flow of spring water, I bring a fragrant leaf first to my nose, then to Willow's. I say a prayer: *Might I be as brave and as wise.*

On our return, an itchy heifer is busy rubbing her ears on a fencepost; another rubs her jaw on barbed wire fencing. Entering the adjoining Red Nose Pasture, Sassy and Ibis rub their bodies—neck and bottom—against two old cottonwood trees. These mares need a good hard scratch today, and I'm happy to oblige. By the time I leave, my fingers are not only sticky with sap but covered in horsehair. Everyone feels the restlessness of the season when winter coats are shed and buds break into blossom.

Were all this to suddenly disappear from my life, it would feel as if I'd lost my soul's compass. Adrift, all over again. Without bearings.

Back in the mudroom, I pull off hiking boots and invite the dogs upstairs. We find Harrison sitting at his desk.

"Hi there. You were gone for a long while. How was it?"

I present a bouquet of yellow balsams with sticky fingers and a kiss. "It is so magical right now. Flowers and birds everywhere. I saw a first robin—maybe it came in with that group we saw on the morning we visited the lek? The mares smell of wild onions. They're by that lower spring just behind the cabin by the creek, where they like to be. The grass there is fluorescent green."

As I talk, Harrison greets each dog. Oscar, then Tula. Airedales and poodles don't shed. Willow's blond hairs migrate to his dark shirt like iron filings to a magnet.

She'll miss Harrison—and everything about this place—as much as I will.

"Did you see anything else?" he asks, not noticing he is covered with hair.

"I saw a new beaver in the pond," I mention incidentally.

"Oh dear." He gestures shooting a shotgun.

"Why can't you just leave it there?" I implore.

"Do you like having those trees around the pond? If he spends all summer there, they'll all be gone." He opens his eyes wide, rubs his hands together, and teases, "Kaboom."

I sigh.

Having scratched each dog, Harrison vigorously scratches his own scalp. Some sort of skin condition? "It's always been so," he tells me. A nervous habit left over from childhood. "I spotted a few mountain goats up at goat haunt," he says. "Come to the kitchen and we can find them with the scope."

Willow's loose hairs take flight like dust dancing in the light as he stands.

"Oh, I forgot to tell you," he says, walking down the hall. "I saw two tiny spotted fawns with their mother yesterday outside the bedroom window, just where we saw those twins last year, near the hawthorns. It's happening."

Note to self: Start bringing leashes on walks with dogs.

Harrison gets me set up at the scope. After pouring himself a cup of cold coffee, he begins scratching his arms.

I look up from the scope, before returning to focus. "Looks like you're all synced up. Scratching like everybody else out there."

THE BRIDGE

We sneak out early for our first float of the year, warm clothes and rain gear in tow. Willow falls sound asleep next to the cooler in the boat. We pass familiar eagles' nests in huge old cotton-woods along the banks. I listen for red-winged blackbirds churring in cattails. Beaver lodges mark our voyage. A fancy kingfisher chitters nearby. The day is breezy. This is our favorite section of the Missouri.

We float just one tiny stretch of this longest river in North America. These same waters travel east and south for over 2,500 miles before flowing into the Mississippi and, eventually, to the ocean. When I fish for two bottles of water in the cooler behind Willow, she opens one eye, raises her head, and sniffs fried chicken. Harrison parks his oars along the inside edges of the boat, and we drink while the current carries us.

Waters are high today, voluminous and expansive. I drop into wonder, contemplating strange whorls and whirlpools, back eddies. A young golden eagle perched high along the banks seems curious. The bird looks to be just the age when its speckled feathers—referred to as "chocolate chip" by one Blackfeet friend—were most desirable for adorning an important headdress. Frogs chirp everywhere.

A family of mergansers hugs the right bank. The male lifts from the water into the sky, as droplets of water fall and flash. From the boat, we listen to the mother talking in guttural sounds to her five ducklings. They skitter upriver along the surface of the water as we pass. Easing downriver, my thoughts skitter too. I imagine the lifespan of my body, flowing like this current. I think of Kelly, how her body changed to accommodate birth, how her infant is changing day by day.

The sound of the oars in the water when Harrison begins to row again is hypnotic—lifting, pushing, pulling. This old river once poured through Phyllis's Shonkin Sag country. Its waters stream from mountain creeks through Harrison's valley. I am now, somehow, a part of all this.

Springtime here is mud season, the time when heavy rains and new snow alternate for weeks on end. Mountain snows melt, creeks rise, and the sound of rushing waters fills every valley. All five small streams in Harrison's valley pour down and flow into Cottonwood Creek until, overnight, it can become a roiling river, far too high and too fast to ford. When we finished building our footbridge last fall near his house, it seemed impossibly high. This spring is its first real test.

We return to the ranch that next Saturday after a long rainy day of running errands in Great Falls. We'd asked Rick to put Willow, Tula, and Oscar in the mudroom. At the final ford, Harrison brakes at high water's edge. In the time we were gone, our ability to cross has vanished thanks to a deluge of cold raging rainwater mixed with snowmelt. We pull on raincoats, turn off windshield wipers, cut off the engine, and abandon ship. In driving rain, we open the back doors of the truck for a first load of groceries.

Like a precarious tight wire, our skinny warped homemade bridge floats a mere two inches above crashing whitecaps. *This* is the Cottonwood Creek that overtook J.Y.'s four-year-old son—rolled him up in tree roots and caused J.Y.'s wife to leave forever. In the torrential downpour, we step gingerly up and onto the impossibly bouncy planks, balance ourselves on slippery wood, and proceed step by step with heavy grocery bags full of milk cartons, eggs, glass jars of almond butter, cans of beans.

Safely across, we have only to trudge up the hill some 250 yards

in sloppy mud and rain. We reach the house drenched, dump our
bags in the mudroom, and shake off like dogs. Our three dry sleepy
friends rise from their beds with wagging tails. We are soaked and
chilled. Laughing at each other with wet smiles, we head out for the
next load.

CAUTION

Harrison calls me at the office to chat one afternoon. I answer, closing the door.

"Did you get that hailstorm in Great Falls a few days ago?" he asks.

"I was afraid it was going to break the windows here in my office. Some of those pellets were the size of half-dollar coins." I shuffle through piles of paperwork on my desk while we talk.

"A storm like that can destroy a farmer's entire crop for the year in a matter of minutes," he says. "I called Tanya over at the Big Sag Ranch, and she was pretty rattled. They drove two trucks and stock trailers along the highway up a blind hill toward home, and when they reached the top, everything exploded. Huge balls of ice breaking windshields, shards of glass and ice flying everywhere, while they tried to keep their vehicles and horses on the road."

"Sounds terrifying. Was everyone okay?"

"Yeah, they made it. She said, 'If I was a drinker, I would be drinking now!'"

"I bet the horses were freaked out." My assistant knocks. I hand her wall texts (object labels) to copy for a meeting in two hours. "I should get back to work here. Things are rolling."

"Okay. But if the weather holds, would you like to help me measure the balls on all my young bulls and test their semen when you're here this Saturday? Doesn't that sound *fun*?"

I get home late, sit down with Willow on the floor of our Bird-house, and tell her how much I'll miss her while Harrison and I are in Scotland. Only a couple months away now. She'll be in good company with Tula and Oscar at the ranch. I still haven't told Harrison about my limited time in Great Falls. First, Scotland. Then, get the exhibition open. Maybe something will reveal itself by then.

On Saturday, instead of holding a copy of exhibition wall texts, I stand at the scales with clipboard and pen in hand while testicles are measured on bulls and electric prods are shoved up their rectums to make them ejaculate. The vet puts the semen under a microscope to assess its quality.

On Sunday, we head down to the barn to saddle horses for a ride. Andre closes his eyes as I brush his back, the length of each leg, his forehead. T nuzzles Harrison before dropping his head and opening his mouth to the bit. It's warmer now, so we keep an eye out for rattlesnakes. But the day is beautiful, and our equine friends seem as happy as we are to be heading out. Crossing through the winter pasture, we bump into an angry coyote mother. She persistently barks at us. Pups in a den must be near. We turn around to leave the area. She follows us, still barking, until she has ushered us and our horses all the way back to the main road. Along Timber Creek, Harrison gives T the *whoa*.

"Hey. Stop. Hear it? That's antelope barking."

He points to the top of a big hill above us, where an antelope is standing, staring down in our direction. A small baby antelope lies next to her silhouetted against the sky. The antelope mother barks aggressively, decides to run down the hill toward us and our horses. Then she moves right into our physical space. Snorting angrily, like the coyote mother, she herds us out of her territory.

During these warmer months when Harrison's bird dogs are not hunting, we usually exercise them in harness. A welded steel-bar extension allows Harrison to hook up all five setters so they can travel down the road in front of his ATV. We all enjoy doing this together. Harrison never asks them to pull. His top speed is ten miles per hour. We travel about three miles along the gravel road, stop for water at the halfway point, and give them a good walk. But this Sunday afternoon, the first weekend in June, we want them to feel like real dogs.

"Let's load up everybody and give them a break."

Nell, Drum, and Dollar burst out of the kennel door and jump straight up into the truck bed. I sweep one-year-old Bec and Bastion into my arms and up into the cab with us. Bec sneaks in some French kisses.

"I'll take them to the winter pasture so they have a nice open country to stretch their legs," Harrison says, as dogs with wagging tails scramble around behind us. Tula, Oscar, and Willow follow along beside the truck.

"It's hot today. Better get rattlesnake shots for everyone when you're in town next week," I say, recalling the injections require thirty days before they are fully effective. "I took Willow in for hers last week."

"Okay," Harrison says. He shuts off the engine and opens the tailgate.

Excited dogs leap to their freedom. I step out with the puppies. They'll chase butterflies and meadowlarks in the grass while we stay by the truck.

Harrison blows a whistle. "Let's go!"

The minute three grown setters take off running through the country, we look at each other in the horror of sudden realization. This is the same pasture where we spotted a mama and baby antelope two days ago. We load Oscar, Willow, and Tula back into the truck, while Bec and Bastion romp nearby. The three older bird dogs cast out, and four adult antelope suddenly appear to handle the situation. They are hiding the baby with their bodies. Two of them move out to distract the dogs, galloping away at thirty miles an hour with dogs in hot—and futile—pursuit.

As we watch them disappear over a distant hill, the two other antelope lead a small (but fast!) baby over a hilltop in the opposite direction. Eventually, three hunting dogs, now exhausted, make their way back to us with the first two antelope right on their heels. I hustle to gather the puppies safe in the truck. The antelope literally deliver Harrison's three setters right to our feet, where our defeated dogs collapse, panting on the grass. The two antelope breathe heavily but stand strong, facing us with heads high. They give us a stern look and loud huff, then turn and trot away. We are duly chastised.

Over two hundred elk return to Harrison's valley each June to graze and give birth. We use the scope to observe groups of cow elk with large bellies. They look ragged after wintering in the breaks below, where hayfields of alfalfa have kept them alive. Unlike the calving of domestic cattle in winter, unfortunately timed for the marketplace instead of following nature's course, the timing of elk births in the wild optimizes calf survival. Born late enough that the risk of cold weather has passed and early enough for their mothers to benefit from fresh grass, elk calves have considerable time to grow strong on mother's milk.

Sitting quietly in the woods one day, Harrison and I spy seventy-five cow elk with a small group of babies in a lower meadow; new mothers are mewing and suckling their young. Mountain lions always watch for easy prey. Pregnant cow elk will leave a herd like this to give birth but will return as soon as possible. There is safety in numbers. One afternoon, a tiny spotted elk arrives only twenty yards away from where we sit. I hold my breath, watching. This calf is new to the world. It plays in a swale, hops in and out of mud puddles, runs around in circles on spindly legs, and kicks up its heels before trotting back to its mother. Such joy. Such vulnerability.

As temperatures rise and flooded creeks subside, we anticipate fires and other dangers during this season of birth. On one hot day in June, we spot four dead rattlesnakes at crossings along the road between the ranch and Geyser. They have left their dens. Triggered by some ancient knowledge, something deep inside their reptilian bodies mysteriously signals to every rattlesnake at the same moment, *Move now!* Like bears and marmots emerging from hibernation. Like migrating birds. From now on, we train our minds, set them to high rattlesnake awareness mode. We don gaiters (snake guards) or wear tall boots for every hike, look twice at every stick's shadow on the road, every movement in the grass. Even so, we have at least three or four close encounters each summer.

One Sunday afternoon when I step outside to head home, a rattlesnake is curled up right beside the house only two feet away. By the time I grab Willow and call Harrison, it has disappeared.

Harrison rushes upstairs another afternoon, white as a ghost. His story spills forth like a fable.

"Rick and I are on our knees on the cement floor downstairs. One of the two French doors is open to the outside while we work to fix the door handle. I look up and see a rattlesnake coming rapidly toward the open door, the cool air of the mudroom beckoning him. Suddenly the snake becomes aware of us and starts to rattle. The rattling, amplified by the hollow mudroom, sounds enormous. Both of us crawl around, without getting anywhere. Rick reaches for a stick. 'Not big enough,' I say. I find a broom handle. I can't really remember which of us killed it. We were in some sort of frantic fog."

The mangled snake leaves a dark greasy stain on the stonework outside the mudroom door. The oily mark remains there as a reminder for the rest of the summer. Experience teaches me that most rattlesnakes don't *want* to strike; they're simply responding when they feel threatened. They're just trying to stay comfortable and avoid trouble. Like everything here.

FALLING IN LOVE
WITH PREDATORS

Summer, 2008. Tula is like a goddess who gleams with humor but can do awful things. A fair amount of my ranch time is spent helping take care of creatures and, sometimes, saving lives. I concede that simultaneously, I am falling in love with two of this valley's predators: Harrison and now Tula. One infamous summer day, heading out for a walk a little too eagerly (leaving water bottle and leashes behind), I *see* just what a beast Tula can be.

Suddenly Willow takes off, triggered by Tula, who is in hot pursuit chasing a spotted fawn. I run after them yelling, try to call them off. Tula tackles the fawn, and I tackle her. I slap and scream, prying her jaws open to release the delicate nape of its spotted neck and shoulder. When I finally push Tula away, the frightened fawn lies frozen, panting in shock. A second twin leaps from tall grass just thirty feet away and flees. When I jump up, my fawn stands and bolts. It runs away in one direction as I run again, yelling, toward Tula, who in a split second has taken down the twin. Willow takes chase on the first. I pull off my belt and use it as a leash to yank Tula away. Hearts pound as I drag her muscular seven-years-strong body across the grass toward Willow. Somehow, I free the other fawn from Willow's hold, grab her collar, and drag them both as far away from the scene as I can, before letting go and catching my breath. As I glance back, both babies seem okay. Shaken but not badly hurt. I walk the disappointed dogs home with a hoarse throat, rattled nerves, and a guilty conscience.

Back at the house, Harrison fills me in on what he has observed.

What seemed like chaos was, in fact, a refined intuitive hunting strategy. To flush a small scentless fawn from the grassy place its mama has told it to stay, Tula watches for deer who linger—who seem confused instead of running away. She then whips around in ever-narrowing circles to create pressure, just like a coyote. When the fawn at last breaks from its grassy hide and flushes to run, she takes it down.

"She's the only dog I've ever seen running shoulder to shoulder with a bloody doe," he recalls.

This same Tula rises from deep slumber to welcome me each Friday night or Saturday morning with Oscar and Harrison. Her pink tongue covers my face with kisses and passionate nose nips until I laugh out loud. We share favorite pastimes as often as possible, lying together in grass (or in snow) under these big open skies. She's overjoyed, as am I, when baby deer and elk are older and she can once again be off leash. Traveling out and up into mountains on hikes, she darts in and out of darkness along hidden animal trails full of scent. I make up songs to sing with Tula's beautiful name. She responds with wolfy smiles. Trotting up beside me, she touches my hand with her wet nose as if to say, *I'm glad to know you. And so very glad you are glad to know me. We belong to one another now.*

NEAR SUICIDE

J ust ten minutes after Harrison and I arrive in town from the ranch one Sunday, his cell phone rings. Something serious. Sounds like he's talking with his best friend, John. This is the younger friend he first met when he got Nell, just a few months before my crash on the gravel road four years ago. He is the falconer. I painted a large portrait of John standing in high grass last year with his prairie falcon, Gretchen. Harrison hangs up.

"What's going on?"

"John's in trouble. We've got to get to his house as fast as we can." He makes a quick U-turn.

"Why? What's happening? Is he okay?"

"He's got a priest there with him right now. He's confused, maybe suicidal."

When we pull up, the priest is leaving. John is a strong church member. Harrison is the only other person he called.

"Wait here," Harrison says, jumping out. He speaks briefly with the clergy, then disappears around the back of the house to find his friend.

After a long while, the two of them emerge. Harrison has his arm around John's waist. John's head hangs heavy. I think of him as a healthy forty-something-year-old man, but he can barely walk. I jump out and open the door. A strong odor of alcohol rolls off his breath. Strange, since John doesn't drink. We head straight to the emergency room. John tries to talk but makes no sense. I pull up, and Harrison takes his friend inside.

I'm in the waiting room for over two hours before Harrison reappears.

"Come on. Let's get out of here," he says. We step through a lobby full of people.

"Is he going to be okay?"

"He's with people trained to handle this. That's the best we can do right now."

Harrison drives me back to my house.

"Can I fix you some tea or something?" I don't want to be alone tonight.

"I should probably get these errands done and get on the road. I still have to feed. You sure you don't want to take off work tomorrow and come with me?" He looks into my eyes and grins. Leans over to give me a kiss before I get out. "I'll call you when I get there," he says. "Chin up."

I blow him a kiss before turning to walk up the stairs to my front door.

Two days later, we talk by phone after work.

"How is John? Have you heard anything?"

"He's in some mandatory program."

"What do you mean? What drove him to this?"

"Evidently, he's hooked on prescription painkillers and can't figure a way out. He'd taken a bunch of pills and was drinking vodka when I arrived."

"Oh dear. So lucky you were in town."

"He's got to go through some program. He'll be all right. He can take a lot of pain."

Our voices go quiet.

"I had a single friend who would call me every day, without fail, sometimes three or four times," Harrison says. "I don't remember anything about what we said that first year after Moira died. It was just the fact that Douglas was on the other end of the phone. He always ended: 'Get a good night's sleep.'"

"I had one college friend who would call me every year, for at least ten years," I recall, "on the anniversary of my father's death, just to check in."

"There was something about the pattern, the regularity of hearing Doug's voice, that did a lot to get me through. That, and the passage of time. You just need to not act when you're in the dark. Just endure and wait it out. Give yourself over to your God."

"Is that what you said to John at his house?"

Harrison swallows, clears his throat. "I told him we'll do whatever it takes. For every miserable moment in life when you're willing to die, you can survive if you get beyond that place, get yourself to that next moment."

The following weekend, we sit on the couch in Harrison's living room after dinner. My feet are propped against his thigh. His hands rest on my calves. Oscar sleeps on the rug beside us. Our lantern over the table lends light. We are both still thinking about John. Harrison called yesterday to check on him.

"During my dark time, after losing Moira, it felt like hemorrhaging."

I understand. I was physically hemorrhaging for two years, back in Atlanta, until a second surgery finally made it stop. It was hell. But it got me to Montana.

"I might have tried suicide had it not been for the boys," he says. "I worried about my mental state, tried to commit myself. But the minute I walked in the door of that hospital, I knew I wasn't insane. I turned around and got the hell out."

He reaches down to pet his sleeping buddy. Oscar's legs are moving; he is running in his dreams. I squeeze Harrison's hand. I constantly worry about his happiness. I was always measuring my father's happiness as a girl. Apparently, this is part of who I am. This is something I do: try to make sad men happy.

"Someone in that condition is like a shocked deer that has been shaken by dogs. Everything is over." He shakes his head. "For me, it was mental bleeding."

We sit together in the kitchen over coffee on a Saturday morning three weeks later. It's already mid-July. John has been gradually getting better. Harrison stands and sets up his latest painting to show me. He has worked on it for eight hours straight. It looks as if a man's body is floating underwater with fish swimming all around him.

"What's this one's title?"

"Grief."

"What's happening?"

"It is a portrait of a man—a Canadian fishing guide friend of mine—who drowned himself after being left by his girlfriend two years ago. Just walked out into his favorite pool, Double Eddy, and waited until he became too cold to swim. Then he just let go without a fight."

We stare at the painting without speaking.

"Was it hard, painting this?" I ask. After staying up half the night, he looks exhausted.

"No. Painting is not hard. You just go." He takes a sip of coffee.

I lean in to examine the portrait more carefully. The man's dead body is floating underwater with the salmon. Or *is* he dead? His face, with wide-open eyes, stares straight at the viewer with an odd expression.

"I was really upset when I heard that Rene had died. I spoke with him about a month before he committed suicide. He told me in veiled words about his pain. I had a chance to be there for him, for someone calling out for help like John. But I didn't say what I should have."

I'm quiet before speaking. "*Always really* listening to others . . . and responding with a level of compassion that can save *even one life* is a noble aspiration," I say. "Let's keep checking in with John, okay?"

SCOTLAND

Geordie Soutar, a silver-haired gentleman with ruddy cheeks and a rich Scottish brogue, meets us at the Edinburgh airport. Harrison has been emailing this Scottish rancher for quite some time. Our two-hour drive carries us northward into fertile countryside, a verdant farming region of rolling hills and open fields. We pass sheep and cattle, eighteenth-century farmhouses of cut stone and beautiful old stone walls. Lambing and calving happened here only a few months ago, so babies are everywhere. Ancient stone castles pop into view like dreamscapes. The Soutars are Aberdeen Angus breeders. We're here to visit their family farm on the outskirts of Forfar in Angus County.

Friendship happens easily with Geordie, his English wife Julia, teenage daughter Louise, and son Duncan. They are gracious hosts. The women of the family are bold with a sharp wit, playful and cheeky. Tall and blonde from Yorkshire Viking stock, Julia says of herself. Like me with Harrison, she is younger than Geordie. Clearly, she is the captain of her brood. To everyone's amusement, she winks and joins me soon after we arrive in calling out Harrison on his platitudes. We poke fun at the boys between far too much cattle talk. Harrison loves it. He is always pleased to be the fool in the presence of strong smart women. We're surprised to find ourselves so instantly comfortable, sitting around the kitchen with this family and their two dogs. They are animal people, like us. Geordie and Louise soon rise and invite us outside to walk their farm and look at livestock, while Julia prepares lunch.

"Geordie, please tell us about your work of saving these old Angus bloodlines," Harrison suggests, as we stroll. "We're here to learn."

"Well, I grew up, you see, as a wee lad familiar with Aberdeen Angus. As a young man, I worked as a trainee auctioneer. That gave me a good opportunity to develop my eye. But it wasn't until many years later, in 1995, that I decided I'd like to find a true native Angus cow. To my great surprise and dismay, an exhaustive search for the last of our old native bloodlines revealed fewer than forty left. Most were old, already sixteen or seventeen years of age."

Geordie turns to me, cheeks fleshy, eyes bright.

"You see, Lynne, what I felt I had to do was to find and acquire as many of those few remaining Aberdeen Angus as I could. Someone needed to make sure their old lines of proven genetics weren't lost forever. It came to me to do the work."

I could listen to Geordie's slow sonorous accent forever.

"And thank goodness you did!" Harrison cheers.

"Well, that's right, Harrison. As it turns out, had I not started in 1995, within two or three years, there would have been no local seed stock left. Of the original ninety-eight cow families of Aberdeen Angus, I've been able to recover four or five so far."

We move from one docile cow to the next. Geordie's daughter, Louise, approaches and pets each one as we speak about them, ready to offer her own informed perspective on any given animal. Louise is tall like her mother, a mature sixteen-year-old with thick, long, wavy red hair and a kind disposition, with her mother's endearing sassiness. She is obviously good with animals and a great help to her father.

"Sadly," says Harrison, "these original bloodlines you're building from here aren't valued by the ranchers I know. The United States has dominated the world with McDonald's genetics. All razzle-dazzle and no *truth*. The cattle you're breeding here are Scotland's grand heritage. As I see it, they're historic treasures, like a cathedral, or anything formed of a single-minded pursuit."

These like-minded souls needed to meet. I notice our two ranchers from different sides of the pond are wearing almost identical plaid shirts and pants. I nudge Louise and wink. We smile. She tells me in a lovely accent about her plans to study and become a veterinarian. She'll be a damn good one.

After lunch with the family, Geordie takes us to visit the tomb of Mr. Hugh Watson, 1787–1865. Watson is recognized as the father of the Angus breed.

"His cow Old Grannie and bull Old Jock and their progeny were the beginning of the first organized herd book. Generations of black cattle were bred over the next hundred to a hundred and fifty years in our local region here, by Watson and others. It was those bloodlines that were then shipped from Scotland in the late 1800s and were disbursed all over the world, including to the States."

Standing at the gravesite while men talk cattle, I wonder how things are going back home with the bison exhibit. I picture the American West during the late 1800s, a century after the "clearances" in Scotland when the Highlanders were forcefully removed. At the same moment black Angus from here were arriving to the East Coast of North America, every aspect of life for Indigenous North Americans was under *full attack*. Millions of wild bison had just been slaughtered. Entire populations of proud independent nomadic people were being violently ripped from everything they knew and valued, forced against their will to live in poverty on oppressive reservations. In that period's unspeakable devastation, Native American men who weren't murdered were effectively emasculated, no longer able to live as warriors or hunters and forced to consider farming as their livelihood, considered women's work by many Native Nations. Children were taken from their parents, many were abused, some died. Traumatized heartbroken Native women could no longer tan hides, go on hunts, move camp, or go foraging. Their response while grieving, with more time on their hands, was to create stunning, colorful, fully beaded objects of magnificent power and beauty.

We take leave of our new friends the next day for an adventure on our own. It begins with a thankfully short drive that is terrifying and hilarious all at once. The steering wheel is on the right instead of the left. "Stay in the left lane, the left!" I exclaim. Harrison heads for a roundabout. Flummoxed, he plows straight over it. We progress slowly through lush green countryside along winding roads that do not appear wide enough for two cars but are. Following the Soutars' instructions, we turn onto a single-lane gravel road that weaves us into a secluded and intimate mountain valley called Glen Clova.

As we enter, everything about this valley reminds us of Harrison's, only it's much larger. We pull up to a lone structure, a charming white-with-black-trim country hotel. This is where we will stay. Just across the road, sheep are grazing by a stream while their lambs play and sleep in the dale. We will share this narrow hideaway, high hillsides on both sides.

Harrison and I stand outside the car to inhale fresh mountain air. We listen to the baaing of sheep calling lambs to nurse. We're still laughing.

"We made it here in one piece!"

"We've dropped into heaven on earth, Harrison."

He smiles and leans over to kiss me as he lifts our bags to carry them inside.

We're not here by accident. Glen Clova is one of five major glens (valleys) where the Angus breed began. These glens finger their way higher still into the foothills of the Cairngorm Mountains and National Park. Even before we arrive, these mighty mountains of Scotland have claimed a place in my heart through Nan Shepherd's stunning descriptions in her book, *The Living Mountain*, penned in the forties. In the craggy hillsides and good draining land of this lovely lower valley, small original herds that numbered only ten to fifteen head were the beginnings of what would become Aberdeen Angus. They lived here on native grasses like timothy during warmer months, the same grasses Harrison's cattle graze in his own "glen." When we check in at the front desk, we're told old cattle droving roads and whiskey smugglers' tracks that course through these glens are now walking and climbing trails, and that this beautiful wilderness extends all the way to Queen Elizabeth's beloved Balmoral Castle.

For dinner at the hotel restaurant, I order venison harvested here. It is served rare, with a classic sauce made of beef stock, red currant or hawthorn jelly, fresh brambleberries, garlic, and red wine. We're offered generous helpings of local carrots and tatties from communal bowls.

"You have so many deer at home, Harrison, but we've never had venison. Now I understand why mountain lions like it so much."

Just beyond where we dine, sheep grow quiet outside as evening comes to the glen.

The following morning, after scones and coffee, we hike together to Loch Brandy. We discover peaty bogs, flowering heather, unfamiliar birds. Though lacking bird dogs, I notice Harrison, who claims to hate hiking, is not complaining. The following morning on an early walk by myself along the gravel road up into the mountains, a lifting mist reveals a large group of red stags not far from where I stand. I stay awhile to admire them through binoculars. These boys are not as big as bull elk but are every bit as elegant and noble. Later in the day, Harrison and I climb a steep grassy hillside covered in heather.

"Look at these strange rock formations," I say, stopping to point and catch my breath. "They appear every so often, and they're running along a line, all the way up. They seem ancient, but they must be man-made."

"Those are old butts for grouse shooting. We hunt sharp-tailed and ruffed grouse. Scotland has red grouse. Driven hunts here are famous. Their season is just about to begin, like ours. Very soon, shooters will be hiding behind these stone blinds covered in moss, waiting for a special grouse that is said to fly low and fast, close to the contours of the hills."

Halfway to the top, we stop for our picnic of bridies: short-crust pastry turnovers filled with cooked minced beef, onion, and gravy. We've brought them from the town of Forfar, where they are said to have been invented in the early nineteenth century. Our lunch view of the valley is breathtaking.

With bellies full, we lie side by side on a sun-warmed hillside, our own bed of purple heather in complete solitude.

"I've . . . been wanting to tell you something." Harrison stammers. "I haven't known how."

Puffy clouds drift overhead. An unfamiliar bird is singing.

"What is it?"

"I love you."

I roll over next to him, all smiles. "I love you too! Boy, that was the longest, most difficult breech birth delivery ever, getting *that one* out!"

He smiles, strokes my face, before sitting up. He is looking into my eyes. "Even seven years after her death, I still feel strange. Allowing myself to love another woman. To say that I love you feels like I'm cheating."

I let out a half-cocked primal scream.

"*We are in love,* Harrison! Can't we share this moment's joy, just you and me?!"

"You're right." He stops speaking to kiss me. "I'm trying to be as honest as I can." He begins picking purple flowers and places them all over me. We can't stop grinning.

"Speaking of honesty," I say, beginning to unbutton his shirt, then helping him as he awkwardly tugs at mine for a roll in the heather.

When we drive down the gravel road out of Glen Clova the next morning, I leave a small bit of my heart behind. This is the place our love finally found its voice. Before setting off to explore the Western Isles, we return to stay one more day and night with the Soutars on their farm.

Away from the beauty of that heathered hillside, something about Harrison's long-awaited words hangs heavy. Even his declaration of love for me was attenuated. Following a grand farewell dinner of beef Wellington with our new friends, I'm relieved to be alone again in their guest house. I invite him to sit next to me on the bed.

"I still don't know why, Harrison. But for as long as I've known you, you've most often spoken about Moira in ways that put up a wall of impossibility. It's so unnecessary. Our being in love doesn't displace or threaten any part of your past. That gift is yours forever. It's difficult to imagine Moira *not* wanting you to find new happiness and love in life."

"That's right," he says, pausing. "I'm sorry I've made it so hard for you. What I had with Moira was something of a subjective fantasy. As I've said, I never learned one thing about taking care of myself. She took complete care of me. And the boys. And she loved us all deeply. Others looked at what she was willing to tolerate and said she was a saint."

He has my full attention.

"All my life, I shut myself off from knowing the world—with a hubris and insensitivity to others. She was everything I needed. I never thought about the value of friendship. The importance of optimism and joy. Then, I was faced with overwhelming pain for the first time, and I had to endure. Alone. I was afraid death was going to eat me, I was so close to its edge."

"Thank goodness you didn't give in, Harrison."

"I know," he says, squeezing my hand. "I'm incredibly lucky. And I'm very happy to be with you. Losing Moira . . . and finding you—it's all forcing me to become a better person."

We rest in each other's arms in bed, embracing the joy and uneasiness, all at once. In Harrison. In me. Even, *and perhaps especially*, in love.

"I heard a beautiful quote yesterday," I tell him. "'Older now, you find holiness in anything that continues.'" [4]

Drawing my body into his, he holds tight. I squeeze back. He pulls away just far enough to look straight into my eyes. "I love *you, Lynne.*"

I smile and close them, safe in our embrace. He already knows what I am coming to understand.

"Everything takes time; give it time," he says. "Nothing of substance happens immediately."

Who perseveres, conquers.

As I drift off in his arms tonight, I picture our lantern: a hanging chrysalis, illuminated from within. Each morning, its armature of willow boughs and translucent skin of yellow-orange prayer flags catching the sun's early light and holding it. Its glowing shape dissolves to become a group of monks in saffron orange robes. They are sitting in a circle with their backs to me.

It has not yet revealed itself.

WOMEN WHO HUNT

F all, 2008. Harrison returns home excited to transform his own breeding program into a rare-breed/seed-saver initiative. With Geordie's help, he will become North America's only custodian of true Scottish doddies (cattle) in his own Montana glen. He arrives on the ranch just in time to work with Rick, giving calves their preweaning shots and banding (castrating) bulls to become steers.

Back in town, I hit the ground running to play catch-up at the museum. Everyone is working against the clock now for the bison exhibit. Our public opening date of December fifth is less than four months away. Long hours of work spill over into weekends. I miss seeing Harrison and helping out around the ranch. When cottonwoods turn orange, Willow and I miss our long treks through grasslands with bird dogs. Closer to home, I'm often too tired at the end of the day to visit Phyllis. I find myself missing her too.

One morning while Willow and I walk the river trail, dressed in orange to be safe, I decide that I'd like to know more about *women's* perspectives on hunting.

I read about early American women hunters late into the night. Waiting in grocery lines, I leaf through contemporary hunting magazines for stories about women in the field. In contrast to the pre-Scotland swirl of Harrison's introduction to guns and men's secret brotherhoods, I explore my own pathway. I seek wisdom from my own tribe.

For the relatively few white women of earlier generations who enjoyed hunting in North America, most found their way into it through men. In 1889, the photographer Evelyn Cameron, having first visited eastern Montana with her new husband for a holiday of hunting and camping, a trip she later recalled as her honeymoon, put it this way:

> For the woman with outdoor propensities and a taste for roughing it, there is no life more congenial than that of a saddle and rifle. Whether a wife shows any liking at all for life in the open, I consider a hunting expedition one of the most desirable ways for a couple to spend a holiday. It is wonderful what comradeship is developed between them. All sorts of cobwebs get blown away in the long days together on windswept prairies, or in the gulches and trails of the Badlands. [5]

It comes as no surprise that beyond the basic practicalities of remaining safe, finding partners to hunt with, as well as procuring appropriate clothing and gear, these women hunters have had to overcome social barriers. *A good woman shouldn't kill things.* This unspoken taboo and cultural upbringing are strong in me. But many pioneer women, including Phyllis's own Italian grandmother, took care of domestic animals and surely harvested their own chickens and geese for eating. Others were capable hunters of wild game. Grandmothers of contemporary Blackfoot women had an informed perspective, with deep knowledge and diverse skill sets that encompassed *everything* necessary to survive in nature. Women's stories are recorded far too seldom. I wonder again about the practical details of how an elder Native woman in the valley where Harrison lives might have managed, living all alone by the creek.

I call Phyllis about my hunting angst.

"Did you ever hunt when you were growing up on the ranch?"

"I never shot anything—couldn't. Daddy was a good hunter and took care of the family that way, but men are hunters and women are gathers and nurturers; that's the way it's always been. We know the pain of bearing life, and we want to take care of it. If you see something in pain, you try and help it, don't you?"

"Of course. Seems like I'm always trying to save something that might be in trouble."

"Sure you are. When we see young lives, like those calves you've been helping, we'd rather take care of them. But I'll eat wild birds or elk anytime a hunter feels like sharing." She laughs. "And I can always use new feathers for hats."

"But you fished a lot," I say, recalling her stories of fishing at Harrison's as a young girl when J. Y. lived there.

"Oh, we loved it growing up, fishing all the time. Sometimes I would feel guilty. But it's just the way things are. I'm sure testosterone and estrogen have something to do with it too. Hey!"—she exclaims over the phone—"I've been reading lately about microorganisms in our bodies. That's basically what we are, you know—it's what the world is: a bunch of bugs, all interconnected, living and dying all the time. Matter is neither created nor destroyed, right?" She laughs with delight. "I think we don't ever really die. Isn't it wonderful?"

At seventy-nine, surely grappling with her own mortality, Phyllis finds ways to see all things full of grace. Maybe what's still gnawing at me is just all those microorganisms, trying to inform me of something they know and I don't.

Before bed, I pull a book off the shelf on Native art of the Northwest Coast. I linger on images of Transformation Masks of the Kwakwaka'wakw, carved and painted wooden masks that kinetically demonstrate one spirit giving way to another. When worn and danced/performed during ceremony, masks-within-masks become animated ancestral spirits and supernatural beings. Animal forms change to human forms. Human forms change to animal forms. They are such brilliant reminders of the potent connections between natural and supernatural worlds, between the visible and the invisible. [6] Returning to my collection of essays on women hunters, I read until I stop cold.

> The tangle of fear over real and imagined predators is accumulated over a lifetime and is a complicated unsnarling. . . . Hunting, in part, can be like stalking fear itself. [7]

I reread this quote several times, before closing the book.

My father feared repeated beatings as a child from his alcoholic father. My courageous mother has felt insecure and fearful most of her life.

Feeling safe was never part of my DNA.

Yet I feel safe with Harrison. I want to keep learning about his wild animal nature. Stalking elk or hunting birds together, I discover more about my *own* animal-self. I catch glimpses of what is visible and invisible in me. No matter what happens, I'm beyond grateful for this rare freedom to finally reconnect—to explore my *own* relationships, *without fear*—with the rest of nature.

THE POTENCY OF PLACE

T he last exhibit labels left to write will describe traditional hunting practices. Personal experiences on these Native lands now lend new perspective to this work. My feet have followed the paths of wild animals. I've hidden in brush, close enough to know the sound of a thirsty bull elk slurping water, cow elk mewing to calves. My heart has felt the raw energy of that moment when an arrow pierces the heart of something wild. Today at the museum, my body recalls the feeling of calm anticipation, sitting quietly with the man I love in the woods where he lives. But traditional communal bison hunts, intended to feed the masses, were something entirely different.

In preparation, Indigenous peoples of the Northern Plains—Niitsitapi (Blackfoot), A'aninin (Atsina), Apsáalooke (Crow), Tsitsistas (Cheyenne), Nehiyawak (Plains Cree), and others—engaged in elaborate ceremonies. Prayers and songs were intended to "call" the bison, to cloud the animals' minds so they were not aware of the traps set for them, and to ensure a successful hunt. Dancing was a part of traditional hunting rituals. Dancers assumed qualities of the bison. Poring through early anthropological journals at work, the thought of what Harrison's hunting dance might look like amuses me.

From the Navajo to the Sioux nations, and for Indigenous peoples around the world, oral traditions of storytelling served as blessing rites, as potent creeds for relating in an appropriate manner with any animal being hunted. [8] There was intimate knowledge of plants. Plants fed the animal. The hunted animal would surrender its life so others could live. (According to Native American friends, Harrison, and several women hunter/writers I've read, sometimes this seems to be what happens.) The remains of the animal's body, all bodies, then return to earth's soil, helping new plant life to emerge. Everything is related, woven into a brilliant endless process of transformation.

I have continued to gather quotes for the walls of our bison exhibition. Today I find two new references that point directly to the sacred exchange of hunting. I anticipate sharing them with Harrison at dinner tonight. The first is from a 1922 interview with a Crow medicine man:

> Once people could not find any game. Big-Ox bade them get a buffalo skull and put its nose toward the camp. In the night they began to sing. In the morning they saw six head of buffalo and killed them. The following morning they again found several head. When they had had enough, Big-Ox bade them turn the skull around, then they did not see any more buffalo. [9]

The second reference describes an anonymous Innu woman almost two hundred years earlier, circa 1750, on the other side of our northern continent in Labrador, who fashioned a beautifully tailored hunting coat made of caribou hide. She painted her coat with bands of intricate pink patterns so the wild caribou would gift itself to the hunter who so honored the animal.

When I arrive at the restaurant, Harrison is already at a table.

"Sorry I'm late. I've been updating my hunting section."

He smiles lovingly while I speak. I tell him about the woman who created a beautiful jacket 250 years ago to honor caribou.

His response: "The way you and I travel animal trails together is what excites me most, tunneling into a place where the mystery of things is felt. The potency of place." Taking a sip of water, he continues. "Almost every time I'm out hunting, amazing things happen, mysterious experiences that seem to come out of nowhere. *How could this have happened?* I wonder. I can give you an example."

"Yes, please."

"Up early one morning, walking in the dark with my bow and arrow, I was obsessed with the idea of a lion near me. Climbing up Saddle Butte, I could see the backs of elk moving in the first light. I was still feeling the sense of danger at my back. I was relieved to arrive at my pine tree, to climb up through thick branches, and finally to be sitting in my tree stand above the ground."

I have heard this story before. And like so many of his hunting stories, I am fascinated to hear it again.

"Not two minutes passed before I heard the sound of an animal approaching. It didn't have the cadence of a deer. I just knew it was a lion. It came up directly underneath me in the darkness. I was twelve feet above it. I felt comforted by the thick branches between me and him."

Harrison continued.

"A short time passed, pregnant, until the first slivers of daylight started to illuminate the branches and enter the place. I looked down and saw the lion walking away, its great long tail behind him."

"Thrilling and strange all at once," I say,

"Experiences like that don't feel normal. There's something more to them."

Our expressions say how much we've missed each other. Whatever this is between us feels thrilling and strange. Definitely out of the ordinary. I throw a quick glance at the menu to break the spell.

"It's frustrating not getting to the ranch these days. I'm too busy! How are Tula and Oscar? How's Dollar?"

"Tula looks for you every time I walk in the door, seems disappointed when it's only me. They're all fine. I'm afraid they're handling your absence much better than I am."

He lifts his eyebrows and fakes a pout. I picture him sitting in front of the television each night with cashews, a bag of chips, and bourbon for dinner.

"But this exhibition *should* be your focus," he says. "You're about to give birth. How long has it been—three years in gestation? And you love what you do. How fortunate you are!"

"No complaints. It's incredibly exciting. I just miss our slower pace. Spinning around indoors all day makes it a lot harder to feel the nuance of things. I miss watching a doe run across the hill with her friends at first light, shaking her body because the air feels good." I pause. "Hopefully, I can steal away next weekend. Are you working on a painting?"

"I can't decide what to paint. Hunting is the only thing holding my interest at the moment. I'm just out there. Waiting for elk. Waiting for you." He winks. "I bet you've got a million interesting details and decisions to keep you busy right now. I'm happy for you. You're good at what you do."

"Indigenous hunters *absolutely* lived in all the nuances—the *spirit* of wild bison, of wild caribou. Their bond was unbelievably deep. Elk come and go from your valley. Nomadic Native hunters were following bison throughout the entire year. They were never far from one another. They lived as close relatives."

After lunch we step outside to go our respective ways. I gather my hair and long skirt, holding both in whipping winds for a goodbye kiss. This is the same gray skirt I wore the day I first met Harrison by the side of the road. Was that really four years ago?

CHINOOKS

Howling gales carry the strong odor of smoke on a harrowing Friday night drive with Harrison. A fire, where?

"You've got a great nose. You're probably smelling the one they've been working on putting out in Carter, one hour away. These winds aren't helping. I had to jump in the truck yesterday and drive full speed across the lower hay field just to catch my hat. It ran like a rabbit."

One hour closer to the ranch, we're relieved to hear the Carter fire is 90 percent contained. But strong winds continue.

It's dark by the time we pull up to the house. Headlights illuminate Oscar and Tula peering out through glass doors of the mudroom. As I open the heavy truck door, a gust of wind rips it from my hands with such force that it bends one of the metal hinges.

Montanans will tell you, "Wind was born here." My first experiences of Chinook winds in Montana were up north on the reservation years ago. In Glacier Park, an empty train was literally blown off its tracks. Back then, I found such demonstrations instructive, something to take seriously when hiking along steep trails on mountain passes with huge scary drop-offs. When I first moved to live here, I noticed people complain a lot about the wind. The ferocity of these Chinook winds, which arrive each year like clockwork following the autumnal equinox, is grating.

"I hope that door can be fixed," I say, taking off boots inside.

"I've probably had that happen on every vehicle here. Chinooks are good for this place—they're what warm things up and keep us from being buried for months in snow. But they're unsettling. Being cooped up alone with these winds can feel oppressive." He smiles. "I'm glad you're here."

All through dinner, seventy-mile-per-hour winds howl and push against the house. They blow at home in Great Falls, but not like here. I walk upstairs after dinner to Harrison's library while he paints. A Chinook is a *katabatic* or *descending* wind, one that travels downhill. When conditions are right, as air moves up the western slopes of the Rockies, moisture in that air is lifted and condenses. Condensation releases heat into the atmosphere. Warmer, drier gusty air masses race down the eastern slopes that lead to places like this valley. As compared to other parts of the state that are cold snow holes all winter, the force and warmth of Chinook winds makes this part of Montana a relative banana belt.

Similar winds, I learn, blow all around the world. The same phenomena in Switzerland are called Schneefresser, meaning "the snow eater." In the Andes of South America, the name of foehn winds describes their superhero-like power: Zonda. Wherever they blow, there are tales of extraordinary happenings. Sudden temperature changes caused by the arrival of these violent warm winds have been known to crack windows and split wood.

I head downstairs and find Harrison in the kitchen. "Did you know that the town of Loma once recorded a hundred-and-three-degree change in temperature, from minus fifty-four to plus forty-nine within twenty-four hours? That's not far from here!"

"Yeah, they hold some kind of record for extreme shifts. It was minus twelve degrees here two days ago, before these winds arrived. Now it's thirty-three," he says, searching cabinets for something to eat.

Water boils for tea. Windows rattle and shudder. The phone rings. A truck driver heading this way across North Dakota to pick up a load of Harrison's cattle calls to say his empty rig has been blown over. While Harrison talks, I stroll toward the bedroom, listening to high-pitched shrieking and wailing sounds as air pushes into the deepest seams of the house. I pass the west-facing open courtyard, which is taking all the force like a catcher's mitt.

On nights like this, Harrison and I sometimes imagine we are on a ship at sea. The roof clatters like sails. Will we be smashed against rocks, pulverized by what sound like crashing tidal waves? No. We are snug and safe. We are together.

When daylight arrives the following morning, nothing has changed. I watch from living room windows as top layers of snow are scoured and ripped from surrounding hillsides. Multiple ground blizzards and rising cyclones of swirling snow emerge one after the next, animating the hills and mountains of this valley like a symphony, grand and turbulent.

Later in the day, I sit cross-legged in bed with eyes closed for a challenging attempt at meditation. Harrison's bedroom, with its three walls of glass, projects westward toward the Highwood Mountains, straight into predominant winds.

At times, my mind's ear hears rolling thunder. At other times, it imagines one hundred huge sheets being snapped and shaken out to dry. They pound and beat, smash and rip. Eventually, I discern distinct layers of sounds—the distant humming roar of mighty wind channels as they pour down the mountains past the Red Nose cabin, across the valley, long before reaching us. It's like listening to distant locomotives rolling through a tunnel.

The mares are standing steady and still on the other side of the creek when I open my eyes. The Red Nose cabin is their partial windbreak. But they are *in* this windstorm: viscerally experiencing what I am only hearing and seeing. Gray Halcyon flashes bright among her darker sisters. The group is quiet. Nothing in their behavior indicates they are disturbed.

When high winds at last stop the next day, the stillness is shocking. Venturing out, I notice the habit of my upper body leaning forward, always marching onward. The mares feel fresh. They take off in a canter across the top of a hill above the cabin. Deer come out to graze. In the heifer pasture, restless young Angus are playing. I slow my pace, lean back, and inhale the sublime pleasure of strolling easily with dogs in calm quiet mountain air.

EMERGENCY ROOM

F inal preparations for the bison exhibit are well underway. The lower floor of the museum is like a busy hive of worker bees. Each day's soundtrack is the buzzing of saws and hammering of nails. Open storage drawers made of wood and large glass display cases are being built and filled. The various components of my full-scale diorama have all been delivered and are now being assembled in the largest gallery: the mannequin of a young Native hunter; the life-size sculpted horse; the native grasses, dried and preserved; the bison bull, posed by the taxidermist to look as if he is running at full speed across the prairie.

A local electronics shop is due to put the finishing touches on a Sensurround room designed to allow visitors to feel the power of thousands of running bison in their bodies. They'll find themselves surrounded by filmed images of a stampeding herd, while the floor beneath their feet rumbles and shakes and speakers project the sounds of grunting and roaring while bison hooves pound the earth.

On a cold October night at my Birdhouse, I start to feel a stomachache. Pain intensifies. It escalates, more and more quickly, until I am doubled over on the floor and can hardly breathe. I counsel myself: I've endured excruciating abdominal pain before. How often did I grit my teeth and bear it during those two years of bleeding back in Atlanta?

But this is *worse*.

I crawl to the phone while gripping my torso to call 911.

Between gasps, I describe what is happening. "What . . . do you suggest I do . . .?" I'm desperate.

"Get yourself to a hospital. We can send an ambulance."

"No. Thanks," I say, doubled over, barely able to get words out. It's nearly midnight. I know I can't wait for help.

I grasp at keys and grab a winter coat, though I'm sweating. Turning the doorknob, I lean for support. The hospital is a straight shot. Only thirteen city blocks away. Somehow, I make it to the car and pile my torqued body into the driver's seat. It's a struggle to jam the key in and start the engine.

I set off with a grimace, knees pursed as close to my stomach as possible, upper body draped over the steering wheel like a corpse. One block to the next, I keep accelerating. Must get there before I pass out. I run a red light, swing into the hospital lot, and park like a drunk driver. Hunched over with pain, I make it to the main entrance in the dark.

The fricking doors are locked! I nearly collapse in the cold. The only option is to drag myself around the side of the building to the emergency entrance. I'm almost crawling by the time automatic doors ease open. I enter the waiting room weeping out loud, in mind-numbing pain. Doubled over the front desk, I beg for help. I can hardly speak.

I am ushered in immediately. But no one will give me anything for the pain. A doctor tells me they must take X-rays first to determine the cause. While I lie there alone, in agony on a cot with white sheets, I try to remember how I dealt with the mental torment of strong winds. My body drops into its own version of Lamaze breathing. These labored rhythms are the same I remember Kelly using during labor. By the time I'm brought back from being held up by two people for X-rays, I am out of my mind with pain. Finally, the doctor returns.

"These images show all the characteristics of a colon twisting itself into knots. Something called volvulus is causing your discomfort. That's when a loop of intestine twists around itself. And the lack of blood supply to tissues in those twists can very quickly cause necrosis, which means we need to operate immediately."

Another surgery?!

Post-traumatic shock slams through me like a violent blast. In a single moment, all that I thought I had left behind is upon me again.

"But . . . I want someone who lives far away to be here *with* me," I plead through tears.

"How long will it take him to get here?"

"One and a half hours." I weep, still trying to breathe through the pain.

"That's too long. I'm sorry. We have to operate now. What's the number?"

The doctor stands next to my bed with a phone and dials the number. He hands the phone to me when it begins to ring.

But no answer comes. Only a pre-recorded message.

"Harrison, I'm at the hospital in Great Falls. I'm about . . . to go into emergency surgery. They say I can't wait until you get here." I whisper into the phone, "*I love you*, Harrison."

The surgeon preps on the other side of the room. I imagine myself an inconvenience.

"I'm sorry," I say. "You were probably having a nice evening at home . . . with your family until I showed up."

The surgeon turns and walks rapidly across the room, places his hands on the blanket over my feet. He looks straight into my eyes.

"Listen to me. Do not apologize. There is nothing for you to apologize for. You need help from a doctor. That's why I'm here. Now let me go get the anesthesiologist, so we can help you with your pain and get going."

Five hours later, lying in the recovery room, I begin to regain consciousness. When I open my eyes, Harrison is beside me, holding my hand in his.

IV.

EARTH

(2009)

DIFFICULT NEWS

Winter, 2009. Harrison insisted I come here to the ranch with Willow for my six weeks of recovery. I feel shell-shocked. He shows up for me as he did for Dollar, with unconditional love and no expectations. He brings me hot tea and toast, props up my pillows, keeps me company, feeds our finches, and cares for Willow as I would myself. When I am able, I gladly return to feeding Willow and all our gray-crowned rosy-finches each morning. He encourages me to spend time outside with the horses, knowing they, too, will help me heal.

By mid-November, I feel strong enough to return to work. I reenter an environment full of stress just four weeks before the exhibition's December opening. Part of me would rather have remained with Harrison and the horses, feeding birds back at the ranch. But after three years in the making, everything has come together, thanks to many talented people and a true collective effort. We share the credit for this grand collaboration.

Here I am, standing at the podium to welcome everyone at the official opening, as our beautiful new gallery spaces fill to capacity with hundreds of visitors. I wish Harrison was here tonight to see all this. But Rick is off the ranch, so Harrison is home tending to animals. He made me promise: "If you have the energy, call when you get home, no matter how late."

My heart leaps when I see the first children opening "discovery drawers," finding replica rawhide rattles they can pick up and shake, beaded moccasins they can touch and try on. Crowds stop to examine objects made from almost every single part of a bison. Painted bison robes, bone tools, hide war shields, bison fur-lined winter moccasins. Beautiful cups, spoons, and ladles fashioned from bison horns. A full-sized bison-hide tepee with strips of bison meat drying outside its entryway (inspired by Phyllis's fake laundry hanging out to dry at Lonetree) over an imaginary fire that uses bison dung as fuel. Visitors learn that glue was made from bison hooves, powder from bison bones, soap from bison tallow. An adjacent area describes traditional Indigenous Northern Plains hunting practices and the central role bison played in the spiritual life of many Native Americans.

> The Buffalo was part of us, his flesh and blood being ab-sorbed by us until it became our own flesh and blood. Our clothing, our tipis, everything we needed for life came from the buffalo's body. It was hard to say where the animals ended and the human began."
>
> —John (Fire) Lame Deer, Oglala [10]

I watch with anticipation as visitors enter, one by one, into our sensory chamber where they *hear* and *see* and *feel* the power of a bison herd, stampeding and grunting in filmed footage that plays all around them, with speakers booming, the floor shaking beneath them.

Now bison have come alive! These visitors' hearts are open and full of wonder. I see awe in their eyes. *They, too, now care* about bison before entering what comes next. Stepping into the second gallery, everyone stops cold in their tracks. Their gasps are audible. A floor-to-ceiling, black-and-white 1870 photo presents a towering twenty-foot-high pile of bison skulls. Two white men in the image, one standing on top of the pile, demonstrate its immensity. Actual bison skulls placed at the foot of this pile bring the shock of the photo mural to life. A caption overhead asks: *Once there were tens of millions of bison, then almost none. What happened?*

The intensity of this all-out slaughter is complex. Visitors learn in this gallery about the multiple factors of a perfect storm that centered on white racism and expansionism.

"Kill the buffalo and you kill the Indians."

—General Philip H. Sheridan, 1866

"The civilization of the Indian is impossible while the buffalo remains upon the plains."

—Columbus Delano, US Secretary of the Interior, 1873

By 1884, some fifty million wild bison had been reduced to a few hundred captives. They were hunted almost to extinction in a matter of decades.

"Nothing happened after that. We just lived. There were no more war parties, no capturing of horses from the Piegans and Sioux, no buffalo to hunt. There is nothing more to tell."

—Crow Warrior Two Leggings, 1919

The exhibition's spacious third and final gallery honors the persistence of bison as an American icon. It also celebrates the enduring relationship between bison and Native peoples. Sensitized visitors are drawn to its centerpiece: our full-scale diorama of the brave young Native hunter galloping on horseback, bow drawn, in pursuit of the magnificent bison bull.

Six-foot-high glass cases surrounding this centerpiece display gorgeous hand-beaded and elk-tooth dresses, long-flowing feathered headdresses, horse masks and embellished horse tack, war shirts embroidered with porcupine quillwork. Brilliant works by contemporary Native American artists tell their own stories. In looped video interviews, members of contemporary Indigenous Nations talk about their growing tribal bison herds and how reservations are seeing diabetes disappear when bison meat is reintroduced as a diet mainstay.

Teachers at the opening make a point to say how thrilled they will be to bus children here from the reservation. Three Native women artists express their joy and gratitude at finally having this access to study the works of their ancestors. Back at the ranch the following day, Harrison presents me with a work of art by our friend Kevin Pourier, a contemporary artist who is Oglala Lakota. A crescent-shaped bison horn is covered with small figures of many individual bison, all carved in relief and moving together as a herd across its polished surface. It has been blessed and filled with sage by the artist.

January snowflakes are falling outside the third-floor window nearest my bed five weeks later when I open my eyes. It's morning—a morning that unfortunately I seem to be reliving, again and again. I trace the IV tubes and color-coded wires connecting my body to machines. I watch green numbers change on my heart monitor, take slow deep breaths to practice lowering my beat. When I think about seeing Harrison tomorrow, the beat jumps.

In a recent post-op exam, imaging showed cystic ovaries. No sign of cancer, thank goodness. But I have opted to have them removed. I kept them only to postpone menopause after the partial hysterectomy seven years ago. This time around, it's no big deal. Harrison brought me to the hospital, sat in the waiting room, and was beside my bed in recovery when I awoke. Today, he is back at the ranch working with Rick to prepare for calving. Phyllis called yesterday to check on me. Our laughter hurt my incisions. It will be good to see the horses soon. Especially Halcyon, Harrison's gray mare.

Halcyon's drama and arresting beauty re-excited my awareness of her when I was convalescing at the ranch this past fall, like the thrill of seeing a first lightning bug on a pitch-dark night. When I was strong enough to travel in the truck last year, Harrison took me to visit the mares. Halcyon's flashiness stunned me. The elegance of her outbursts tickled my heart. She was a vision at a time when I felt empty.

I have no choice but to rest today. It's exactly what I need. When I get back to the museum, I'll begin the process of wrapping things up, preparing to start all over, once again, somewhere else. *Are all these health troubles the result of holding myself (and others) to such impossibly high standards over the past forty years?* I'm weary just thinking about it.

Snowflakes are still falling outside the window. Reaching for a glass of water, I drop back in time to consider my father's last experiences. Was it snowing that day too? He suffered a heart attack, at just forty-seven years old, while jogging on that cold November day. Parts of the story remain a mystery. Who found him lying there, motionless on cold ground near his church? Did he die quickly? How long was he there all alone? He was one year younger than I am now. Some part of me always imagined I would die at the same age.

I roll back the bed sheet and lift my hospital gown to examine new scars. My belly looks like a war zone. My finger traces the longest incision, where a kind male surgeon sliced me wide open three months ago. And the one beneath it, where years earlier in Atlanta, a good woman surgeon returned twice, trying to save my uterus, before years of bleeding finally ended. Multiple places where layers of flesh have been stitched back together, where parts of what was inside me have been cut out, where holes in my heart and my gut have never fully healed.

Like a huge bend in the body of a river, the sudden loss of my father caused everything after it to flow differently.

I soldiered on, as *we all do.*

That was twenty-seven years ago.

Back on the ranch now, I'm lying next to Harrison. He wants to examine my belly. He is particularly fascinated by the five-inch incision from October that runs vertically from my belly button down, where it meets the horizontal scar below.

"Here, if you're really gentle," I say, "you can rub on vitamin E. It's supposed to help reduce scarring."

"Oh, boy!" He sits up with excitement.

Willow lies next to the bed beside me. Her wagging tail taps the carpet.

Harrison pours the sticky liquid and, using two fingers, moves slowly. He comments on the larger scar as he works. "This one is really good-looking."

"It's horrible. I hate it."

"No, not at all," he says. "Look again." He traces its outer edges all the way down to the oldest scar. "The way these two meet, it looks like you've got a beautiful anchor drawn on your belly. Scarification is much cooler than any tattoo."

I get up in the night for pain medication but can't fall back asleep.

In the morning, Harrison asks, "Why didn't you sleep?"

"Fear," I answer.

"I didn't sleep either."

"Why not?"

"Misery." He laughs. "What are you afraid of? Keep resting. You'll heal. You're good at this. Get back to taking short walks. Andre and T and the mares will be happy to see you again."

Willow's tail beats again against the carpet.

"Maybe it's a very old fear of loss," I say with a sigh. I tell him my spotty memories of dad's death, the crazy guilt and shame I've carried my whole life.

"And ever since Scotland, I've noticed fear popping up about losing you," I continue, trying to stay strong. I haven't yet told him that I'll soon be leaving Great Falls.

"Come here," Harrison says. He kisses my cheek and curls up next to me. "The minute you care about anything or anybody, it involves pain," he says. "That elusive feeling of closeness is what everyone is looking for. And so many people never find it. When it's real, it always hurts."

We lie together for a long while without talking. I think of my father; Harrison's loss of his wife, his best friend, and his father eight years ago; the mare, Brise; Max's cow elk; the bull elk Harrison harvested last November; the bison.

I turn to look deep into blue-gray eyes. "I'm so glad last fall was not my time to leave this world."

"Me too," he whispers, holding me.

RUB MY BELLY

I n subsequent days, I find solace watching our flock of gray-crowned winter finches as they lift with great energy and gather in murmuration. We share *zugenruhe,* the experience of migratory restlessness. Soon they'll be leaving to fly north to Alaska and the Aleutian Islands. As the whirling energy in my own life lifts, I wonder, *Where will I fly?* I anticipate the toll that a next move and new job—wherever I end up— may exact. I haven't told either Phyllis or Harrison yet. But I always hear Phyllis's voice in my ears: *Life is for the living!* If these resilient finches find the strength to survive our Chinook winds and frigid Montana winters, then so can I. They travel in large flocks. They've got each other.

And I've got Willow.

Back home at my Birdhouse, I call Phyllis.

"How wonderful that Harrison has helped you through all this, Lynne."

"He stepped up to do the right thing," I say. "His aunt Rebecca would be proud of him. He still drives me crazy sometimes. But he's a man of integrity."

"I knew a handsome man like Harrison in Hawaii once, when I was working as a nurse. A senator came into the hospital and fell head over heels in love with me. Six months later when I told him I was moving, he arranged for a whole entourage to meet me at the airport right there on the tarmac. I had leis up to my eyebrows!"

We both laugh. Willow is asking to go out. "I need some inspiration, Phyllis," I say, opening my back door. "What are you painting these days?"

"I decided the Square Butte 'Country Club' bar near our ranch needs a makeover," she reports with pride. "I'm painting on fabric to make new window treatments and tablecloths. I'm doing portraits of all the regulars at the bar there too. Won't that be fun?"

I examine the uninspired dusty old plastic blinds on my kitchen window. I pull the cord to lift them, to watch Willow, to let in more light.

"I decided to start with a portrait of Bill Beckett. He's a relative of mine. He said he didn't want me to paint him because I'd make him look like an ass. I've got him standing here on my easel right now in his jeans and cowboy hat, next to his horse, with his back end facing me. Do you think he'll appreciate my little joke?" She laughs. "Hey! Did I tell you my sisters are here? We all went over to the 'Country Club' last night for dinner."

"What fun."

"We walked in the club with our hats and jewelry, and all the regulars at the bar—including Bill Beckett—turned around to give us the hard look. 'What are you staring at?' I asked. 'Half of you are my relatives!'"

She laughs, then asks, "Why don't you and Harrison come visit us this weekend?"

Phyllis greets us from the porch, stepping down the stairs with a big wave.

"Welcome, welcome! How about some limoncello?" she says.

Entering the Meriwether, we inhale the aroma of a garlicky Italian pasta sauce her sister Connie is stirring on the stove and fresh bread that her sister Mitzi has just taken out of the oven. Pavarotti's voice swells, an exquisite note suspended in midair.

After a grand meal, seated next to Phyllis, I take her hand in mine to admire a silver ring with many little bezels of turquoise.

"See this," she says, pointing to one. "I just lost another little piece of turquoise the other day. Yesterday at the studio, I mixed up the right color and painted a new one, and it's good as new. I bet you didn't even notice! Speaking of painting, one of my signs up the canyon needs a touch-up. Why don't you come and help me dress it up a little with fresh color?"

Harrison, Connie, and Mitzi linger with libations while Phyllis and I sneak away to grab some paint and brushes. We take our time, heading up into the deep canyon, past the old stage stop house where she and her sisters grew up, until we stop in front of my favorite sign. I trace the painted words with my finger. THIS LAND IS DEEP WITHIN ME. I CAN FEEL IT IN MY BONES. IT IS MY ROOTS AND MY SOUL.

"It's beautiful up here, isn't it?" she says, handing me a paintbrush before loading hers with bright blue enamel paint. "What are you working on at the museum, Lynne, now that your big exhibition is such a success?"

I tell her my news.

"I have no idea where I'm headed next," I confess, tearing up. Holding a paintbrush in one hand, I give her a fierce hug. "I'll miss you *so* much, Phyllis. I love you."

"I love you too, Lynne. Have you told Harrison? What does he have to say about all this?"

I shake my head, wiping a tear.

"Well, *why not*?!" Hands on hips and head cocked, two pheasant feathers wiggle on her hat. "He *might, at least*, like a chance to surprise you at the airport, don't you think?"

Phyllis always encourages laughter. Harrison's love has an equal but different effect. Back home in my Birdhouse, I stroke Willow. It's hard to believe she's already six years old. In the time since I got her, the love Harrison and I share for this world's beauty has woven us together. Our root systems have become entwined—so much so that it feels inconceivable we might ever part. I've grown so, so tired of living alone.

At the ranch next Saturday, I finally find the courage.

"My darling, I've got to look for a new job. I can't wait any longer. I don't want to leave you. I don't want to leave any of this. I love you! But Great Falls isn't the place where I want to grow old."

His only response is a long stare and a hug. "I love you too. And I don't want you to go."

I wait for more, but he goes strangely silent.

On the drive back to town with Willow, I gird my loins. It's migration time. At home in bed, I encourage my armored body to remember how good it feels to lie next to Harrison, to share a meal with him, to laugh with Phyllis until we weep with pleasure, to sit quietly in the woods with Harrison until we become invisible and feel a part of everything, to gaze out his bedroom window and count the mares grazing on the hillside, until we are sure everyone is together.

To *belong*.

Willow jumps down in the dark, stretches her legs, and walks over to the water bowl. I listen to the familiar sound of her three-count drinking: *lap lap lap, lap lap lap, lap lap lap.*

Be grateful for small intimacies, a voice whispers. *Loosen your hold on the world. Listen to your heart.*

I recognize the voice as my own. It trickles up through me like clear spring water.

You are almost fifty years old. What haven't you tried yet? Keep exploring that uncharted territory of the heart.

Three weeks later, on Easter Sunday morning, I sit down next to Harrison on a park bench along the banks of the Missouri River. We've spent a romantic night at the Grand Union Hotel here in Fort Benton. I look down and notice two of his lower shirt buttons are undone. Were they that way before? He's acting nervous. He refuses to button them.

"Put your hand in there," he implores.

"What?" People are walking by us along the river trail. "Why would I want to rub your belly *here, now*? You *never* want me to touch your stomach."

"*Please.*"

Covertly I insert my hand into his unbuttoned shirt.

"*Deeper,*" he insists.

Feeling inside, running my hand all around his soft belly, a hidden ring box falls into my fingers.

Slowly, I open it and find a ring of two stones intertwined: a white diamond and a blue Montana yogo sapphire. I'm stunned.

Harrison begins to confess how hard it still is to stop feeling as if he's cheating. How this ring has been burning a hole through his pocket for weeks now. How he told his boys first.

"I don't want to live my life without you, Lynne. Will you do me the great honor of having me as your husband?"

I look at him with tears in my eyes. We hug without saying a word.

He places the ring on my finger. I'm silent for what feels like a very long time.

Nothing has ever felt like this.

Yes.

A HUSBAND

Spring, 2009. He agrees to wait a week before we share our news with anyone else. I am cautiously overjoyed. But the reality is a lot to digest. This moment is worth savoring—with Harrison, and on my own. We are both old enough to understand the imperative: make the most of every single day we have left together. At the ranch, I take special care feeding our gray-crowned rosies in their final days with us before they migrate north. Like every animal here, they, too, now will become family.

It's hard to be objective about such a consequential decision. I have agreed to marry an older man whose favorite childhood book was *Tarzan*. (Mine was *Where the Wild Things Are*.) Harrison O'Connor has lived most of his life in nature. At sixty-one, he still feels embarrassed to say his own first name out loud. Yet he is deeply attuned to beauty and to the tenderness of life.

My husband-to-be has a Roman nose and crisp lips, with brilliant blue eyes. His forehead drops off precipitously into a deep ridge at his eyebrows, like the sudden grooves and coulees hidden in the landscape of these sprawling grasslands. I tease him, "Your features are the perfect mix of a great elite and a cave man." He looks pleased.

At his core, he is generous, forgiving, kind. He knows how to stay calm and patient in any storm. His steadiness is good medicine for me. And he is more fully the animal than anyone I have ever known.

He jokes to imagine his own gravestone with a quote from Dracula:

THERE IS MUCH TO BE LEARNED FROM [THE] BEASTS.

I recall the words of Chief Seattle:

"What is man without the beasts? For if all the beasts were gone, man would die of a great loneliness of the spirit."

This man I will marry climbs trees half-crazed and walks home in the pitch-black of night when lions and coyotes and bears are active. Autumn is the season when Harrison most embodies his animal-self. Like his bird dogs set loose, he cannot but follow scent. Like the bucks and bull elk he seeks, he is highly evasive and prefers to remain hidden.

But Harrison's hungry heart has finally forced him out into the light of day.

And mine has told me this is where I belong.

We decide to get married in late September, hunting season.

The season of mating.

My tenure at the museum will officially end in early June. In just a few months, I will spend all my time on the ranch. We enjoy our fifth summer of floating and camping together along the river. We plan for the fall wedding in our favorite town, where he proposed. Established in 1846, Fort Benton is one of the oldest settlements in the American West. It was the farthest point upriver along the Missouri where steamboats could navigate to transport many tons of bison hides downriver to St. Louis and beyond. We'll celebrate at its grand old hotel. In front of the hotel, in the center of town, is a large bronze memorial to a dog named Shep. Whenever we bring along Willow, Tula, and Oscar, they respond to the giant statue as if it were real.

As the legend goes, the herding dog Shep appeared at the Great Northern Railway station one day in 1936 when a casket was being loaded onto a train in Fort Benton heading east. When the train left, Shep kept coming back to the station for the arrival of every incoming train. Station employees eventually realized that the body in the casket was probably Shep's owner, and that the dog was showing up for each train hoping to reunite. Shep continued his daily vigil for almost six years until he slipped and was run over by a train. A few days later, the dog's funeral was attended by nearly everyone in Fort Benton. The granite base for Shep's statue by the Missouri River came from the granite quarry once owned by Phyllis's parents near Lonetree. The large heroic bronze figure of Shep is titled *Forever Faithful*.

THE GOLDFINCH

One spring weekend, while making wedding plans at the ranch, I hear a small thud. I rise to look out the windows. Something bright yellow lies still in white snow in the courtyard. I throw on a coat and gently scoop up a small goldfinch. I cradle him in my hand. His beak mechanically opens and closes with shock. His eyes remain closed. He is rattled and helpless, but he is alive. Moments later, his eyes open briefly. His beak becomes quiet. I touch soft yellow feathers on the back of his neck.

"It's okay," I whisper, sitting down on a bench with him. "I'll take care of you." His eyes close again.

It takes twenty minutes for his eyes to stay open and become alert. Fluttering a bit, he rises just enough to perch on my pointer finger, where he remains for another twenty minutes.

This tender black and yellow bird stays with me long enough that my awareness moves beyond the visual wonder of its presence. I close my eyes while he perches on my finger, noticing if I can still perceive something so delicate, so light. The only way I know my friend is still with me is when a slight breeze rustles and his tiny body adjusts itself ever so slightly to keep balance. Finally, he flutters again and lifts from my finger, only far enough to perch on a finger-limb of this courtyard's single aspen tree next to the bench. We remain together like this for a short time more, before the goldfinch takes leave.

Not able to sleep one starry summer night, I lie in bed listening to the charming song of a bird outside our bedroom window. Who sings so beautifully in the dark of night? While Harrison sleeps, I record the

song so I can send it to my birder friend Kelly. She writes me the following afternoon: "That's a catbird!" I was only familiar with the call
for which they're named—sounding just like a cat. I am thrilled, now,
to know this nighttime serenade.

Two weeks later, a catbird bangs into a glass door at the end of the
hallway. I hold it in my hands for thirty minutes, as I did for the
goldfinch, encouraging it to live, as we do with sick calves. I care for
this dark gray bird with its black cap and long black tail all the more,
realizing this might be the very one who brought me such joy with its
night song. When it recovers and flies away, I am grateful to have held
something wild for a time. I am happier still when, three nights later, I
hear the catbird's enchanting song again outside our window, this time
under a brilliant full moon.

HALCYON

HALCYON:

1) denoting a period of time in the past that was idyllically happy and peaceful.

2) a mythical bird said by ancient writers to breed in a nest floating at sea at the winter solstice, charming the wind and waves into calm.

The dogs and I strike out one warm morning in mid-July for a walk over to the Red Nose Pasture to visit the mares. I find Halcyon rolling on the ground. Her white hair is covered with dirt and grass. I walk closer and try to get her up, but she continues to roll. The muscles of her body look shiny. Tight. I cannot catch her gaze. I move as fast as I can to get help.

"Harrison! Something's wrong with Halcyon," I shout, hustling, out of breath, toward his desk.

His blue eyes squint and glare, drilling right through me. "If she's rolling, that means colic," he says, pushing his cattle book aside. His tone is severe.

"What's colic? What can we do for her?"

"There's a halter in the back of the truck," he says. "Let's go. Colic is what happened to you."

Oh, God.

"It's not that uncommon for horses," Harrison says, zooming up the valley. "When they have pain in their stomach, they paw, sweat, kick at their sides, and roll. Rolling is dangerous because their intestines might twist."

My skin prickles.

"She might be impacted. We need to get her up and moving. See if that helps."

When we arrive, she's still on the ground. "Not good," Harrison says, jumping out. The other mares are grazing nearby. Harrison grabs a halter. He flares his arms walking toward her, barks at Halcyon to get up. I speak to her with quiet urgency. I recognize the look of her glazed eyes, the belly taut as a drum. She's not registering. She's in the fight.

When finally she stands, her eyes remain anxious. We move closer, speak gently. She allows Harrison to put the halter on. I place one hand on her chest, wipe grass from her sweating neck and back. She lifts a hind leg to kick at her gut. Everything in me feels empathy. She knows she needs help. Just as I did.

Immediately he leads her to walk out slowly, around and around, while the others continue to graze. Halcyon pulls to stop and begins folding her front legs as if she's about to go down. Harrison tugs on the halter, and I get behind to urge her on.

"See how she's trying to kick at her belly," he says. "We need to get her some Banamine. If we can get the pain down and keep her walking, this might solve itself."

Halcyon stops to paw the ground with a front leg.

He says, "There's a plastic box inside the cabin with first aid things. Under the sink to the right. See if you can find a white tube of Banamine in there."

I hustle fifty yards over to the cabin, nerves buzzing.

When I return, he stops Halcyon just long enough to squirt the white paste into her mouth, then compels her on. This walking seems endless. Their path has worn a track through grass.

"Can I spell you and take a turn?" I ask.

"The Banamine should kick in soon. Here," he says, handing me the lead rope. "Just keep her moving. Don't let her go down."

I speak quietly as we walk. After walking some twenty-five minutes together, I notice Halcyon licking her lips. Her head begins to drop. Her steps slow. I feel my own rapid heart rate drop with hers. The painkiller is taking affect.

We stop. She stands still, head low.

"We'll need to keep an eye on her for a while now," Harrison says. "Let's walk her down to the barn and put her in the corral there, near the trailer."

We meet Rick as three of us walk slowly along the road to the barn, Harrison on one side of her and me on the other. Rick follows, then stands with us in the corral to observe Halcyon. Both men have seen colic before. Harrison holds the lead rope while she rests, head still lowered.

"Come closer," he says to me. I watch him place his right hand on the back part of her gray flank toward her stifle. "You can feel for any gurgles or activity in her digestive track. That would be a good sign. Another thing we're wanting is for her to take a shit. That would be a good indicator she's not impacted to the point of needing a vet."

I bring both hands next to Harrison's, rest them on her grayish-white body, moist with sweat. Pressing lightly, I feel for movement in her gut. I listen for sounds.

Ten minutes later, I am standing with Halcyon and see her lift a hind leg to stomp. Harrison and Rick are talking nearby, I call out for help. When I step closer to stroke her back, she lifts her head like someone suddenly snapping out of a stupor and begins folding her front legs again to go down. I yank hard on the lead rope and the three of us get her to move forward and start walking again. We have been walking her now for almost two hours. I look at Harrison through tears.

"Just keep her up and moving," he orders. He turns his back and walks away from us toward the gate.

"Where are you going?" I shout.

"To hook up the horse trailer so we can get moving," he yells.

Rick stays while I walk Halcyon. A few minutes later, we load her for the hour and a half ride into town. Harrison ties her so she remains upright.

Two hours later, we stand on a cement floor with our suffering friend in a small cool room inside the vet's barn. Harrison is steady, attentive. Halcyon is given a sedative, then led into a metal horse chute. We remain on either side of her as the vet inserts a long, flexible hose into her nostril to the pharynx, the structure that serves as the entrance to the esophagus and the trachea. We stroke the front of her neck, encouraging her to swallow before he guides the tube down into her stomach. White foam bubbles from her nostrils. She can barely stand because of the sedatives and exhaustion.

Fluids begin to gush out of the tube from her stomach—a condition called reflux—and splash onto the cement floor and down the drain. The vet takes a finger to his nose to smell the fluid; sourness suggests an intestinal obstruction. This uncomfortable process continues for a while. The vet tells us Halcyon needs to stay for further observation. Three hours after we leave, we get a call. She is in severe pain again and needs immediate surgery.

When she is well enough to return to the ranch a couple of weeks later, Halcyon has white and blue bandages and surgical tape running the length of her underside. These must be cleaned and changed on a regular basis. She also wears a huge cloth body armature that attaches with Velcro strips around her middle to hold everything together. She must be kept in a stall for several more weeks to limit her activity until the incision heals. Hay must be soaked in water. She will need periods of limited grazing and gradually increased exercise. It will be four to six months before she is fully healed.

For many weeks to follow, Halcyon and I help each other rehabilitate. She, with her belly scar. Me, with mine. Harrison helps me fill her hay bowl with water and carry water buckets to her stall. I spend time brushing and stroking her. When she is ready, I hand-graze her for fifteen minutes each day. Then thirty minutes each day. Then an hour each day. I listen to the sounds of her pulling and chewing grass while I stay with her. I discover the calming effect grazing has on my own body. She teaches me about different grasses. One day, I lead her to a certain spot where I imagine the grass might be tasty. But her knowledge is far deeper than mine. She shows me exactly what she likes and doesn't like.

I hold her lead rope while I lie in the grass one sunny day in early August and again recall sitting in tall grasses outside Browning with a friend who is a member of the Confederated Tribes of the Colville Reservation and lives in Alaska. We spent hours together that afternoon, many years ago, running our fingers through the sacred hair of Mother Earth. I learned how to distinguish the qualities of fragrant sweetgrass from other grasses, lost myself to discerning the distinct and subtle characteristics of each different blade (the hard spine through the middle of one grass, another smooth on one side and sticky on the other like a cat's tongue), appreciating how grasses taste and smell differently. Quiet intimacies like this are innate for animals like Halcyon.

My beautiful mare friend stands patiently by my side each day as I pour water into a bucket for her. She stays still and sniffs me while I change her bandages and then reattach the noisy Velcro strips of the wide girdle-like belt she does not like. Before her colic, Halcyon was so passionate and reactive. Coming to know her during my recovery last October was like befriending something truly wild.

Sitting over tea one afternoon, Harrison tells me Halcyon was high-strung and reactive from the time she was born.

"You've seen it in her sister Hess. She's excitable too. Their mother and grandmother were the same way."

My mother, who often seemed irascible and erratic to me when I was a child, tells me I was born a colicky baby with clenched fists and endless bouts of crying. I think of Harrison's descriptions of Nancy's violent temper; how he grew up in his own maelstrom of intense emotional disturbance. When he proposed to me on Easter morning—a holiday of new beginnings—we agreed: the one thing we want most in our life together is peacefulness.

Lying on the ground, I listen to the sound of Halcyon eating. I inhale her warm grassy breath as she brings her muzzle to my face. We speak for a moment, nose to nostril, before she returns to grazing. I surrender to the ease of this day.

RITES OF PASSAGE

F all, 2009. Harrison has told me for weeks how nervous he is about the whole ceremony. I've been too busy making plans and caring for Halcyon to feel nervous. I'm sorry my mother won't be attending due to health issues. Harrison's mother approves of our union but is too old now to travel.

Five days before our big weekend, Phyllis calls.

"We want to come visit you two at the ranch tomorrow. Let's meet over at your new Red Nose painting studio. Will two o'clock in the afternoon work?"

Harrison and I are there at the cabin, waiting and curious, when the three sisters pull up. Phyllis steps out first. We talk, while Mitzi and Connie unpack two large objects and carry them inside. We're told to stay put until they're ready for us.

"Okay, you can come on in!"

Next to my painting easel on the far wall of the cabin, we find a three-foot-long table and painted stool. The table is similar to the funky, homemade furniture of branches and leather I've admired at the Meriwether. I turn to look at the sisters, speechless.

Mitzi says: "Phyllis painted the stool. We all made the table."

Under its glass top, they have placed a historic photograph of J. Y. Warren, as well as a photo of their entire Fontana family of Italian immigrants, taken when they first arrived in Montana. At the center of these early images, linking our personal history with this special place in the world, is a copy of our wedding invitation. A note, tied with a bow, hangs from a branch at the top of the table: "If you'd prefer, you can always exchange this for a toaster!"

"This is the best wedding gift ever," I say, hugging all three at once.

"Hey," Phyllis says. "You two are hosting your out-of-town guests here at the ranch in a few days; they'll be here one day before the wedding, right?"

I nod.

"We'd like to help. Do you think some of your friends would enjoy a tour of the Meriwether?"

My heart jumps.

"We'll have an open house at Lonetree for anyone who might be interested in seeing the old stagecoach and quarry. How does that sound?"

The day before the wedding, when guests arrive, the ranch is dotted with luminous groves of yellow aspen. It's not unusual to get a first winter storm during this last weekend of September, but luck is with us. Vibrant cottonwoods wind their way down the center of the valley along Cottonwood Creek like a tangerine-colored silk ribbon. The air is cool; the sun is warm. We serve lunch outside in the courtyard.

At some point, Harrison catches my eye from across the courtyard. He motions for me to join him, then stands and clinks a glass.

"We're so happy to have all of you here with us today. I have a special wedding gift I'd like to present," he says, smiling nervously, eyes down. "This is something a true artisan has been working on for the better part of a year, just for this occasion."

From behind his back, he hands me a five-foot-long slender object slipped inside a cloth bag. I loosen the drawstring at one end and pull a light curved piece of wood from its sleeve.

"My very own bow?!"

I lift the handmade traditional longbow high in the air for everyone to see. Its carved surface is like silk. Its weight, perfect. My hands explore its patterned layers of laminated blond and mahogany-colored woods.

Harrison is grinning when I turn to hug him.

"What a gorgeous work of art!"

He wiggles away. "You'll also need these." He hands me a string for my bow and a rawhide quiver with a leather strap. The twelve arrows it carries have bright yellow and purple feather fletchings.

My city friends look intrigued as Harrison strings the bow. *Why would she want a bow and arrows?* I imagine many have never seen a traditional bow before, let alone tried to shoot one. A few look puzzled. *When did our friend become a she-hunter?*

We adjourn to grab more bows and arrows. Curious friends take turns practicing on a series of targets we set up last month among cottonwood trees along the creek near the house. Harrison and I offer instructions.

"Now stand really close this time, and don't even worry about hitting the target. Close your eyes as you draw back. Just feel it in your body," I say.

I haven't seen some of these friends for a very long time. I hear my confidence and surprise myself. When I take aim with my wedding bow and release a first purple arrow, the bow comes alive in my hands.

A group of our visitors soon gathers for their tour of another local ranch. They are climbing aboard a yellow school bus sent by the sisters. We wave goodbye as it fords the stream. What a surprise these friends have in store. Imagine their delight as that yellow bus winds its way around these beautiful Highwood Mountains, then pulls up into a steep hidden canyon with tepees and soaring granite cliffs. And Phyllis steps off the porch to greet them.

The next day, our wedding day, a mix of guests—artists, hunters, scholars, local ranchers—assemble at Fort Benton's small stone church of St. Paul's. Just a few blocks down the street from the hotel along the Missouri, this is Montana's oldest Episcopalian church in continuous operation. Its masonry was built by Phyllis's grandfather, Christopher Fontana, in 1881. I see Harrison's three sons with their children as they arrive. Dutiful and polite, they are here today as good men supporting their father while still blind in their own grief, dragged into suits to move forward in ways they aren't ready for yet. Their anguish still feels deep and painful—at times, misplaced. But I see their father in them. He convinces me to stay strong; to trust that they will come around, as he has, in their own ways and time. And they do. My sister is present with her family to support me. Our friend John is here. Kelly is here with her red-headed one-year-old boy, Ellis. Phyllis, Connie, and Mitzi enter the church in their fanciest hats with shiny silver conchas and long dancing pheasant feathers.

Austin, my twenty-one-year-old nephew, is standing in for my father to walk me down the aisle. I slip my arm through his as we wait together outside the church on the front lawn, watching as three maids of honor walk in first, arm in arm with each of Harrison's three sons. Harrison's young grandchildren enter next with their mothers, sprinkling yellow rose petals, carrying the ring.

"Here we go," I say, squeezing Austin's arm when the music changes.

My entrance as the center of attention in this small, packed space is instantly uncomfortable, so much so that I forget Harrison is even here. I grip Austin's arm while everyone stares. One step at a time, finally, I remember Harrison at the altar. Our eyes lock. His gaze holds me steady under pressure, as it has so many times before. When we arrive, he thanks my nephew and folds my hands into his.

A few minutes into the ceremony, Pastor Val, our minister, gets to the part, "Should anyone present know of any reason that this couple should not be joined in holy matrimony, speak now or forever hold your peace." Harrison breathes an audible sigh of relief and thinks the ceremony is over. He motions for the musicians to start playing and turns us toward the congregation.

A small band revs up with celebratory music as my antsy husband-to-be pulls me to start walking out. But we've not yet taken our vows. I turn to Val, confused.

326   LYNNE SPRIGGS O'CONNOR

"Are we finished?"

"No!"

Harrison and I begin waving arms at the band. As they joyfully play on, Harrison rolls his eyes and shrugs his shoulders. Everyone in the church breaks out laughing.

Finally, the room grows quiet, the ceremony resumes. Harrison says his vows. I fight back tears to say mine. Val turns to Harrison.

"Do you have the ring?"

He is visibly caught by surprise, searches both pockets wildly. More laughter rises from the pews. I take his arm and point to his three-year-old grandson, little Harrison, who is seated nearby, holding the ring he carried in as ring bearer. Big Harrison returns to center stage with the ring, waves it in the air to show the crowd. Cheers erupt.

In the drama of that perfect moment, he turns to me. I am weeping and now laughing with exasperation. He pulls a Kleenex out of his breast pocket.

Everyone sighs.

When the ceremony *really is* over, there is great applause.

Our photos are taken on the banks of the Missouri, standing beneath giant orange cottonwood trees, with Shep looking on.

DROPPING ANCHOR

We drive down the gravel road a few days later toward Leroy's, dog trailer in tow. Nell, Drummy, and Dollar, as well as Willow and two-year-old Bec and Bastion are on board. This will be the first day in our fifth year of bird hunting, now as husband and wife, and the first season of hunting adventures for Bec and Bastion. The air is sweet. The light is soft. If we're lucky, Hungarian partridge and sharp-tailed grouse will be on the wing.

As we follow Nell and Bec on foot, traveling along hillsides and ravines between Square and Round Buttes high above lower hayfields, the vista stretches out for miles and miles to the Arrow Creek breaks and open plains far below. Four mountain ranges rise blue in the open distance around us—the Little Belts, the Snowies, the Moccasins, the Judiths. We follow our canine friends straight to the foot of Square Butte.

"Look," I notice. "Nell is on point!" Harrison picks up his pace. I follow.

We watch Bec move in to back Nell. Her tail lifts and points, imitating her mother, standing perfectly still. Guns are loaded. I carry mine in a ready position as we move closer.

"Go ahead. Walk in, just ahead of Nell. This one is yours," Harrison says. Willow stays at a distance while he reaches down to encourage Bec, rubs her white-and-orange-ticked hair from back to front: "Whoa. Whoa."

Everything in my body is focused, steady. I step out slowly through dried grass, notice where Nell points with her eyes. In a sudden whir of flapping wings to my right, eight huns lift and rise. Safety switch off, I focus on one bird's movement and, with a loose swinging action, pull the trigger.

A bird falls from the sky.

"You did it!" Harrison calls out. "You got your first hun! Nice shot." He walks up, slips his arm around me.

I stand frozen in place, head down. My shotgun hangs in my right arm. I press the palm of my left hand against my heart.

I leave him without a word to find my bird.

The partridge lies in the grass where it fell—still, unmoving. Barred feathers, streaked with red-and-white patterns, suggest the bird is a male. I drop the gun to hold his warm body in my hands, feeling the ballast of his weight. A patch of chestnut brown colors his pale belly. A momentary movement of legs and feet presses against my fingers. Blood stains his mouth. He grows still again. Harrison arrives.

"Aren't they beautiful?" He pats me on the back.

I cannot smile.

I have taken a life.

The full weight of it registers. I am horrified. Humbled. In today's world, a rare experience: I feel what it is to assume full responsibility for procuring what I eat. I know now what it is to receive such a gift. Cupping my hands around the bird, I say a prayer of profound thanks.

Bird dogs have moved on.

"You can take it now," I say, head still down.

Harrison squeezes my shoulder, slips the quarry into his orange hunting vest's back pocket.

For the rest of our hunt, I don't reload. I have held several injured songbirds in my hands by now. Today's experience is entirely different. Back home in the kitchen, I give deeper thanks than ever before. Tonight, this bird I shot will feed us.

Will I find a way to do this more than once?

I am still conflicted when we head out with bird dogs one week later. My decision to bring a shotgun is not an easy one. This time Dollar is on point. Again, I feel the apprehension involved in taking my turn. Harrison gestures with encouragement. I take one step at a time until a covey of huns suddenly takes flight, red tail feathers flashing. My right eye zeros in on a single bird and follows it as I swing and pull. It falls to the ground. Dollar is thrilled! Willow helps find my quarry, and only reluctantly does she allow me to remove the limp body from her jaws.

Harrison and I cheer for Dollar. "Good girl," I say to Willow.

Following Nell and Bec, we remark about the annual uptick of traffic along the gravel road. So many trucks and men with guns in orange jackets. We always make a point to give a Western wave to these strangers visiting our "neighborhood." It's customary around here. The majority cruise by without reciprocating. Driven hunters on a mission, too busy for cordialities. It is unfortunate this seasonal sport so often engenders feelings of entitlement and avarice. *Am I, too, now a hunter?*

"Look," Harrison shouts. He motions for me and Willow to follow. Nell is on point again just ahead of us, with Bec backing. Harrison approaches and walks forward following their gaze, the covey rises, and he shoots. When a sharpie falls from the sky, Nell and her daughter race forward. Each grabs one end of the bird in her mouth, both refusing to let go.

"Ha!" Harrison laughs. "Don't think for a minute that the behaviors of greediness are just in humans! Look at that passion. How wonderful."

One year from today, I will decide hunting is not for me and never shoot another bird.

Intimacies with wild birds will continue to teach me about resilience, danger, love, and hope. I will continue to embrace the fact that hunting is who my husband is, even as *his* relationship with it changes.

Back in town, it's moving time. One by one, I gather up each special object from my Birdhouse's makeover with Phyllis two years ago. I've moved more times in my life than I can count. This bubble-wrap-and-cardboard-box job of repacking everything is all too familiar. But this is different. Harrison is here with me, my partner. There's someone beside me to help with the heavy lifting.

Where is all this stuff going?

Harrison's sense of aesthetics is something I love about him. His house is decorated elegantly, like a beautiful museum. We agree: my things wouldn't fit at all with its formality. The Red Nose cabin, on the other hand, has a much wilder, more folksy feel to it. And it's about the same size as my Birdhouse.

"You've got your easel and painting supplies set up," Harrison says. "The sisters' table and stool look great there. I love your feather spirit catchers; why don't you keep going? If you like, we can take your things over there and you can make it even cozier."

"Great idea!"

Before a first box is even unpacked, I throw on my smock, mix paints, and cover the entire surface of the Red Nose cabin's old plastic refrigerator with eye-dazzling patterns and colors.

The closing on the sale of my Birdhouse in Great Falls happens three weeks later. With the addition of painted furniture, art objects, my carved box of feathers, special trinkets from around the world placed in a "cabinet of magic objects," and shelves of books on art and culture, the Red Nose cabin becomes our favorite spot on the ranch. Phyllis is thrilled when she comes for a visit—I have a creative oasis of my own. Harrison prepares a celebratory dinner for the three of us: succulent braised quail (from a Texas hunting trip) with apples, fresh cream, and butter, a recipe from a 1937 *Derrydale Cookbook of Fish and Game*. Our prayer flag lantern hangs overhead like a jewel.

There is shock and wonder in such radical changes. At nearly fifty years old, familiar pressures are gone for the first time in my life. I no longer eat most every meal alone. Living paycheck to paycheck is over. Each morning when I wake and each evening when I sleep, someone I love and trust is here beside me. We are outside every day, caring for and living with animals. In nature. Together.

The backdrop for *everything* now is the sweet embrace of these beautiful mountains, this hidden valley, and all that belongs to these wide-open and wind-filled spaces—the grazing horses and bugling elk, the finches in the daylight, and the owls in the dark. The shape of my scars has led me here. My spirit has finally put down anchor. I am home.

END NOTES

1. E. B. White, *One Man's Meat*, 1942, page 16.

2. *North American Journals of Prince Maximilian de Wied*, August 1833 (Fort McKenzie): 33.

3. Historic references to Elk medicine among early Native people of the Northern Plains are found in the writings of Clark Wissler, 1905: 261–269; John Ewers, 1958: 40; Robert Lowie Reports in 1912: 221.

4. Naomi Shihab Nye.

5. Evelyn Cameron, courtesy of Prairie County Museum and Evelyn Cameron Gallery, Terry, Montana.

6. For an excellent window into Blackfeet perspectives on these relationships, see Rosalyn R. LaPier's *Invisible Reality: Storytellers, Storytakers, and the Supernatural World of the Blackfeet*, 2017, University of Nebraska Press.

7. Geneen Haugen, "Stalking Fear" (2000), page 44 in *Heart Shots*, 2003, Mary Zeiss Stange, editor.

8. In her essay entitled "Deerskin" (1984), pages 23–28 in *Heart Shots*, Terry Tempest Williams offers a beautiful passage from Claus Chee Sonny, a Navajo medicine man, describing part of the Deerhunting Way he learned from his father, who obtained it from his father, passed down by Claus Chee's grandfather and teachers before him.

9. Big-Ox, Crow medicine man, 1922, interviewed by Robert Lowie.

10. *Lame Deer Seeker of Visions*, with Richard Erdoes, 1972.

ACKNOWLEDGMENTS

This book never would have happened without the stalwart and compassionate guidance of Page Lambert. Every step of the way, her intuitive approach—as a teacher, editor, author, and dear friend— has fostered my courage to tell this story. In similar ways, I remain eternally grateful for the deep kindness Suzanne Preston Blier extended over thirty years ago, when she took me under her capable wings at Columbia University. She and Aldona Jonaitis opened my eyes to the distinct honor and complex responsibilities inherent in studying Indigenous cultures. The venerable George Horse Capture deepened my education as a mentor and friend throughout the years of his own ever-expanding legacy.

Thank you to David Penney for his steady encouragement and the gift of serving as his research assistant on a first major exhibition: *Art of the American Indian Frontier: The Chandler-Pohrt Collection.* To be welcomed into the Pohrt family became a personal blessing. Richard Pohrt, a consummate collector who had traveled to Montana's Fort Belknap Reservation in the 1930s, shared firsthand stories while examining objects together. Tom Pohrt, a beloved self-taught illustrator and storyteller, allowed me into his world of meticulous watercolor paintings and travels with Barry Lopez on their *Crow and Weasel* book tour. I devoured the reading lists of Karl Pohrt, a true visionary and the legendary owner of Shaman Drum Bookstore. Over my summers on the Blackfeet Indian Reservation, Elouise Cobell, Molly and George Kicking Woman, Darrell Kipp, Carol Murray, Darrell Norman, Ernie Pepion, and others were my esteemed teachers and friends. Darnell Rides At The Door also has guided me as a Blackfeet matriarch, knowledge carrier, and bundle keeper. I am grateful to all these wise souls, to my father and my incredible mother, for instilling in me the foundational perspectives that flow through this story.

A rainbow of thanks to the artists of this world for shining their bright and generous light, especially those of you I have had the good fortune to work with over the years. To *all* my friends and advocates along this winding path: but for the grace of your love, I could not have persevered. Special thanks to Natasha Atkins, Janet Berlo, Nancy Dickenson, Lisa Easton, Courtney Fuchs, Jenniphr Goodman, Meredith Johnston, Alice Kehoe, Andrea Leeb, Kelly Lynch, Linda Musser, Nani Power, Ellie Rodgers, Elizabeth Tucker, Sara Walsh, and S. Kirk Walsh, who were kind enough to read versions of my manuscript and respond. This finished work is better because of you. In 2003, Mary Zeiss Stange edited *Heart Shots*, a powerful collection of essays by women writing about hunting. These sister-voices have inspired me.

Writing X Writers provided a first experience of writers in community and refreshed my confidence to keep going. Towards the end of *Elk Love*'s twelve-year gestation, Pam Houston's feedback was invaluable, helping to lift my story ever closer to where it wanted and needed to be. I am indebted to John Gritts and Dakota Hoska for their generosity in reviewing discreet passages for issues of cultural sensitivity. John, a full-blood member of the Cherokee Nation, has worked in higher education with Tribal Colleges for nearly 40 years. Dakota, a citizen of the Oglála Lakhóta Nation, is also an accomplished artist and educator. She currently works as assistant curator of Native Arts at the Denver Art Museum and has her M.A. in Art History. Deep gratitude to Brooke Warner, Lauren Wise, and the entire staff at She Writes Press for your professional expertise. I am incredibly fortunate to have you in my corner.

I would be remiss if I did not voice my daily appreciation of the many good souls here in Montana. Since this story began twenty years ago, I have come to know my doctor and my hairdresser, our mechanic, and our family of ranch hands as cherished friends. Our postmistress.

Our amazing veterinarians. Kindness brings buoyancy in a shared dedication to this lifestyle and a pride in work well done. In the tacit solidarity among our neighboring ranchers, the same principles hold true. I am extremely lucky to live in a rural community where hard-working people devote their entire lives to caring for animals and to helping one another in times of need.

The bedrock of this love story is the generous heartbeat of Mother Nature. I owe a debt of immense gratitude to the autumn love songs of elk; the welcome company of spirited gray-crowned rosy-finches each winter; early spring's blossoms of colorful pasque flowers, mountain goldbanner, arrowleaf balsamroot, and shooting stars; the flowing waters of the Missouri River that have carried me each summer. As one of many inhabitants in this remarkable valley, I bow to the power of Chinook winds and mountain lions, to the friendship of dogs, to the unspeakable beauty of horses and cottonwoods, and to all that knits us together. To Harrison O'Connor, my husband and partner in all things, the deepest gratitude of all. Twenty years have passed, and I love you now more than ever. *Thank you for walking me home.*

ABOUT THE AUTHOR

Lynne Spriggs O'Connor spent ten consecutive summers on northern Montana's Blackfeet Indian Reservation while pursuing fieldwork for her Ph.D. in Native American Art History at Columbia University. After moving to Montana in her early forties, she curated a three-year project called *Bison: American Icon,* a major permanent exhibition of Native American art for the C. M. Russell Museum on bison in the Northern Plains. O'Connor previously curated exhibitions of folk and self-taught art at the High Museum in Atlanta. She also worked in the film industry as production coordinator for Spalding Gray and Jonathan Demme on the iconic *Swimming to Cambodia.* For the past fifteen years, she and her husband have lived on a cattle ranch in an isolated mountain valley in northeastern Montana, where her life centers on writing, animals, and family. *Elk Love* is her first memoir.

SELECTED TITLES FROM SHE WRITES PRESS

She Writes Press is an independent publishing company founded to serve women writers everywhere. Visit us at www.shewritespress.com.

Available As Is: A Midlife Widow's Search for Love by Debbie Weiss. $17.95, 978-1-64742-237-0. When Debbie Weiss lost her first and only true love at fifty years old, she went through an intense period of grieving—and then dove headfirst into online dating. This is her full-hearted, darkly funny, unvarnished account of learning to be alone at middle age—and finally becoming her true self.

Burning Woman: Memoirs of an Elder by Sharon Strong. $16.95, 978-1-64742-377-3. At sixty-five, artist, writer, and psychologist Sharon Strong claims the next decade to trek the Himalayas, build massive sculptures for Burning Man, and meet the love of her life—and to find a way, when a raging wildfire destroys twenty years of artwork, to persevere. This passionate love story about the adventure of aging will guide others through times of creativity, destruction, and transformation.

Here We Grow: Mindfulness through Cancer and Beyond by Paige Davis. $16.95, 978-1-63152-381-6. At thirty-eight years old, after receiving a breast cancer diagnosis, Paige Davis ventures into an unlikely love affair of a lifetime—and embraces cancer through a lens of love rather than as a battle to be fought.

The Memory of All That: A Love Story about Alzheimer's by Mary MacCracken. $16.95, 978-1-64742-417-6. Deeply in love, Cal and Mary brave divorce, marry, and help each other succeed in their work—Cal becomes a renowned inventor, Mary a best-selling author—only to be faced, years later, with their biggest challenge of all: Alzheimer's. It's a battle they can't win—but Alzheimer's doesn't win either, because Cal and Mary's love persists throughout and beyond their battle.

Miracle at Midlife: A Transatlantic Romance by Roni Beth Tower. $16.95, 978-1-63152-123-2. An inspiring memoir chronicling the sudden, unexpected, and life-changing two-year courtship between a divorced American lawyer living on a houseboat in the center of Paris and an empty-nested clinical psychologist living in Connecticut.